D0612968

The New Prosperity

Investment Opportunities in Long-Wave Economic Cycles

Jake Bernstein

NEW YORK INSTITUTE OF FINANCE

Library of Congress Cataloging-in-Publication Data

Bernstein, Jacob, 1946-
    The new prosperity : investment opportunities in long-wave
economic cycles / Jacob Bernstein.
        p.   cm.
    Bibliography: p.
    Includes index.
    ISBN 0-13-540279-4
    1. Investments. 2. Long waves (Economics)   I. Title.
HG4515.B47 1988
322.6--dc19   88-29377
                                                                   CIP

This publication is designed to provide accurate and authoritative information in regard to
the subject matter covered. It is sold with the understanding that the publisher is not
engaged in rendering legal, accounting, or other professional service. If legal advice or other
expert assistance is required, the services of a competent professional should be sought.

*From a Declaration of Principles Jointly Adopted by
a Committee of the American Bar Association and a
Committee of Publishers and Associations*

Printed in the United States of America

10 9 8 7 6 5 4 3 2 1

New York Institute of Finance
(NYIF Corp.)
70 Pine Street
New York, New York 10270-0003

To Linda, Becky, Eli and Sara

Contents

Chapter 6

Is War Inevitable? 137

Chapter 7

Saved from the Brink: Preparing for the Future..... 151

Chapter 8

How to Prepare for Each Stage of the Long Wave.. 165

Chapter 9

Long-Term Cycles: An Overview 203

Preface

Since 1972, my career in the stock and futures markets has taken me throughout the world as a speaker at numerous investment conferences and seminars. I have presented my ideas and analyses to a large diversity of audiences, ranging from knowledgeable and sophisticated professional traders to those who are essentially ignorant of basic investment and speculation concepts. What has impressed me most about the people I've met is that while their motivation to succeed in the investment world is high, their knowledge of economic history is pitifully low. While they share an interest in learning how to profit from various investment programs, market indicators, and trading or investing systems, they lack the historical structure and knowledge that can facilitate the performance of these systems, methods, and indicators.

Investors, traders, and businesspersons are all primarily concerned with forecasting trends and prices. This is, indeed, an erstwhile concern. Clearly such knowledge can frequently predetermine the direction of their investment goals. However, the future is not predictable to the extent or to the degree of precision required for consistent success. Within gross limits we can forecast trends and prices. The longer the term of our forecast, the less accurate it is likely to be. In their never-ending search for more accurate ways in which to predict the future of prices, trends, and economic changes, the majority of investors, investment managers, and economists have all too often overlooked the two things we do know for certain: the present and the past.

They are frequently too concerned about tomorrow to see the relationships among the past, the present, and the future.

History is the basis of my work. Repetition, patterns, cycles, similarity, and correlation are the ingredients of my approach to market analysis and trend forecasting. Without an understanding of how prices, trends, cycles, politics, international conflict, and market forces all fit into the panorama of economic life, your view of long-range economic trends will be myopic. Tunnel vision will prevent future-oriented thought. You will be driven by the same illusory goal that motivates most investors and market analysts: the need to forecast the future. Yet you will be inhibited by an incomplete understanding of the past and, therefore, an incorrect analysis of the present. The future will be difficult to forecast, even with a moderate degree of success.

My hope is that this book will help provide you with a framework within which you can evaluate and understand current and projected economic trends. Unfortunately, I cannot supply you with every piece of information you will require in order to avoid economic crises in the future. However, this book will provide a strong starting point from which you may choose your next direction of study. My goal in what follows is to introduce and briefly analyze as many concepts as possible in the most basic and understandable terms possible. To do justice to every topic and concept in this book would require several volumes. Yet economic history is not occult. It is readily available to all who seek it. If what you are about to read makes sense to you or arouses your interest, then I urge you to pursue a serious course of study in economic history, cycles, and patterns.

Finally, remember that this book was researched and written with the average investor in mind. Within these pages you will not find the erudite analyses of a doctoral dissertation. Nor will you be attacked by a barrage of statistical analyses, formulae, or abstract concepts. Rather you will be guided slowly, carefully, and in plain English through the maze of theories and facts that comprises long-wave economic history. But the journey does not end with an introductory tour. Rather, it continues until history has been transformed into an understanding of current economic realities and anticipated economic trends. What you will achieve is a broad perspective—a structure, within which you can interpret the present and forecast the future.

If you find my approach too basic, then let it be the stimulus for further study. If you find my approach too complicated, then let it serve as a warning that perhaps you do not know enough about the subject at hand. Regardless, let my book be your starting point rather than your ending point. This book may answer many questions; however, a thorough reading should stimulate the inquiring mind to seek many more answers than I have provided herein.

Finally, a brief comment about accuracy. The process of writing this book has been long and laborious. I suspect that by the time you read this over one year's time will have elapsed since I started writing, and it may be several months longer before the final product has reached you. Some of my charts, graphs, and comments may be slightly dated, yet it is not the primary purpose of this book to give forecasts. Rather, it is the intent of this book to teach structures that will allow virtually any event, expected or unexpected, to be analyzed and understood. If you can put day-to-day events into their framework, understanding their *sub-rosa* meaning as opposed to their surface symptomatology, then you will have achieved a valuable understanding of *holistic* economics . . . , one which I am certain will serve you well for years to come . . . one which should lead to very few surprises.

Jake Bernstein
Northbrook, Illinois
February 1989

Acknowledgments

I wish to express special thanks to the following for permission to reproduce charts and/or text from their services and publications.

Commodity Research Bureau
30 S Wacker Drive - Suite 1820
Chicago, IL 60606

Commodity Quote Graphics
PO Box 758
Glenwood Springs, CO 81603

Commodity Price Charts
219 Parkade
Cedar Falls, IA 50613

Cycles
Foundation for the Study of Cycles
3333 Michelson Drive - Suite 210
Irvine, CA 92715

The Kondratieff Wave Analyst
Donald J. Hoppe, Editor
Box 977
Crystal Lake, IL 60014

Chapter 1

It Can't Happen Again

Credit Is Sound, Reynolds Says

That forced selling is pretty well over is the belief of Arthur Reynolds, Chairman of the Board of the Continental Illinois Bank and Trust Company. Mr. Reynolds said that he has been advised that selling orders have been cleaned up and that there is now substantial buying power.

"Current stock prices have attracted purchasing from many different quarters," Mr. Reynolds said, "particularly from concerns that could invest for a period, such as insurance companies and others of this nature."

—Arthur Reynolds
Chairman
Continental Illinois Bank and Trust Company

While Jack Kerouac was hitting the road and Bob Hope was flashing his toothy smile on the road to Bali, the roots of a new economic order were threading their way through the subsoil of America. Still fresh from triumphs of World War II, America was now free to dedicate its resources and energies to domestic growth, as it had done on four previous occasions, each following a war. The 1950s found America abundant in many of the ingredients necessary for substantial and sustained economic growth. Interest rates were bottoming, and commodity prices were low. Land and real estate prices were comparatively low; government was pro-business and expansive. Social attitudes were liberal but not radically so, and the business climate was positive because of pent-up consumer demand following the war. The stock market was still only several years into the upswing of its nine-year cycle. Yes, memories of the Great Depression were still reasonably fresh, but they were overshadowed by the greater horrors of war. A new age beckoned with its promise of "unlimited" atomic power, peace, and scientific progress.

The U.S. economy was about to embark on a twenty-five-year upswing that would bring with it the inescapable yin and yang of economic cycles. But the ride would not be without its rough spots. The period just ahead would usher in the best of times as well as the worst of times. Today, more than thirty-five years after the fact, we can examine history with the aid of 20:20 hindsight. We can look back with scientific detachment, formulate conclusions, carefully retrace the sequence of events, and confidently explain to high school history classes what brought about the greatest era of growth known to humankind. Yet, in the 1950s there were few who could forecast with confidence either the magnitude or extent of the coming trend. To do so would have taken considerable foresight, a keen knowledge of economic history, and the emotional fortitude necessary to withstand the almost certain storm of ridicule that would have followed.

Yet the lessons of history were all too clear. American and European economies had experienced numerous periods of cyclical growth and contraction since the 1600s. Though not carbon copies of one another, each period of growth was characterized by essentially similar social, political, economic, and religious themes. Each cycle or period followed a generally repetitive pattern of growth, crest, downturn, and decay. Most of the "long-wave" economic cycles measured approximately fifty to sixty years in length from their start to their finish.

In spite of the seemingly obvious similarities shared by each cycle, the common threads could not be discerned by those in the heat of economic battle. An understanding of long-wave cycles could be acquired only by taking a distant stance. The myopia that afflicts many of us after the age of forty clouded the view of economists and politicians who looked at economics from close up. Even the so-called "macro economists" were too entrenched in their theories to see the facts from afar. Save but a few brave souls whose work is still looked upon askance today, the eyes of the world were too closely riveted on events to see trends. Each cycle turn took many of the "experts" by surprise. Economic trends, like the work of the great impressionist painters, must first be studied from a distance. The blobs of color are interesting but unintegrated from close up; yet from several yards away they take on rich and flowing meaning. They transmit information to the senses and energy to the human brain. Once the total picture has been experienced, the viewer can step closer, closer, and closer still without losing the meaning of the whole. Then the parts take on new life. What on first glance was meaningless acquires new and subtle definition upon each successive examination. The whole is greater than the sum of its parts, and the parts are greater than the sum of the whole. The cyclical view of socioeconomic life is, in many respects, like the work of the impressionist painters.

Although the lessons of economic history were clear, there were those who were either standing too close to see, who were standing too far away to see, who were too biased to see, or who were altogether blind. When the U.S. economy embarked upon its long-term cyclical upswing of the 1950s, it was the general impression that new challenges were soon to be encountered. And the impression was correct! What many failed to realize was that the coming years would bring a replay of previous issues and trends. The story would be the same; "only the names" would change.

At first on an unsteady footing, the U.S. economy began to regain its strength. The uncertain 1950s brought with them recession, the threat of nuclear destruction, fallout shelters, seeds of the race for space, and the promise of better times to come. The 1950s set the tone for trends in virtually every facet of life for the next three decades. From the abortive struggles of the French in Vietnam grew a war that carved a deep and irreparable rift within America, and between the "superpowers." Prompted by the civil rights movement, the 1960s, '70s, and '80s brought women's rights, gay rights, and student rights. From Chuck Berry grew the Beatles, and from the Beatles, "acid rock" and "heavy metal." The beatniks of the 1950s became the hippies of the 1970s. The mescaline experiments of Huxley gave us Timothy Leary, pot, magic mushrooms, and LSD. LSD spawned STP, DMT, and a host of hallucinogens. Those who "tripped" in the 1960s graduated to "snorting" in the 1980s. The quest for spiritual enlightenment, self-development, social improvement, and sexual freedom grew from its childhood in the 1950s to full adulthood in the 1970s. By the late 1970s, liberalism had reached its pinnacle, the Vietnam War was over, the dead and MIAs were still being counted, and the "mind expanding" drugs, as they were called, had been abandoned for "recreational" drugs.

By the 1970s, it was clear that every aspect of life in America and the "free world" was slowly changing. The process that had begun in the 1950s had grown to maturity by the early to mid-1970s. By 1979, the growth cycle had become geriatric. It was turning gray, losing its hair, and losing its strength.

Those who had earlier theorized and researched the long-wave economic cycles were about to have their ideas tested. Juglar, Kitchin, Kondratieff, Schumpeter, Van Dujin, Forrester, and Dewey, all economists or students of cyclic theories, had written extensively on the repetitive nature of economic phenomena. Those who discounted the long-wave economic theories, such as the proponents of Keynesian economics, were also about to see their systems and theories challenged as never before. By 1980 it was clear, even to the most optimistic observers, that there were serious problems in the U.S. economy. Would the cycle run its course, bringing the economic downwave forecast by the cyclical theorists, or could we "spend" our way out of disinflation as suggested by the Keynesians?

Following a steady decline from 1980 through mid-1982, prompted by sharply rising interest rates and a variety of international incidents, stock prices began an upward move that was to become the most significant rise in all economic history. Prices on Wall Street pushed higher and higher, eclipsing one record after another. The market rose on good news, and it rose on bad news. Every selloff was a buying opportunity. Forecasts became more and more bullish. Stock index futures soared. Speculation in futures options, OEX options, and interest rate futures set new volume records. Respected market technicians dissected their price charts, figuring the next levels of resistance, estimating how high stock prices could go, determining how much of a price correction was reasonable, knowing that the madness had to reach its end but doubting that the correction would be a major one. Mutual fund managers and pension fund managers who knew the lessons of history advanced reasons for having some funds on the sidelines, but they were in the minority. Although the U.S. dollar plunged on overseas markets and the federal deficit soared, stocks remained in a world of their own, oblivious to the news. Seeing only the obvious plethora of chronic economic symptoms, most analysts were confused about the etiology of the persistent stock market uptrend. The cycles, however, which did not deal in causes, had clearly and unmistakably predicted the bull market as well as its imminent collapse.

In the 1900s, Edwin LeFevbre, alias Jesse Livermore, anticipated a crash in stock prices:

> Finally there came the awful day of reckoning for the bulls and the optimists and the wishful thinkers and those vast hordes that, dreading the pain of a small loss at the beginning, were now about to suffer total amputation—without anesthetics. [*Reminiscences of a Stock Operator*, American Research Council, Larchmont, NY, 1965, p. 110]

And then, almost 58 years later, there came yet another "day of reckoning." On October 16, 1987, stock prices lost more than one hundred points. Following a weekend during which traders and investors had time to ponder the market's recent losses, Standard and Poors futures opened sharply lower on Monday, October 19. The decline seemed, at first, to be a reasonable follow-through for a Monday after a weak Friday. Within several hours there were bargains galore. A market maker at the Chicago Board Options Exchange told me "when the Dow was down 100 points we thought prices were cheap; we started buying. When the Dow was down 200 points we bought more. When it was down 300 we got worried. At 400 points lower we sold out our positions and took the losses. We watched the last 100-plus points totally mesmerized, anesthetized by the avalanche of sellers, the lack of liquidity, and the worst selling panic in stock market history."

Yes, in spite of the litany that "it can't happen again," it did. Ignoring the charts, the buyers, the speculators, the government, and the bargain hunters, the beast of Wall Street unleashed a market purge, the implications of which are still not fully known. Those of us who had been preaching and warning about the coming decline were vindicated, but not happy. Those who took maximum advantage of leverage, options, stock index futures, and their various combinations either gained handsomely or, failing to act quickly enough, were caught in the mass exodus, price skids, illiquidity, trading halts, margin calls, margin selling, or frozen assets. Donald J. Hoppe, publisher of *The Kondratieff Wave Analyst*,[1] had been warning of an imminent crash in stocks for several years, based on his cyclical studies. After the "Crash of '87," he observed:

---

[1] Hoppe, Donald J., *The Kondratieff Wave Analyst*, Box 977, Crystal Lake, IL 60014.

Well, it has finally happened. The Great Crash I have been predicting and expecting for the past three years is now a terrible reality. I feel vindicated, but certainly not happy. I do not rejoice in the world's misfortune. It is sad that we few "prophets of doom" could not make the great majority recognize the disastrous course they were following. But we tried our best. My personal vindication, however, is of no importance. What really matters is that Kondratieff wave theory has been confirmed beyond all doubt. . . .

I warned repeatedly that a crash was not only inevitable, but that it would come when least expected. I also said that very few would be able to get out at or near the top with a significant part of their paper profits, and that the great majority would be trapped in the collapsing market, unable to get their sell orders filled except at ruinous losses. I said that hundreds of billions of dollars (and ultimately trillions) would simply disappear into a "black hole" of collapsing prices, and there was little that the Administration or Fed could do. . . . [Vol. II, #11, November 1987, p. 12]

But Hoppe was not alone in his forecast. Several well-known market analysts had been warning, well in advance of the crash, that all was not well.

In the Standard and Poors futures trading pit, the usual insanity became mass confusion on October 19, 1987. Futures traded one-hundred-point ticks, twenty times their usual fluctuation. Not too many months earlier, the exchange had suspended trading limits, consequently S&P futures couldn't halt their decline at limit down. Sell orders poured in from everywhere. Bids were scarce, offers plentiful. Under the circumstances, it was impossible for floor trades to maintain an orderly market without slashing prices one hundred S&P points at a crack in order to balance the bids and offers. Selling prompted more selling. The holocaust raged all day, spreading into all financial and commodity markets. Brokers, fearing they would be held liable for margin calls customers might be unable to meet, encouraged their clients to sell out. When clients couldn't be reached to satisfy intraday margin calls on stock index futures, their positions were liquidated for whatever price they would bring. This stimulated more panic liquidation. Brokers and floor traders left the exchange buildings in Chicago and New York like drugged psychotic patients leaving an old-time electro-shock treatment session. During the evening and early-morning hours, international stock markets trembled to their very foundations as the shroud of emotional selling enveloped the financial centers of the globe. The "Crash of '87," now a reality rather than a book title, came some fifty-eight years after the "Crash of '29." Both crashes came in October. Both crashes were preceded by an already declining market. The effect of each crash was felt the world over. Following both crashes such "experts" as the president of the United States declared their faith in the U.S. economy and in the stock market. The *New York Times*, on Wednesday, October 30, 1929, reported: "On Friday last the President stated that the fundamental business of the country, that is production and distribution of commodities, is on a sound and prosperous basis."

And following in the tradition of U.S. presidents, Ronald Reagan after the "Crash of '87" affirmed his sentiment that the U.S. economy was sound and that the stock market was healthy. He assured the nation that "the economic fundamentals of this country remain sound."

Within several days, trading advisors, politicians, and market analysts were in general agreement that the "Crash of '87" was merely a bull market correction, one that was long overdue. The long-term impact would be positive, they agreed. The consensus was that damage had, indeed, been done to the bull market, but that the correction was necessary. Now that it was out of the way, it was felt that investors should turn their attentions to picking up stocks at bargain levels. Roger Babson had warned of the 1929 crash and its possible consequences. The *Chicago Tribune* reported as follows on October 26, 1929:

Market Will Work Lower, Babson Says

New York, Oct. 25—Roger W. Babson, the statistical expert who along about Sept. 3, when prices were at their highest on the stock exchange, predicted with dire accuracy that they would decline from 60 to 80 points, today in a statement to a New York newspaper foresees a period of inactivity in trading, with prices gradually working their way lower.

"Crazy markets such as we had yesterday must be followed by a resting up. As to the future of common stocks, I would say that each issue should be considered on its own merits and according to its yield. Speculative buying for profit is over for a while. The buying from now on will be of a legitimate investment nature. This means that prices will be determined by yield rather than by prospects."

Both in 1929 and 1987 there were efforts to minimize the expected effects of the crash. While the wreckage was still smoking, market analysts lifted their heads out from under their hands in order to take stock of the carnage. Once the damage reports had been obtained, their tongues began to wag afresh. "We saw the crash coming," many of them told the public. "We got our clients out before the crash," they boasted. "We got out close to the top," they affirmed, taking forecasts out of context and statements out of sequence. But there were few true heroes. The clear fact was that very few analysts had predicted either of the two crashes. Fewer yet were in for the ride; and still fewer, even in their worst nightmares, dreamed that the crashes would be as bad as they were. The uninformed public as well as a surprising number of market professionals rejected comparisons between the Crash of '29 and the Crash of '87. They cited, among other things, the fact that in 1929 stocks were selling at a 10 percent margin. Yet they failed to recognize that in 1929 there were no stock index futures, and there was no program trading to accelerate the decline. The lack of historical knowledge and perspective so painfully evident in the American educational system became obvious as traders, investors, and market analysts demonstrated their ignorance of the events leading to and subsequent to the Crash of '29 and previous U.S. stock market crashes. Many investors felt that previous stock market crashes had "caused" the economic recessions and depressions that followed them. In fact, they had not. Taken out of context, the previous stock market crashes lost their meaning. Taken in their historical perspective, they were all symptoms of economies in trouble, of fiscal cancers run amok.

Half a world away, the Siberian tundra holds the frozen remains of Nikolai D. Kondratieff. If interviewed from the icy depths of his grave Kondratieff, who in 1926 wrote "Die Langen Wellen der Konjunktur"[2] (Long Waves in Economic Life), would have regarded the Crash of '87 as *prima facie* evidence that his theory was, indeed, correct. But for the exiled Russian economist who died in a Soviet labor camp, the end came before his work had progressed to its final proof. Left in the lurch, without solid statistical validation, Kondratieff's long-wave theories were criticized, ridiculed, and rejected, not only by his Soviet leaders but also by academicians the world over. With the exception of a few market analysts and/or economists such as Jay W. Forrester of M.I.T., Don Hoppe, Julian Snyder, I, and a handful of others, the theories of

---

[2]Kondratieff, N.D., "Die Langen Wellen der Konjunktur," *Archiv für Sozialwissenschaft und Sozialpolitik*, Vol. 56, 1926, pp. 573–609.

Kondratieff have received limited attention or constructive contemporary research.

For those of us who have studied cycles in prices, economics,
history, political science, and social science, there is no doubt whatsoever that cycles are real, reliable, and predictable. There is no doubt
that most stock and commodity markets move in fairly regular and
demonstrable cycles and patterns. Although this premise is not widely
accepted by economists, politicians, or the public, the fact that economic history has repeated itself—not once, or twice, but many times—is
inescapable. Those who know the cycles and, moreover, their ramifications are not surprised by even the most extreme of economic events.
Rather, they are prepared, well in advance, to survive and, perhaps,
even profit during times of economic upheaval and disruption.

It is the purpose of this relatively brief but thorough analysis to
provide the reader with a descriptive analysis of the long-wave economic cycles and patterns, with an overview of the historical parallels,
with a set of guidelines to help prepare for the best and worst of times,
and with the tools necessary to arrive at a fairly reliable forecast of the
future in everything from stock prices, to interest rates, precious metals,
real estate, politics, and economic trends. In achieving these objectives
I will make every effort to be as specific as possible and to explain the
basis for each of my suggestions and conclusions. My presentation will
reach the following conclusions:

1. that the history of prices and price trends in many markets is
   repetitive and, within limits, predictable,
2. that trends are more readily predictable than are specific prices,
3. that the ability to forecast the approximate timing of a given event
   or events is considerably more important than is the ability to
   predict or forecast the exact price of a top or bottom in any given
   market or economy,
4. that economic fluctuations are influenced by the sum total of fluctuations in prices, mass psychology, and social, political, and religious phenomena,
5. that economies fluctuate in cyclical movements, the most important of which are the "long waves,"
6. that long-wave economic cycles, like all cycles, consist of several
   specific stages or phases,

7. that there are numerous social, political, and religious correlates of economic phase or stage, and

8. that there are various strategies, investment alternatives, and preparatory actions that investors and businesspeople can take in anticipation of and in preparation for the various long-wave cycle stages.

In spite of the fact that I am firmly convinced of the validity of the ideas to be presented herein, I do not expect the reader to accept my conclusions on faith. Therefore I will, throughout the course of this book, provide compelling supporting evidence—some scientific and statistical, some historical, and some anecdotal. Unfortunately, several of the ideas and theories I will discuss are still difficult or impossible to validate scientifically. The reasons for this will be explained.

Finally, I will make every effort to provide the reader with an understanding of economic and market cycles that is uncluttered by technical jargon, esoteric concepts, or arcane philosophies. Instead, I will focus on the pragmatic, the here and now, and the observable. I won't trouble your mind with debates about such things as money supply, Keynesian economics, supply-side economics, or the complex workings of the international monetary system. Ultimately we all need to know several simple facts that, as elementary as they may be, are difficult to ascertain. I will attempt to answer the following questions:

- Where do we now stand in the long-term economic picture?
- Where are world economies going?
- What can we learn from the lessons of economic history and the long-wave cycles?
- How do various markets fare in different stages of the long-wave cycles?
- Are there specific cycles and/or patterns in the major markets, and, if so, what are they?
- What evidence supports the cycles and patterns?
- What are the criticisms of the cyclic theories?
- What investment strategies have been effective in the past?
- Will they work in the future? If not, what other options do we have?
- Can government prevent or control a financial collapse and/or panic?

- How serious is the world economic situation?
- What do the next twenty-five years hold in store?
- How will each of us be affected?
- What can we do to survive and profit during the economic storms that are imminent?
- How confident can we be in our forecasts?
- Do current government actions represent the will of the people?
- Is a new economic order about to unfold, and, if so, what might be its basis?
- What are the political, social, economic, and religious correlates of the long-wave cycles, and what can they tell us about the future?
- Are we destined to experience a "new prosperity" following the end of the current long-wave downswing?

I am not an economist. I am only one of the millions whose quality of life is daily affected by the machinations of those in positions of economic and political power. I share the concern, fear, and horror that have been prompted by the ghastly and foreboding worldwide events of the past fifteen years. Yet my study of history has also taught me that the present, the past, and the future are, in many respects, one and the same. I know, therefore, that to fear the future is not rational, that to hide from the inevitable is unreasonable, and that to ignore the facts is to be unprepared. Whether rich or poor, we will all be significantly affected by the events of the next two decades, perhaps more so than has been the case since the early 1950s. It is my fervent hope that my understandings and expectations will spare my readers the financial affliction which will be unleashed by the economic plague that is now becoming pandemic.

Chapter 2

What the Waves Are All About

*. . . when the world financial crisis began so unexpectedly with the October
1929 . . . market crash, nothing turned out as expected . . .*

—Donald D. Hoppe
The Kondratieff Wave Analyst
Vol. II, #8, August 1987

It is difficult to know what inspired Samuel Benner to publish his book
of business prophecies in 1875. In fact, it's hard to know much about
the inner workings of the man whose forecasts were so incredibly
correct, and whose ideas were so revolutionary in their day. Whether
history buffs or professional economists, few individuals have ever
heard of Samuel Benner. Until recently, his book *Benner's Prophecies of
Future Ups and Downs in Prices* (1888) was out of print. I acquired my
copy fortuitously. In fact, upon seeing it for the first time, I placed it on
a bookshelf, only to leave it there gathering dust for more than ten
years. When I finally took the time to carefully study this most amazing
little book, I chastised myself for not having done so sooner. For in the
pages of this brittle 181-page volume are contained some of the most
specific and accurate forecasts ever made by any individual whose task it
was to forecast the future of business conditions and prices. One might
think that Benner had had extensive training in economics or business
to make his forecasts. In fact, he was skilled as an iron worker and raised
hogs and corn on his Ohio farm. Based on a combination of weather,
astronomy, price patterns, and historical observations, not only was

Benner's work exceptionally accurate, but it also pre-dated many of the basic concepts espoused today by those who study and apply the basics of price cycles.

On page 15 of his book, Benner wrote:

Panic

I predict that there will be great depression in general business, and many failures in the years 1876 and 1877, and that there will be a commercial revulsion, and a financial crisis in the year 1891.

The forecasts were correct. In fact, by 1880, the U.S. economy was in the throes of an economic decline that—save for brief periods of recovery, also correctly forecast by Benner—was due to last through economic lows of 1890–96. While it is certainly interesting to study the forecasts and their outcome, it is more interesting to understand the theoretical basis of Benner's work. This is best described in Benner's own words:

Theory

We have had to hunt down Price Cycles by establishing periodicity in high and low priced years; the length of the different periods in which they have repeated themselves, and by indisputable dates, facts, and figures, demonstrating their regularity.

The writer does not claim a knowledge of the causes and conditions under which they occur, and the reasons why they occur; meteorological scientists have been laboring and exploring the records of all ages to discover a Meteorological Cycle—the great desideratum of the age.

The cycles of 11 years in the price of corn and hogs, 27 years in the price of pig-iron, and 54 years in general business, can not be accounted for upon any known theory in the operations of trade. Therefore we must look elsewhere for a cause and solution of the problem.

The fact of the existence of these cycles is patent to any close observer, and as to whether any hypothesis or theory would be of practical utility when not a demonstrated and verified truth, is for the reader to determine.

We have not the daily or monthly prices for corn and hogs, so as to ascertain if there are fractions of a year in our cycles; if there should be, they would be found to be small. We know there are fractions in the cycles for pig-iron extending over four months from 1837 to 1845, and in other cycles from one to two months, but not sufficient fractions in any cycle within the past forty years, and will not be before 1891, to change the number of years in any high priced year cycle of either hogs or pig-iron.

Conclusion

In view of the immensity of the interests involved, and the magnitude of the gains or losses incurred in the advance and decline of each price and panic cycle, and the consequences of the effects upon all business and trade, well might we be surprised and astonished at the opportunities afforded for accumulation and the chances for disaster, that by rule of cycles we are compelled to predict.

It has only been a short time before the present century, that if any one had predicted the crossing of the ocean in a vessel driven by steam, or of conveying news by electric agency around the earth, over the land and under the water in advance of time, or of daguerreotyping the human face on a metallic plate by the light of the sun, and then chemically fixing it there; or of forecasting the future of the weather; production and prices by the rule of cycles as regulated by providence; such persons would have been considered visionary, their predictions regarded as contemptibly absurd; their authors the most disingenious [sic] of men, and their theories and systems treated with persecution and ridicule. [p.130]

Benner's forecasts were made possible by the use of historical price tendencies or cycles. The tendency of prices to repeat their trends with a fairly high degree of regularity is the basis of cyclic theory and analysis. In spite of their accuracy, these ideas have never been widely accepted. This, perhaps, explains why the Benner prophecies are not well known, and why his book, until recently, has remained out of print. (Now published by Robert Clarke & Co., Cincinnati, OH.)

About fifty years after the Benner prophecies were published, his basic cyclic periods were still essentially accurate, although several of his forecasts did not fare well. Figures 2.1 through 2.3 depict the Benner forecasts in various markets. It takes little thought or understanding of economics, business, or international trade to see that the periods of rise and fall in the prices and trends shown have been rhythmic. But can the Benner work be applied to other markets, to economic trends, to financial data? The work of Edward R. Dewey and many others suggests that it can.

Edward R. Dewey and his Foundation for the Study of Cycles have been a major force in the research and publication of scientifically validated cyclic studies, in everything from economics to Java tree rings. In spite of the voluminous findings supporting the existence of cycles in virtually every area of science, economics, physics, and biology, there are still very few practitioners who apply cycles in a productive

Figure 2-1. *The cycle in "pig-iron" according to Benner. This chart, taken from Benner's original work entitled* Benner's Prophecies of Future Ups and Downs in Prices, *shows his analysis of the cyclical tops and bottoms in pig-iron prices (the past) and his forecast (the future).*

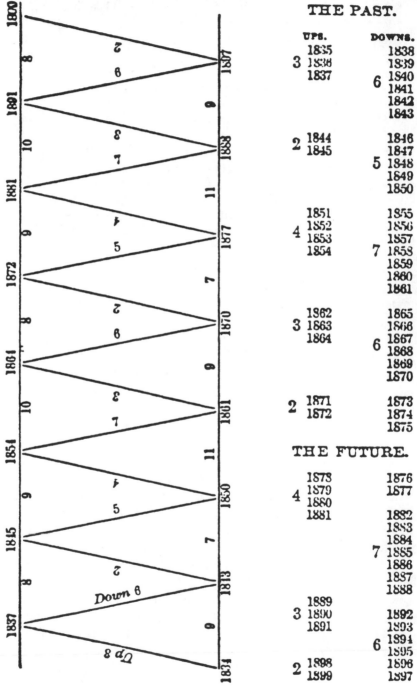

Figure 2-2. *The cycle in hog prices according to Benner. Note that the low and high years are from 5–6 years apart in a pattern of 5, 6, 5, 6, etc. The 5- and 6-year cycles added together yield a longer term 11-year cycle.*

HOGS.

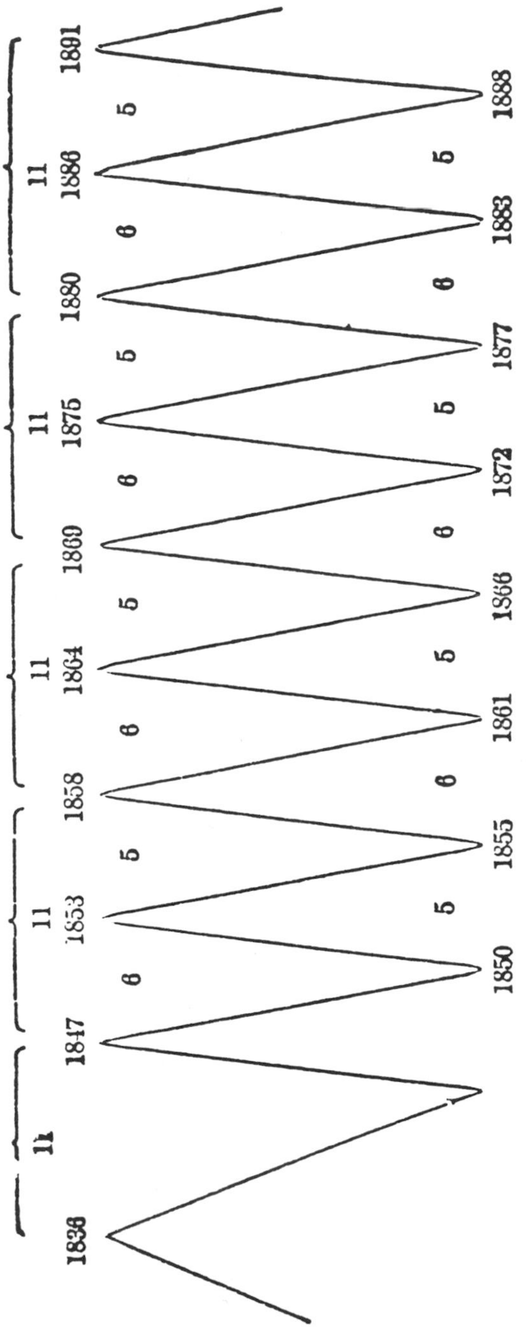

PAST.

UPS.	DOWNS.
1856	1859
1857	1860
1858	1861
1862	
1863	1865
1864	1866
1867	1870
1868	1871
1869	1872
1873	
1874	
1875	

FUTURE.

1878	1876
1879	1877
1880	
1884	1881
1885	1882
1886	1883
1889	
1890	1887
1891	1888

17

Figure 2-3. *The cycle in cotton prices according to Benner. Note that the cycle is shown as 11 years by Benner. The 11-year cotton cycle is still a viable cycle in today's markets.*

Year	Price (¢)		Year	Price (¢)	
1821	16c.		1855	8c.	
1822	16		1856	9	
1823	11		1857	12	
1824	15		1858———11——		
1825———20——			1859	11	
1826	12		1860	10½	
1827	10		1861	16	
1828	10		1862	41	
1829	10		1863	74	
1830	9		1864	1 05	11
1831	9	11	1865	57	
1832	9		1866	40	
1833	11		1867	23	
1834	12		1868	26	
1835	16		1869———29——		
1836———16——			1870	20	
1837	14		1871	17	
1838	10		1872	22	
1839	14		1873	19	
1840	8		1874		
1841	10		1875		11
1842	8	11	1876		
1843	6		1877		
1844	8		1878		
1845	5		1879		
1846	7		1880———————		
1847———10——					
1848	7				
1849	6				11
1850	11				
1851	12				
1852	8	11			
1853	9				
1854	9		1891———————		

fashion. Although this is truly unfortunate, it is, perhaps, a sign that humankind is not yet ready for cycles. Even after Van Leuweenhoek's discovery of microbes, 200 years passed before medicine could benefit from his startling discovery.

As you can see (Figures 2.1–2.3), Benner's forecasts and analyses of pig-iron, cotton, hogs, and general economic trends were highly specific. They pinpointed years during which trends were likely to reverse. If correct, Benner's theory would have far-reaching implications for business, government, economic theory, politics, and investors. Today, almost one hundred years after Benner's prophecies, cyclic analysis is still not considered a scientifically valid approach to economic analysis. In spite of highly convincing evidence in support of cycles (to be presented later in this book), cyclic forecasts frequently fall on deaf ears and cyclic theories of economic and market behavior are not the mainstay of either investors or economists.

Those economists who, through the years, have supported cyclically based theories have not found favor either with their peers or with their superiors. Yet, it is quite clear that the cycles have achieved an admirable record of predictive validity.

In order to understand the importance of cycles in economic data and in economic trends it will be necessary to cover some basic concepts relating to the theory and application of cyclical analysis and forecasting.

THE STRUCTURE OF CYCLES

The length, or period, of a cycle is measured in units of time. Generally, cycles are measured from one low point to another. A cycle of 9.6 years, therefore, refers to the tendency of a given event or variable to make lows, on average, about 9.6 years apart. In order to arrive at the 9.6-year figure, one observes and measures many individual cycles. The time length of all cycles is mathematically averaged in any of several ways. Although most cycles will be about the length of the average, some will be significantly shorter, others longer. Yet a good majority of the cycles will cluster around the average time span. Typically, when one cycle has been shorter than the norm, the next cycle or the one after the next will be a bit longer to "correct" for aberration. Some cycles are more reliable than others. Research has shown that cycles tend to cluster around certain time spans. Edward R. Dewey has isolated a number of significant time spans as prominent in many different markets and phenomena. Figure 2.4 shows some of the more popular cyclic time spans and the various markets and phenomena that

Figure 2-4. *A listing of cyclic time spans and phenomena.*

Phenomena and Current Time of Ideal Turning	
Phenomena	Current Ideal Time of Turning[a]
A. THE 16⅔-YEAR CYCLE	
Iron Prices England, 1277–1918	1958.16
Java Tree Rings, 1514–1929	1958.3
Nile Floods, A.D. 641–1451	1960.6
Arizona Tree-Rings, A.D. 900–1939	1962.4
Average	**1959.9**
B. THE 17⅓-YEAR CYCLE	
English Precipitation, 1727–1929	1963.0
New Haven Temperature, 1781–1940	1964.0
Stock Prices, U.S.A., 1831–1954	[b]1964.0
Population, U.S.A., 1790–1954	1964.5
Wheat Prices, Europe, 1500–1869	[b]1965.0
Cotton Prices, N.Y., 1731/2–1939/40	[b]1965.3
Nile Floods, A.D. 622–1962	1968.6
Saki Varves, 2295 B.C.–A.D. 1894	1969.1
Sunspots, Alternate Cycles Reversed, 1749–1938	1969.6
Average	**1965.9**
C. THE 17.7-YEAR CYCLE	
Temperature, Germany, 1884–1919	1956.85
Pig-Iron Prices, U.S.A., 1784–1951	1957.0
Arizona Tree-Rings, U.S.A., 1100–1897	1958.25
Cotton Prices, U.S.A., 1731/32–1953/54	1958.8
Bituminous Coal Production, U.S.A., 1800–1961	1960.0
Chinese Earthquakes, A.D. 54–1651	1960.16
International and Civil War Battles Inverted, 600 B.C.–A.D. 1957	[b]1962.82
Panics, 1819–1873	1963.5
Business Failures, U.S.A. 1857–1950	1964.16
Average	**1960.17**

[a]Crest (top) unless otherwise indicated.
[b]Trough (bottom).

Figure 2-4. (cont.)

D. THE 18.2- OR 18.3-YEAR CYCLE	
Marriages in St. Louis, 1886–1934	1960.0
Nile Floods, 641–1451	1960.9
An Industrial Company, 1872–1939	1961.0
Immigration, U.S.A., 1820–1962	1961.2
Sunspots, Alternate Cycles Reversed, 1749–1938	1961.4
Industrial Common Stocks, 1854–1951	1961.5
Construction in Hamburg, 1885–1935	1961.7
Real Estate Activity, 1851–1954	1961.8
A Public Utility Company, 1903–1939	1962.0
Pig-Iron (years not specified)	1962.2
Loans and Discounts (years not specified)	1962.2
Many Industrial Companies (years not specified)	1962.2
Residential Construction, 1856–1950	1962.7
Building Construction, 1830–1936	1963.1
Panics, 1819–1873	1963.5
Java Tree Rings, Inverted, 1514–1929	[b]1964.4
Average	**1962.0**

Source: Dewey, 1964.

fall within these more common time frames. Research by Dewey, Kitchin, Juglar, Schumpeter, and others suggests that about six cycle lengths appear to be particularly important. A review of these cycles along with specific examples of markets and economic phenomena falling into each category follows.

1. *The 50- to 60-Year Cycles* have received considerable attention. Lord William Beveridge in 1922 isolated an approximate 54-year cycle in European wheat prices that, with the assistance of historically re-constructed data, he traced back to the 1200s. There is evidence that 50- to 60-year cycles were present in other phenomena as well. Records of the Mayan civilization suggest that its economy fluctu-ated in approximately 50-year cycles. The Aztec Indian calendar was based on an approximate 50-year cycle. Nikolai D. Kondratieff, a man whose work will be discussed in considerable detail later, advanced the notion that capitalist economies have fluctuated on an approximate 54-year cycle. The Kondratieff cycle, long wave, or "K-Wave" (I will use the terms interchangeably) has been analyzed

Figure 2-5. *The approximate 25- to 27-year cycle in U.S. interest rates, 1857–1988. Arrows show cycle lows.*

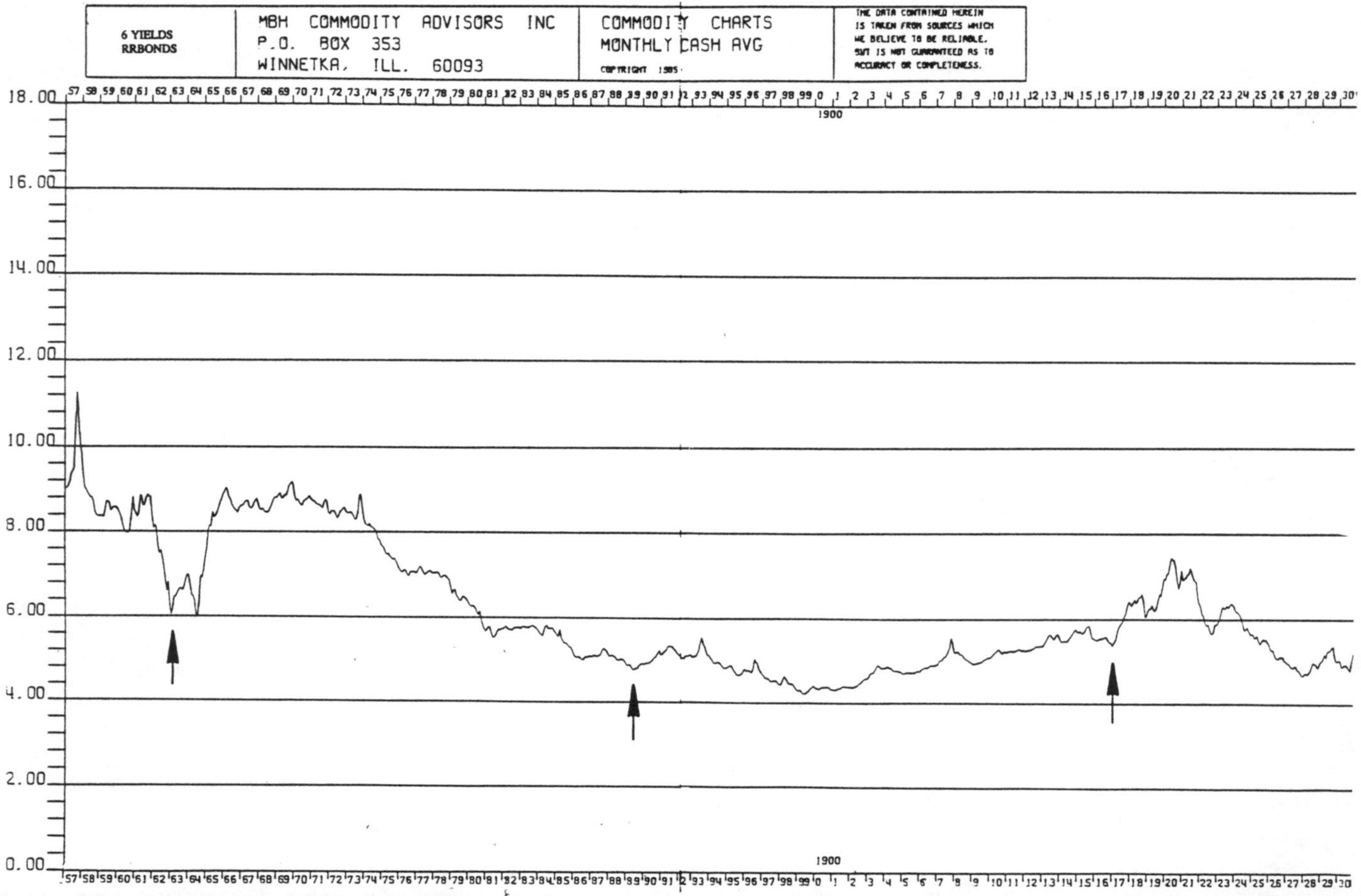

22

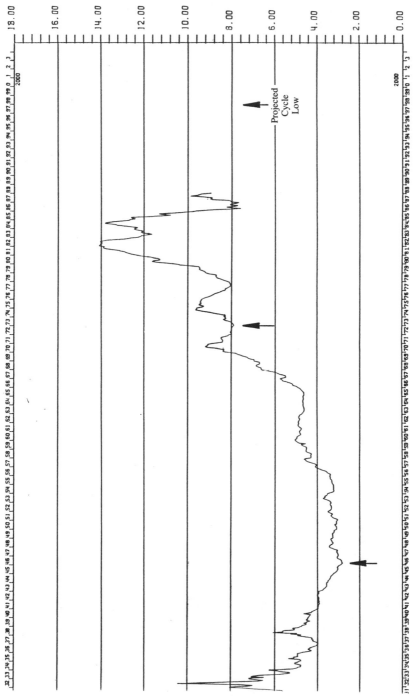

using extensive statistical modeling by Jay W. Forrester at M.I.T., who asserts that the K-Wave is, indeed, a valid and reliable cycle.

Although the approximate 50- to 60-year cycles are the most important ones we will examine, they are cycles whose existence and reliability are difficult to demonstrate statistically, for a variety of reasons. Although there are many who support the long-wave theory of Kondratieff, there are those who find fault with it for reasons that are, indeed, valid. I will discuss the challenges to this work in greater detail later.

2. *The Approximate 25- to 27-Year Cycles* are also important for long-term and economic application. They are more readily testable than the approximate 50- to 60-year cycles. You will note that the approximate 25- to 27-year cycles are about one-half the length of the approximate 50- to 60-year cycles. Corn prices, wheat prices, interest rates, and various other economic phenomena have clearly identifiable cycles of from 25 to 27 years on average, from low to low. Figure 2.5 illustrates this cycle in interest rates from 1857 through 1988. You will note how predictable and regular the cycles have been in long-term interest rates. Consider, for a moment, the immense investment value of knowing in advance the approximate time frame of major turns in interest rate trends. Can you make an educated guess as to the future course of this cycle?

3. *The Approximate 16- to 20-Year Cycles*, however, are much more important to economies and investors than are the approximate 25- to 27-year cycles. You will observe that these cycles are about one-third the length of the 50- to 60-year cycle. It is interesting to note that Dewey's Index by Cycle Length suggests the existence of 16- to 20-year cycles in more than 100 different phenomena, including such things as coffee prices, population, building construction and permits, wheat prices, temperature, weather, sunspots, interest rates, stock prices, business failures, panics, lumber prices, and so on. The ramifications of these cycles are vast. They are so important that I state categorically: *Any investor or businessperson who is not familiar with this cycle, when it made its last approximate peak, its current trend, and its projected low, is missing a highly significant piece of the economic puzzle.*

4. *The Approximate 9- to 10-Year Cycles* are not only about one-sixth the length of the 50- to 60-year cycle, but their influence is evident

in virtually every market, economy, price, and other phenomena. Whether it is the price of stocks, wheat, interest rates, beef steers, or bank deposits, this is, perhaps, the single most important grouping of cycles in the area of economics. Later, I will demonstrate the immense value of these cycles in your planning of such vital things as stock investments, real estate transactions, and borrowing. Figure 2.6 shows this cycle in U.S. long-term interest rates. Can you appreciate the value of this cycle in making major investment and mortgage decisions? Can you think of some correlates of this cycle?

Whereas the statistical significance of 50- to 60-year cycles can be questioned, the 9- to 10-year cycles have been the subject of voluminous research. The cycle in stock prices has run just slightly under 9 years, low to low, on the average. The Foundation for the Study of Cycles has documented the approximate 9-year cycle in stocks back to the year 1854. Two of the most important markets in the U.S. economy, interest rates and stock prices, have fluctuated on an approximate 9- to 10-year cycle.

5. *The Approximate 3- to 4-Year "Business Cycle"* is of considerably shorter term than any of the cycles or waves mentioned heretofore. Originally proposed and researched by Joseph Kitchin in 1923, this cycle is also called the "Business Cycle" inasmuch as it appears to exert a major influence on many components of business. The Foundation for the Study of Cycles reports cycles ranging in length from approximately 3 years to approximately 3.83 years in stock prices, automobile sales, business activity, commercial paper rates, commodity prices, bank debts, business failures, production, steel production, and sales.

The work of Kitchin was very thorough. (His statistics are shown in Figure 2.7 in their original form.) He studied prices in the United States and Great Britain from the period 1890 through 1922, discovering a cycle of approximately 3.20 to 3.36 years in length, measured from low to low. Figure 2.7A shows the Kitchin cycle in graphic form. Kitchin drew the following conclusions regarding his work:

> This statement is the result of a study, by no means confined to clearings, prices, and interest, which has covered a wide range of Great Britain and United States factors extending back to 1810 and 1860, respectively, and covering prices of commodities, trade, in-

Figure 2-6. *The approximate 9- to 10-year cycle in long-term U.S. interest rates.*

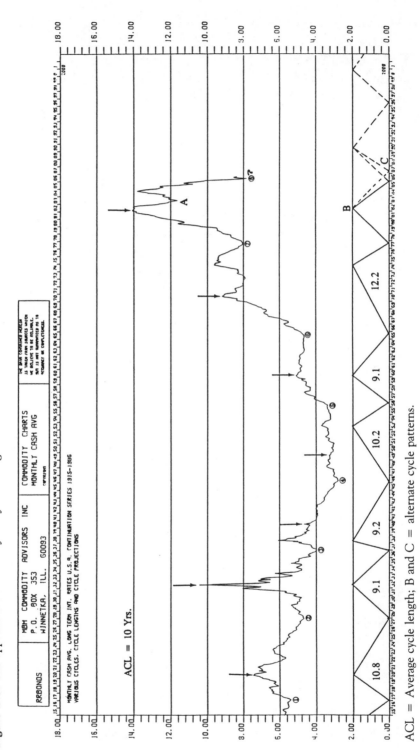

ACL = Average cycle length; B and C = alternate cycle patterns.

26

comes, wages, interest, banking, quotations of stock exchange securities, and quantity or volume figures in considerable variety, based partly on monthly data, but mainly, from the necessities of the case, on annual averages. This work has been sufficient to convince the writer that the theory can be demonstrated in the great majority of cases. [*Review of Economic Statistics*, Vol. 5, #1, 1923, pp. 10–16]

Although the approximate 3.3-year business cycle is a very important one from the standpoint of economic planning and investing, it is not the primary economic cycle. There are approximately 16 repetitions of the 3.3-year business cycle within the approximate 54-year cycle. About 6 to 8 repetitions come on the economic upswing of the long-wave 54-year cycle, and about 6 to 8 repetitions come on the downswing of the long-wave cycle. If the various cycles discussed so far were represented schematically, they would appear as shown in Figure 2.8. You can readily observe that all of the important cycles falling under the 50- to 60-year cycles are fractions of one another. In fact, even the approximate 3.3-year cycle, observable in so many markets, can be divided into approximately 4 cycles of 9 to 11 months each. The existence of cycles averaging 9 to 11 months in a great majority of futures markets is well known (see Bernstein, J., *The Handbook of Commodity Cycles*, Wiley, New York, 1982). The 9- to 11-month cycles are exceptionally regular in some markets. The meat and livestock futures markets, as well as stock prices, have shown highly reliable 9- to 11-month patterns for many years. Figures 2.9 through 2.11 illustrate the 9- to 11-month cycles in several markets. As you can see, the trader or investor who is ignorant of this cycle has missed out on some very valuable information!

Clearly, cycles are present in virtually every market. Whether used for short-term speculation, long-term investment, financial planning, or business planning, cycles should hold an important place in the analytical repertoire of every investor, speculator, or businessperson. Alas, they do not. The reasons for this will never be entirely clear to me; however, it is certain that those who should be using cycles for analysis and forecasting are not. Perhaps the greatest culprits are the governments themselves. Even in the highest levels of government there is almost a total lack of awareness of cycles, their periods, characteristics, and pragmatic applications. This is, perhaps, the single greatest reason for the compounding of economic blunders that has characterized "free-world" economics for so many years. But more about this later. Now let's take a look at the anatomy of cycles.

Figure 2-7. Kitchin's 3.20- to 3.36-year cycle—original statistics.

SCHEDULE OF MAXIMA AND MINIMA, 1890–1922

The ideal dates have their origin at the beginning of 1800, the maxima being placed 3.33 years apart and the minima midway between. Dates of minima are placed in italics. The dates of maxima and minima are years and fractions of years, representing monthly averages, except for Great Britain's prices and interest, which are end-monthly. Where virtual instead of actual monthly maxima or minima are selected, they are indicated by *.

The figures below each date are index numbers on the basis of 1900–13 = 100 for the following factors for the United States and Great Britain, respectively:

United States bank clearings—1900–13 monthly average, $11,750,000,000. Charted in units of $100,000,000.
Wholesale prices of commodities—Bureau of Labour 1900–22 as revised from 1913 (index 90 for 1900–13 on present basis of 1913 = 100), and 10 commodities 1890–99, as given in *Review of Economic Statistics*, vol. 3, p. 369, but condensed to agree approximately with Bureau of Labour annual figures.
Interest rate on 60- to 90-day commercial paper, New York—1900–13 average, 4.82 percent.

London bankers' clearing house returns—1900–13 monthly average, £1,037,000,000. Charted in units of £10,000,000.
Wholesale prices of commodities—Sauerbeck-Statist. 1900–13 average of 75.5 charted as 100.
Market rate of interest on three months' bills, London—1900–13 average, 3.26 percent.

Ideal Dates	United States Clearings	United States Prices	United States Interest	Great Britain Clearings	Great Britain Prices	Great Britain Interest
1890.00	1890.37 / 49	1890.62 / 90	1890.87 / 170	1890.54 / 69	1890.83 / 96	1890.83 / 177
1891.67	*1891.62 / 35	1892.37 / 82	1892.45 / 61	1891.62 / 49	1892.75 / 88	1892.49 / 27
1893.33	1893.04 / 51	1893.12 / 89	1893.54 / 202	1893.20 / 56	1893.16 / 91	1893.66 / 96
1895.00	1894.71 / 30	1895.20 / 74	1895.45 / 55	1894.71 / 44	1895.08 / 79	1895.57 / 17
1896.67	1895.79 / 45	1895.79 / 82	1896.79 / 178	1895.79 / 71	*1895.71 / 84	*1896.83 / 100
1898.33	1897.12 / 31	*1898.96 / 77	*1898.45 / 67	*1897.45 / 56	*1898.83 / 84	*1898.49 / 31
1900.00	1899.20 / 74	1900.20 / 93	1899.96 / 122	*1899.54 / 80	1900.58 / 101	1899.91 / 173
1901.67	1900.71 / 49	1901.45 / 88	*1902.12 / 83	1900.71 / 64	1902.00 / 91	*1902.49 / 75

Intervals in Years Between Maxima and Minima, Respectively

United States Clearings	United States Prices	United States Interest	Great Britain Clearings	Great Britain Prices	Great Britain Interest
2.67	2.50	2.67	2.66	2.33	2.83
3.09	2.83	3.00	3.09	2.25	3.08
2.75	2.67	3.25	2.59	2.55	3.17
2.41	3.76	3.00	2.74	3.75	2.92
3.41	4.41	3.17	3.75	4.87	3.08
3.59	2.49	3.67	3.26	3.17	4.00
3.59	2.92	3.75	3.50	2.67	3.84

1903.33	*1902.79 / 96	1903.12 / 96	1903.71 / 124	1903.04 / 89	1903.25 / 93	1903.75 / 121	3.91	3.34	3.33	4.00	2.49	3.08
1905.00	*1904.62 / 68	1904.79 / 92	1905.45 / 78	*1904.71 / 75	1904.49 / 92	1905.57 / 56	4.25	4.67	4.25	4.00	4.16	4.16
1906.67	*1907.04 / 128	1907.79 / 108	1907.96 / 166	1907.04 / 116	1907.41 / 109	1907.91 / 188	3.50	3.83	4.00	3.91	4.67	3.92
1908.33	1908.12 / 75	1908.62 / 100	1909.45 / 67	1908.62 / 87	1909.16 / 95	1909.49 / 37	3.00	2.41	2.83	3.25	2.84	2.92
1910.00	1910.04 / 146	1910.20 / 110	1910.79 / 115	1910.29 / 132	1910.25 / 105	*1910.83 / 134	3.59	2.75	2.67	3.00	2.41	3.00
1911.67	*1911.71 / 107	1911.37 / 105	*1912.12 / 78	1911.62 / 109	*1911.57 / 104	*1912.49 / 73	2.75	3.51	2.75	2.50	3.00	3.00
1913.33	1912.79 / 146	1913.71 / 113	*1913.54 / 126	1912.79 / 145	1913.25 / 115	1913.83 / 152	2.91	4.08	3.75	3.00	3.92	2.59
1915.00	1914.62 / 84	*1915.45 / 110	1915.87 / 62	1914.62 / 65	*1915.49 / 141	1915.08 / 46	4.17	3.91	5.17	4.33	4.24	2.74
1916.67	*1916.96 / 233	1917.62 / 210	1918.71 / 124	1917.12 / 171	*1917.49 / 239	1916.57 / 172	4.50	3.67	3.25	4.67	3.84	4.41
1918.33	*1919.12 / 220	*1919.12 / 214	1919.12 / 108	*1919.20 / 182	*1919.33 / 244	1919.49 / 97	3.00	2.75	2.08	3.08	2.84	4.59
1920.00	1919.96 / 360	1920.37 / 274	1920.79 / 166	1920.20 / 353	1920.33 / 352	1921.16 / 208	2.00	2.92	3.50	2.42	2.83	3.08
1921.67	1921.12 / 227	1922.04 / 153	1922.62 / 81	1921.71 / 254	*1922.16 / 175	1922.57 / 55						
Average interval between successive maxima 1890—1922							3.29	3.31	3.32	3.30	3.28	3.37
Average interval between successive minima 1890—1922							3.28	3.30	3.35	3.34	3.27	3.34
Average interval between successive maxima 1800—1913							3.20	3.30	3.24	3.19	3.20	3.29
Average interval between successive minima 1800—1913							3.35	3.17	3.28	3.33	3.14	3.33

Source: 1923, p. 11.

29

Figure 2-7A. *Kitchin cycle in graphic form.*

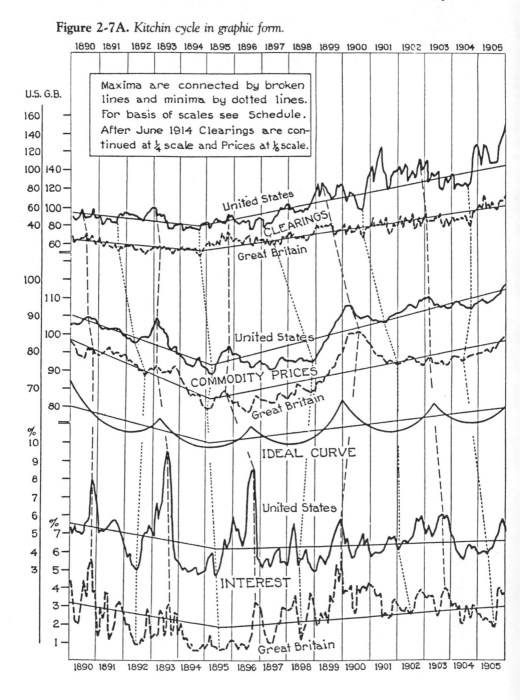

Figure 2-8. *Schematic of cycle lengths.*

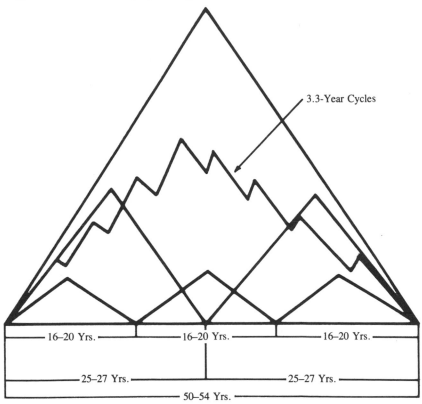

THE ANATOMY OF A WAVE

Just as biological processes exhibit specific stages of growth, so too cycles and economic waves exhibit specific characteristics and stages of growth. Biological systems begin with an initial growth stage. At first, growth is slow. Thereafter, as the organism develops, growth becomes more rapid, reaching its maximum rate of increase. A peak is reached. Growth begins to slow and eventually ceases. Biological systems begin to deteriorate. The system is no longer capable of growth; rather, it is expending all of its energy to maintain current functioning. Eventually, systems begin to falter, and functions begin to decelerate. Finally, life-support mechanisms begin to fail. The organism or system can no

Figure 2-9. *The 9- to 11-month cycle in pork bellies futures. Note the cycle counts (in months) between arrows marking the lows.*

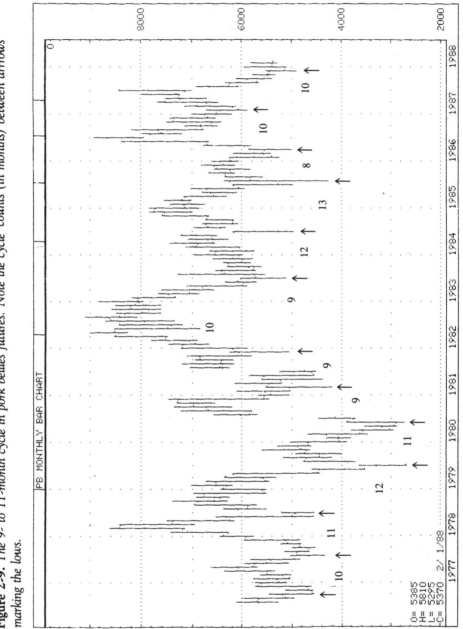

Source: Chart reprinted with permission of Commodity Quote Graphics.

Figure 2-10. *The 9- to 11-month cycle in live cattle futures. Arrows mark cyclical lows and numbers indicate time span between lows in months.*

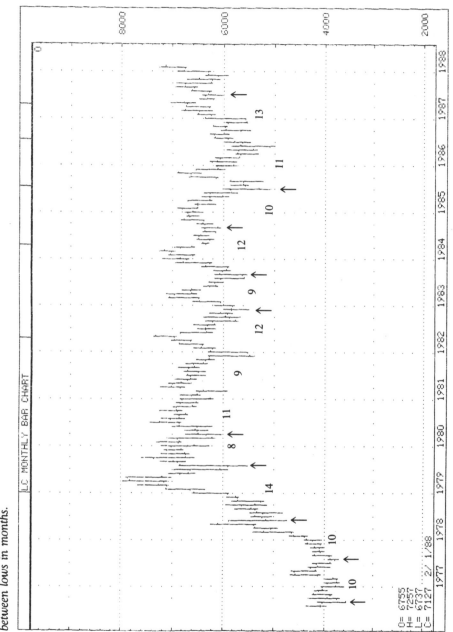

Source: Chart reprinted with permission of Commodity Quote Graphics.

Figure 2-11. The 9- to 11-month cycle in Standard and Poors Stock Index. (Arrows show lows.)

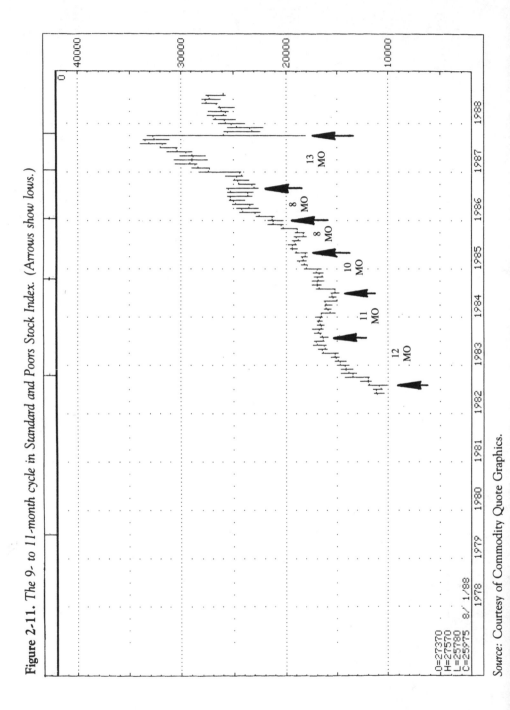

Source: Courtesy of Commodity Quote Graphics.

34

longer fight off prey or opportunistic infections. Functions come to a virtual standstill. Frequently, death is a welcome relief to the suffering.

Cycles in economic phenomena follow the same basic process as do biological cycles. The ideal cyclic price model is presented in Figure 2.12. Whether these cycles are examined in connection with economic data or price data, the fact remains that few trends in stocks, futures, options, or economies spring to life suddenly and die just as quickly. They follow a process that takes them from infancy to maturity and from maturity to old age. After old age comes death of the existing trend, a restructuring, and then rebirth in the form of another cycle. It was Kondratieff who specified the characteristics and time spans of the various cyclic phases or stages. The long-wave cycle was also studied by Van Dujin, whose work yielded slightly different results. Before I enter into a more detailed discussion of the long-wave cycles and their characteristics, let's examine some of the cyclic stages.

Figure 2.13 shows three approximate 9-year cycles in the Standard

Figure 2-12. *The nine stages of the long-wave pattern (not necessarily to time scale).*

THE STAGES OF THE LONG-WAVE PATTERN:
  STAGE 1—THE INITIAL GROWTH STAGE
  STAGE 2—THE SECONDARY GROWTH STAGE
  STAGE 3—THE RAPID ACCELERATION AND INFLATIONARY INCREASE STAGE
  STAGE 4—THE "BLOWOFF" PEAK STAGE
  STAGE 5—THE INITIAL DECLINE
  STAGE 6—THE RECOVERY PERIOD
  STAGE 7—GRADUAL DECLINE AND THE START OF SECONDARY DEPRESSION
  STAGE 8—EXTENDED DECLINE
  STAGE 9—BASE BUILDING

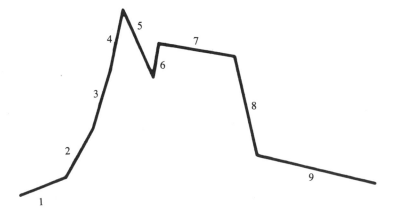

Figure 2-13. Nine-year cycle in stock index showing nine stages of the long-wave pattern. (Also see Figure 2-12.)

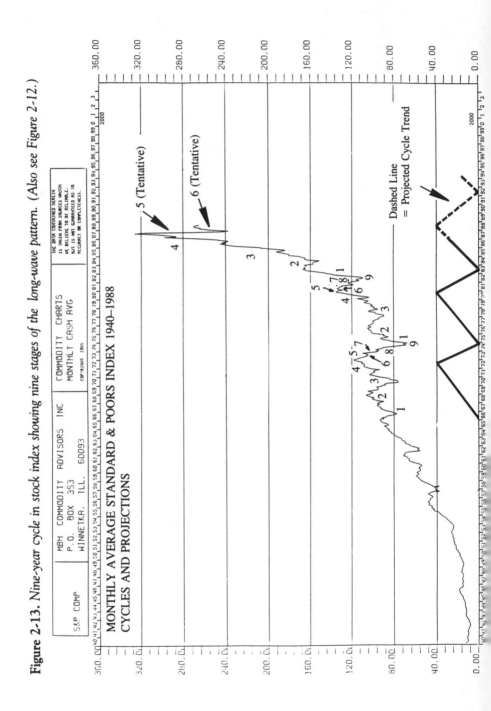

and Poors Stock Index. The cycles are divided into their approximate stages according to the ideal or model presented in Figure 2.12. Although there is no operational definition as to where the stages specifically begin and end, there are some general guidelines, to be discussed later, that relate to price, price momentum, news background, and wave form. In addition to the wave form or acceleration of price itself, there are other correlates that can be analyzed, particularly when one is studying economic cycles. The analysis does not require a degree in economics or mathematics, merely the ability to read about, listen to, observe, and integrate the many different news events of the day. It requires the ability to isolate what is important and what is not.

Now, let's take a closer look at each phase of the cycle. The following discussion refers to the nine stages shown in Figure 2.12. It should be noted at the outset that none of the above stages are rigidly defined in terms of time, length, or placement in the cycle. Transition from one stage to another is usually subtle, imperceptible, and relatively smooth. It is possible, however, to point to specific national or international events, or a series of events, economic and otherwise, that are contiguous with the start of one stage or the end of another.

Stage #1:
Initial Growth

During this stage of a cycle or economy, growth is rather slow. There is a tendency for prices to be low as a carryover from the previous cycle bottom. In the case of a given stock or market, price is relatively low compared with where it had been in recent years. If the cycle being analyzed is an economic wave, then there are a number of specific correlates: social, political, and economic. On the economic level, interest rates tend to be low, and commodity and stock prices are frequently low (*low* will be more specifically defined later). (Note that my economic comments in the analyses refer primarily to long-wave economic cycles of approximately 50 to 60 years, low to low.) Real estate and land prices tend to be low as well. Economic indicators such as the Gross National Product (GNP), Producer Price Index (PPI), and Wholesale Price Index (WPI) also tend to be lower than they have been in some time. Unemployment may still be relatively high as a carryover from the economic low period that immediately preceded this phase.

Value of the dollar (or currency) is still high in comparison with foreign currencies and as a carryover of the economic low period that has ended in the last several years.

Government is usually emerging from a conservative period and entering a more liberal phase. The succession of presidents and Congressional composition from economic low periods to the initial growth stage is usually one of conservatism to liberalism. However, during the previous economic low period, government has usually been forced to become more pro-business and liberal simply to improve business incentives; this, in turn, stimulates employment and, therefore, the economy in general. Business incentives increase, tax liability decreases, regulations are relaxed, and controls are reduced across a broad front.

Social attitudes are slow to become more liberal. Typically such things as negative attitudes toward birth control, strict abortion laws, and racial discrimination, tend to continue as they did during the previous economic decline. Very gradually there is a move toward relaxation of conservative attitudes and opinions. In addition, a gradual decline in religious practice begins to develop.

The directions set into motion during the last stage of the previous cycle and Stage #1 of the current cycle tend to continue. To a certain extent it would be possible to determine the current stage of a long-term cycle merely by examining the major social, political, and economic issues at any given point in time. This will become more evident to you as you progress through the chapters of this book.

Stage #2:
Expansion and Secondary Growth

In the case of a specific stock or other type of market, the secondary growth or expansion phase is marked by an expansion of price range. In other words, prices begin to fluctuate more widely. Stock and futures price movements are generally larger from one time period to the next (*i.e.*, day to day or week to week), and the amount of participation or trading volume increases as more investors are drawn to the market. This shows an increase in demand, which is usually followed by an increase in price, assuming that supply lags behind increasing demand.

The long-wave economic cycle, Stage #2 is also characterized by expansion and broader participation in the business and public sectors.

The public is not generally concerned with ideas of inflation, as growth is slow and steady. Unemployment has usually started to decrease, and interest rates are slowly beginning to inch higher along with GNP (Gross National Product), PPI (Producer Price Index), and CPI (Consumer Price Index). The amount of capital available for borrowing at reasonably low rates is plentiful. Expansion in virtually any industry is possible at a reasonable cost. Social attitudes begin to liberalize very gradually. Government is still responsive and friendly to business; however, the initial seeds of labor discontent are now being sown. Yet Stage #2 does not ensure economic growth. There have been periods of economic contraction during Stage #2. This stage can be, and has been, somewhat unpredictable. Considerable economic "push-pull" is typical in Stage #2. Stage #2 recessions are not uncommon.

During this stage, and during the latter portion of Stage #1, the role of scientific innovations becomes particularly important. In the 1950s, for example, atomic power and a variety of chemical processes developed in the latter part of the 1930s Depression era became important in industrial development. Rocket technology developed during World War II became the core of the American and Soviet space programs. Other examples will be presented later, when my analysis of each stage is more specific. Some theorists have suggested that scientific innovations are the stimulus for new economic growth.

In general, this stage offers long-term investors the most promising opportunities. This is when real estate, stock, land, and most businesses offer "ground floor" opportunities. The potential for profit is greater than it was in Stage #1. The cost of doing business is still sufficiently low to permit a variety of opportunities. Yet, in spite of what seems to be reasonably obvious, all but the most visionary individuals are unwilling to take risk. They would rather wait until "things are clearly better" to take a chance. By the time success appears more certain, however, there is more risk, and the economic peak is closer. Most individuals are still recovering from recent losses and extended economic contraction to take risk without clear and virtually guaranteed success.

It is also during this stage that social mores, attitudes, and opinions begin to move in a more liberal direction. The seeds of liberal social movements are being sown. The days of sexual revolution, equal rights, self-awareness, alternate religious practice, and truly free speech have arrived.

Stage #3:
Rapid Acceleration and Inflationary Increase

Rapid acceleration and inflationary increase mark Stage #3. Inflation becomes a more serious issue as virtually all prices begin to increase. Labor gains a significant amount of power, while business continues to expand. Labor begins to realize less buying power from more wages due to inflation, and there is more labor discontent as well as an increase in union membership. Unions begin to wield more power. Business gladly makes concessions to labor, since profits are expanding. The reasoning of business is logical; it needs employees on the job to meet demand for its products. Every day lost from the job is a day of lost profits. Therefore, negotiations are quick, and labor gets most of what it wants. Everybody seems to get what he or she wants at the expense of the consumer. Issues begin to heat up. Labor continually wants more, while industry begins to feel that too much is being taken. As commodity prices continue to rise during this stage, profit margins decrease. Business leaders soon realize that they have painted themselves into a corner. They cannot cut costs by paying less for their raw products. They must pay whatever the market demands. Even if they have done an excellent job in advance purchases of their goods at lower prices, they will eventually need to come into the open market to buy more goods. Wholesale prices remain high. Wages cannot be significantly reduced, or unions will call for a strike. Employees cannot be laid off or fired; the unions have become too strong. Industry has no choice but to once again pass increased costs along to the consumer. Consumers begin to feel the pinch. They demand higher wages, and again business is squeezed for more money. The vicious cycle continues.

On a social level, discontent continues to grow. Liberal movements have now adopted anti-establishment attitudes. The split between social classes becomes more severe. Ethnic groups are more willing to express their discontent. Factions of all manners and sorts begin to protest in favor of their individual causes.

Political developments are also significant. Government has become ultra-liberal, taking on massive debt through social welfare programs, national improvement programs, and increased military spending. Government goes into debt by printing more money. Yet this is not necessarily the evil that will ultimately cause serious economic woes. Rather, a multiplicity of factors and events will take their toll.

In the meantime, seeds of war have been sown. Slowly but surely, many nations are beginning to prepare for war as international conflict and tensions mount. Each long-wave cycle in the U.S. economy has been marked by the so-called "top war." The top wars since the 1790s have been the War of 1812, the Civil War, World War I, and the Vietnam War. As you can see, not all of the top wars have been international in scope. Yet they have all had in common one element in addition to conflict, killing, and destruction: They have all been unpopular wars. In other words, they have been wars generally unsupported by the public. The timing of top wars is not precise. They do, however, tend to come close to the top of the economic cycle.

The behavior of stocks or other markets (as opposed to an economy) is less complex during Stage #3. It is during this time frame in the cycle that prices begin to accelerate rapidly. The momentum of the given stock, commodity, or market increases rapidly. It is also typical for public opinion to be exceptionally positive or bullish regarding the future. Upon close examination of price, however, the analyst will clearly see that inflation has taken hold, that price and underlying value are clearly out of adjustment, that value is much lower than price. Yet there is sufficient momentum to force prices higher. Reason, good sense, rational economics, and conservative investment planning have taken a back seat to mob psychology, greed, and the fear of being left out of a major upmove in prices.

Stage #4:
"Blowoff" Peak

The key features of this stage are panic buying, very rapid price increases, and peaks in many segments of the economy. This is the most dramatic of times in many years. Events worldwide and domestically are moving at a rapid pace. It seems as if everything affects the economy. In short, a crisis is developing. There are numerous characteristics of prices, markets, society, religion, politics, and economics during this stage. They will be discussed in considerably greater detail later; for now, however, the following relatively brief discussion will suffice. On a political level, government has typically been liberal at or during the blowoff top, followed by a more conservative government after the top.

I remind you once again that the various scenarios presented herein are ideal. There is no one long-wave economic cycle that will conform to the ideal stages 100 percent of the time. In the most recent cycle, for example, there were some fairly lengthy periods of time that did not conform precisely to expectations of the ideal model. In 1958, a year during which Stage #2 growth was ideally supposed to be in process, the economy was weak. There are many other specific examples of deviations from the norm. A good number of these will be mentioned. The essence of this ideal analysis is to provide you with a structure of long-wave economic cycle phases. Once this has been done, I will outline the similarities and differences between what is expected and what actually occurs. If you understand the ideal structure and aspects of each cyclic phase, you will be able to evaluate each situation individually, recognizing what is merely a temporary deviation from the norm and what is a more serious or lasting deviation from the long-term trend. The weak economy of the late 1950s and early 1960s would have been seen as a temporary phase, one likely to reverse itself within several years as prices returned to their upward trend in line with the long-wave cycle.

Society is also in a state of considerable agitation during Stage #4. There is often marked polarization of attitudes and opinions. In the early 1970s, for example, just prior to the blowoff peak in commodity prices, there were "hard-hat riots" on Wall Street as the American working class attacked students, because students were viewed as liberals or radicals in favor of destructive change. These changes were perceived as a threat to the recently found prosperity of the working class. Tensions are brought about by affluence and the threat or fear of its withdrawal. As it becomes clear that prosperity may end because of reckless government policies, high interest rates, and high retail prices, public protests increase, and with them social unrest.

It does not necessarily follow, however, that stock market prices are at their peak. In fact, it has been fairly typical for stocks to peak a number of years after peaks in commodity prices and the economy. The 1929 peak in stock prices was preceded by a 1919–21 peak in commodity prices. The 1987 peak in stock prices was preceded by a 1974 peak in commodity prices.

It is also at this time that liberal social attitudes are at their peak. Study the 1970s and you will recall the moves to legalize marijuana, the liberalization of abortion laws, the sexual revolution, major advances in civil rights and women's rights, and so on. Just as the 1970s were an era of liberal social mores and attitudes, the "Roaring '20s" preceded the stock market crash of 1929, and an era of liberalism preceded the economic peak of 1864.

As I've stated previously, this is the most dramatic and violent period in the long-wave cycle. Though there are many problems, concerns, fears, and panics to follow, Stage #4, the blowoff, is the most volatile. A sense of the extreme price volatility associated with this stage can be obtained by an examination of Figures 2.14 through 2.16. You can readily observe that the price volatility during Stage #4 overshadows virtually everything seen for many years previous.

Stage #5:
Initial Decline

The excesses and unrest of the blowoff stage are followed by an initial sharp decline and recession. After the extremes that are so common in Stage #4, the initial recession comes almost as a welcome relief. The initial decline is a response to the top war. Stage #5 recessions have occurred in the U.S. economy after the Seven Years War (approximately 1766), The War of 1812, the Civil War, World War I, and the Vietnam War. It is most peculiar that during the top period of each cycle there has been a political scandal, often reaching into the highest levels of government. During the time frame of the 1760s and the Seven Years War, Patrick Henry was accused of treason after protesting the royal disallowance of Colonial Laws. Following the 1814 economic peak, the Federalist Party was accused of treason for protesting the War of 1812 and, as a consequence, lost the election of 1816. The 1864 economic peak was followed by the impeachment of President Andrew Johnson in 1868. The Teapot Dome scandal came on the heels of the 1920 economic peak, and President Richard M. Nixon was forced out of office in 1974 following the Watergate scandal.

Stage #4, the initial decline, is more than a mere reaction to the excesses of the top war and the period of inflation that usually precedes it. It has almost always been a harbinger of deflation, a warning that the economic top has been seen, an advance indication that investors should prepare for bad times ahead—times that will ultimately end in the "bottom war." But well before the bottom war, a period of panic, disinflation, and/or depression is likely to occur.

The reader should note that about fifty-one years previous to the economic peak of approximately 1764 in the U.S. colonies came the

Figure 2-14. *Blowoff top in sugar prices at Stage #4, 1974.*

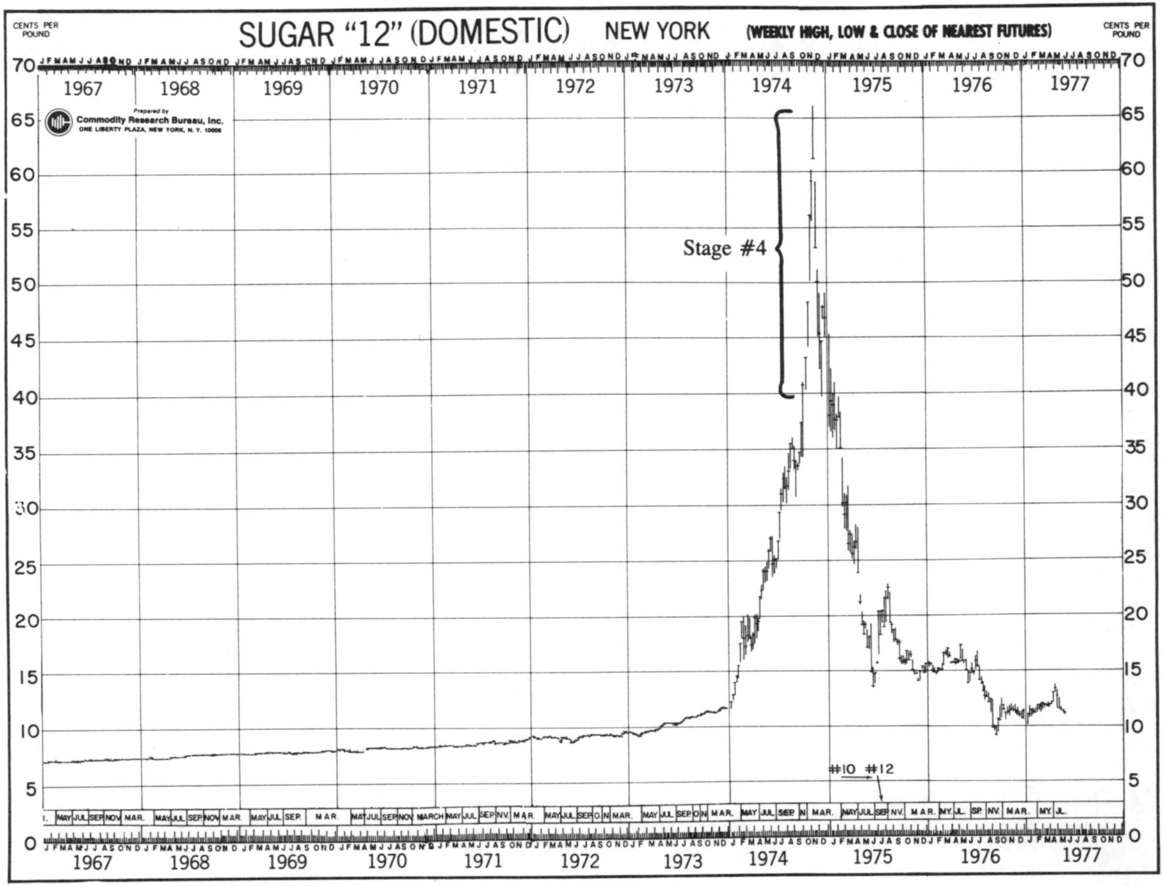

Source: Reprinted with permission of Commodity Research Bureau.

War of Spanish Succession, which ended in 1713. A long-wave cycle decline started, continuing through approximately 1735. Subsequent to the initial economic recession in the 1708–10 time frame in British America, a brief recovery took place, only to be followed by a general disinflation through the 1735–45 time frame. Approximately fifty years following the 1735–45 economic low came the lows of the late 1780s in America.

Stage #6:
Recovery Period/Top Test

In the U.S. economy it has been typical for a period of recovery to follow the initial decline of Stage #5. A recession followed the Seven Years War, after which a period of recovery preceded the American Revolution. A Stage #6 recovery was also seen after the War of 1812. The Era of Good Feelings was a Stage #6 recovery, as was the Reconstruction period following the Civil War. The "Roaring '20s" recovery followed the 1920 economic peak, and the greatest bull market in American history followed the economic peak of approximately 1974.

During the period of recovery, or top test, government becomes acutely aware of the existing economic crisis. By now the economic disease has usually become chronic, and it is difficult to know what steps are appropriate. In the interim, there has usually been a move toward trade protectionism. The feeling is prevalent that foreign competition is to blame for domestic economic problems. Clearly, in the current cycle we blame the Japanese for their "unfair" practices in virtually every business from automobiles to computer chips. As domestic economic woes intensify, there is frequently a trend toward increased trade protectionism and tariff legislation. Whether this takes the form of Congressional action (as it has usually done) or the form of permitting U.S. dollar debasement (this would mean that foreign goods could not compete as effectively), the fact remains that protectionism occurs on various levels. Specifics of efforts to legislate against foreign competition will be given later. This period has also witnessed consumer boycotts of foreign goods.

Various attempts are made to regulate money supply, interest rates, domestic spending, and the tax structure. Ultimately, the net effect is a move toward conservatism.

Social tends change dramatically. In the 1980s we saw a clear shift in attitudes, mores, and behavior. The sexual revolution of the 1960s

Figure 2-15. *Blowoff top in pig-iron prices previous to economic tops of 1814 and 1864, A and B respectively.*

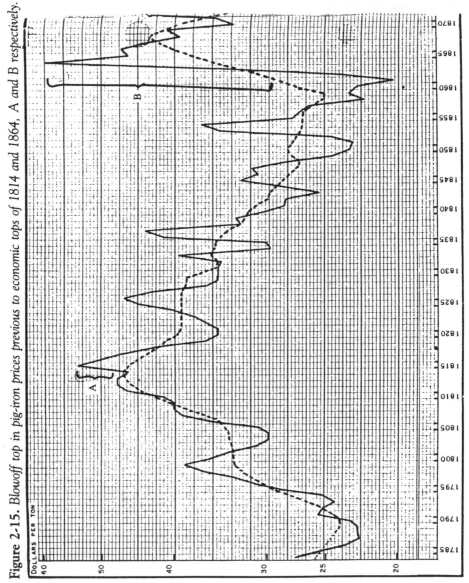

Source: Dewey, p. 546.

46

Figure 2-16. *Blowoff top in wrought-iron prices prior to 1764 economic peak.*

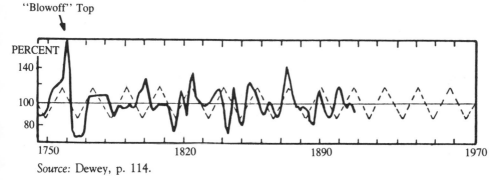

Source: Dewey, p. 114.

and 1970s is a relic of the past. Strong voices are being raised against homosexuality. The AIDS epidemic has caused sexual behavior to change markedly from casual to greater selectivity and increased monogamy.

Composition of the U.S. Supreme Court has slowly changed. In the late 1980s, the Court was dominated by conservative judges. New right-wing voices are being heard every day. It has become increasingly difficult for labor to triumph over business. Business can no longer afford to pay the price as profits begin to diminish partially as a result of the seemingly excessive demands of labor. Strikes are longer lasting and more violent. Concessions to labor are slowly but surely diminishing. A wave of conservatism is clearly and unmistakably sweeping the United States and the balance of the capitalist world, as the economic "recovery" is clearly falling short of the previous economic peak. The top is being tested, but the test is not being passed.

Stage #7:
Gradual Decline and Start
of Secondary Depression

Following the recovery period and unsuccessful tests of the economic peaks of previous economic cycles, the economy usually slides into a period of decline, disinflation, and eventual depression. This is the most difficult time for the economy, the public, government, and individual markets. At first, prices begin to drop slowly. Demand declines, wages decline, unemployment increases, bankruptcies increase, banks fail, and interest rates decline persistently. Commodity prices fall across a broad front. Farmers suffer as prices for their goods drop almost without hiatus. The decline can erase as much as 80 percent of the previous long-wave gains. Figure 2.17 will give you an idea of how severe a decline was seen in farm prices during the last disinflationary period. Figures 2.18 through 2.20 show Stage #7 declines in various markets. Take some time to study these charts. You will observe that the declines are persistent, severe, and precipitous. Prices tend to lose from 75 percent to 80 percent of their value by the time Stage #7 has drawn to a close.

Figure 2-17. *Prices paid to farmers 1910–1933. Note comparison of 1920 and 1933.*

| Index Numbers of Prices Paid to Farmers for Food in the United States, 1910–33* 1910–14 = 100 | | | | | | | | | | | | |
Year	Jan.	Feb	Mar.	Apr.	May	June	July	Aug.	Sept.	Oct.	Nov.	Dec.	Average
1910...	104	105	107	108	105	103	101	101	102	100	99	98	103
1911...	99	94	91	88	87	87	90	93	92	92	94	95	92
1912...	96	99	99	102	105	104	102	101	98	98	97	97	100
1913...	95	97	99	100	99	101	102	100	100	103	104	105	100
1914...	105	105	105	103	103	105	105	105	108	106	105	105	105
1915...	107	111	109	107	112	112	106	104	101	101	103	102	106
1916...	106	111	111	112	116	117	116	117	124	128	138	143	117
1917...	142	152	165	173	200	202	191	192	187	191	191	190	181
1918...	193	195	199	195	202	195	198	204	204	206	206	209	200
1919...	211	205	201	211	230	230	229	227	209	199	203	206	213
1920...	215	217	216	219	233	241	234	218	208	198	183	160	207
1921...	155	146	139	130	124	120	121	128	124	122	120	119	130
1922...	116	117	123	121	126	128	125	119	115	118	123	126	121
1923...	125	123	124	124	128	128	124	120	124	123	122	121	124
1924...	119	120	117	118	120	121	125	131	130	135	137	140	126
1925...	148	146	150	148	151	154	157	158	150	149	159	159	152
1926...	157	156	154	158	161	161	156	147	148	148	151	150	154
1927...	145	145	142	143	146	149	148	145	146	147	147	145	145
1928...	143	142	143	147	157	156	156	151	154	148	146	143	149
1929...	141	146	150	149	152	154	158	159	156	153	151	147	151
1930...	145	143	137	139	137	136	124	121	126	120	117	108	129
1931...	104	97	99	100	96	91	89	88	84	80	83	74	89
1932...	70	67	68	66	64	61	67	67	65	61	61	57	64
1933...	54	51	53	58	70								

*Warren, G. F. and Pearson, F. A., Farm, Wholesale, and Retail Prices of Food in the United States, Farm Economics No. 42, p. 616, February 1927.

The commodities were weighted in the following manner: corn, 5; wheat, 16; rye, 1; oats, 1; potatoes, 4; chickens, 4; eggs, 9; milk, 10; butter, 11; veal calves, 2; beef cattle, 17; sheep, 1; lambs, 1; and hogs, 18. The prices paid to producers are those reported by the United States Department of Agriculture, except for milk, which is the net pool price of 3.7 percent milk at Utica, New York.

Source: Warren and Pearson, p. 187.

Figure 2-18. *The Stage #7 crash in corn prices.*

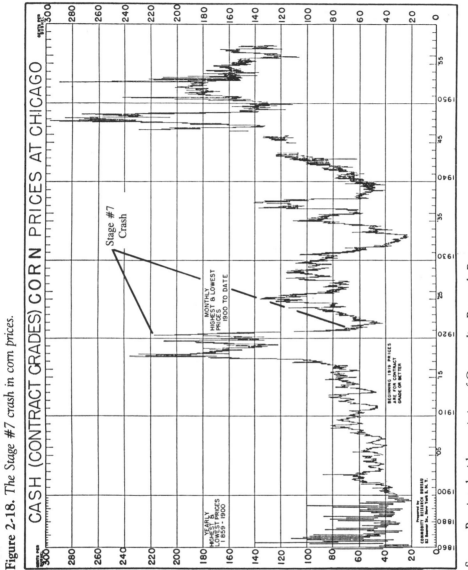

Source: Reprinted with permission of Commodity Research Bureau.

Figure 2-19. *The Stage #7 crash in silver prices.*

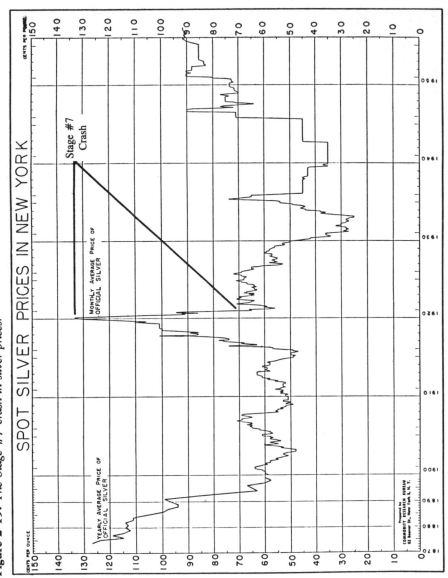

Source: Reprinted with permission of Commodity Research Bureau.

Figure 2-20. *Two Stage #7 crashes in cotton prices.*

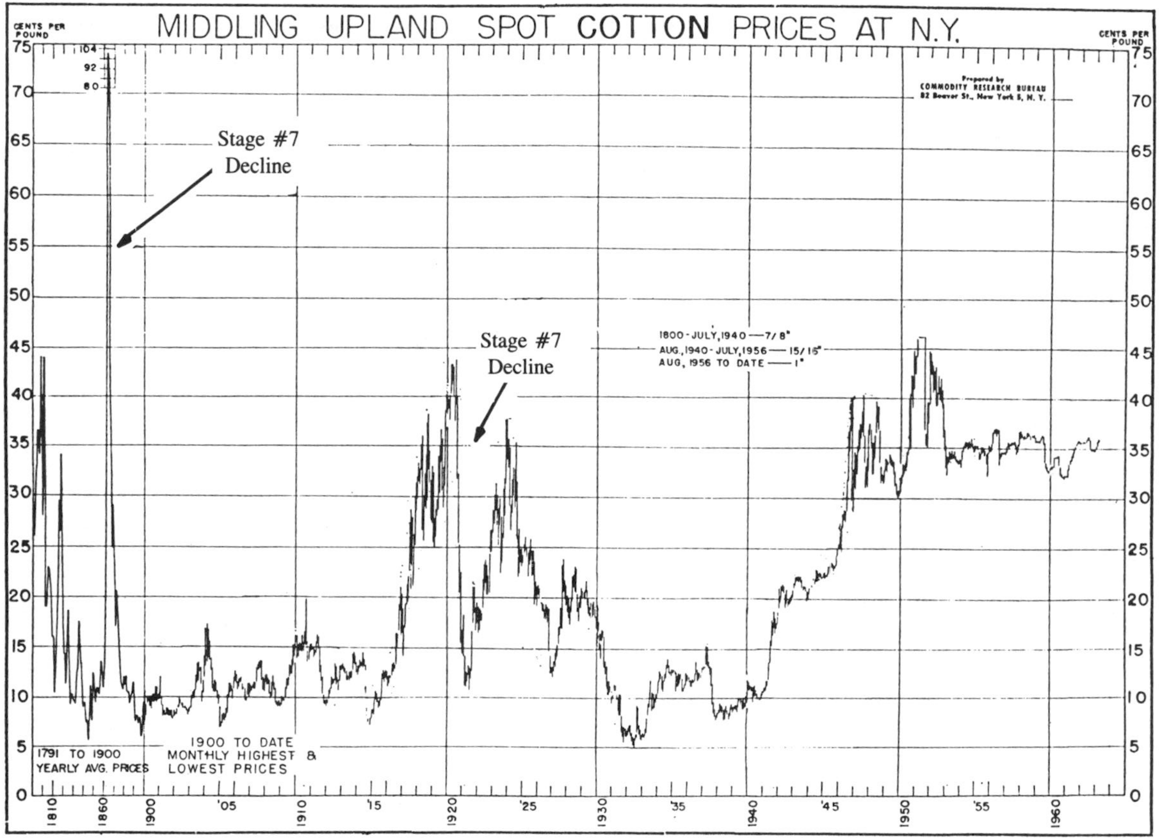

MIDDLING UPLAND SPOT COTTON PRICES AT N.Y.

Source: Reprinted with permission of Commodity Research Bureau.

Stage #8:
Extended Decline

After the secondary decline has taken hold, bringing persistent price deterioration in most markets, the downmoves tend to slow in magnitude but often continue for a period of years. The precise length of Stage #8 is not fixed. It can be fairly short (perhaps several years), or it can run for as long as ten years. During this stage the economy is recovering from the panics, bankruptcies, and severe economic contraction of the previous phase. In fact, Stage #8 is actually a continuation of Stage #7. The only perceptible difference is that the decline tends to slow, and that recoveries are typically shorter.

Social attitudes, opinions, and behavior during this stage continue to reflect increased conservatism. Religious practice is likely to be on the upswing. There is a "return to basics" attitude throughout the country, as people are forced to adjust to a more simple lifestyle, one uncomplicated by the availability of surplus capital or extravagant needs.

Political struggles continue as various efforts are made to solve the problems of recession, disinflation, and/or depression. There is a tendency for isolationism to increase. This trend will eventually lead the country into a war (known for the purposes of this analysis as the "bottom war").

Virtually all prices continue on the downswing. Interest rates continue to decline. Money is no longer in great demand, since expansion is no longer a source of demand. Few individuals or firms are willing to go into debt, inasmuch as the perceived incentive to do so is minimal. Few industries flourish, and many businesses fail. Eventually, the dark days of this stage bring with them increased conflict—at times domestic, more often international.

A most interesting aspect of Stage #8 is the fact that technological discoveries made during this period are often those which help fuel the next long-wave upswing. More about this later.

Stage #9:
Base Building

The last stage of the long-wave cycle has had its unique characteristics as well. Though it is commonly believed that prices at the end of the long-wave cycle stagnate, moving sideways for many years, this is not necessarily the case. Figures 2.21 through 2.24 show on a number of

Figure 2-21. *Stage #9: base building in cash wheat prices, 1928-1932.*

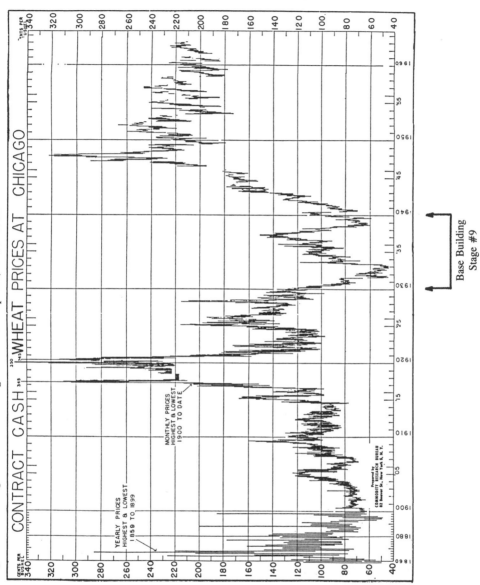

53

Figure 2-22. *Stage #9: base building in bond yields during the economic low period of 1893–1899.*

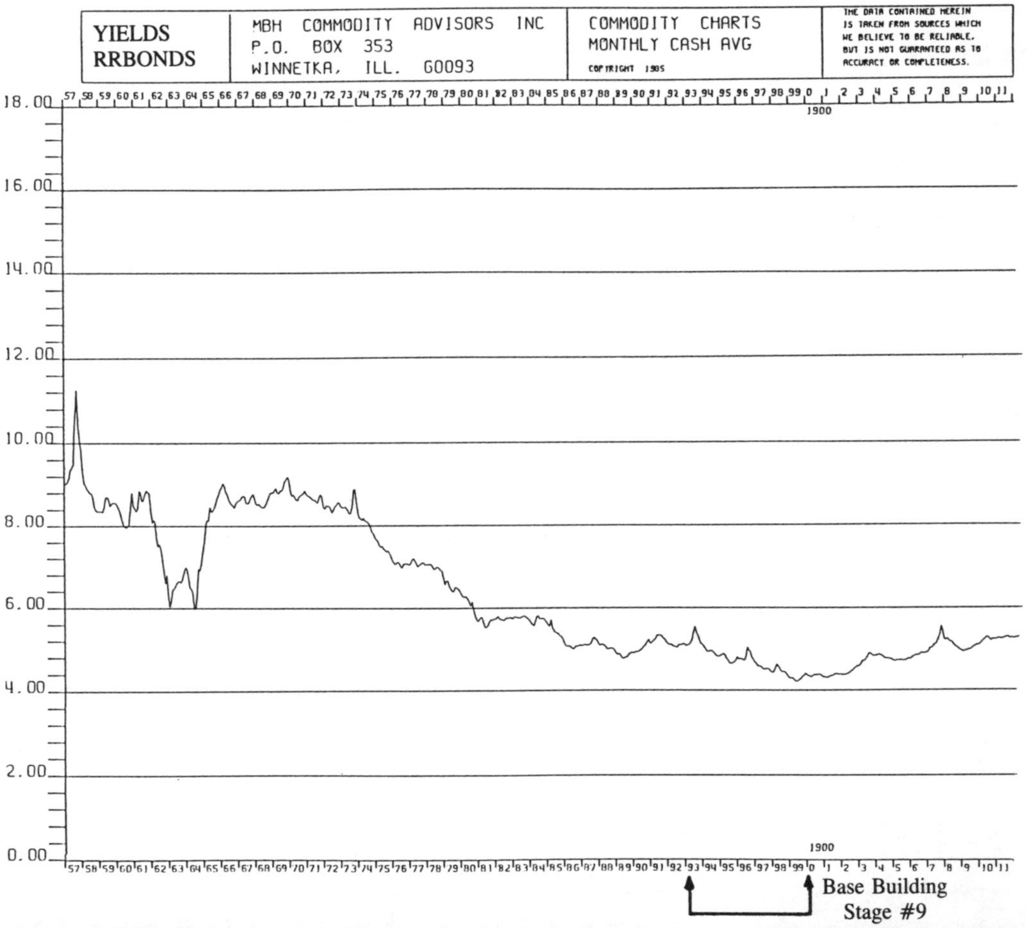
YIELDS
RRBONDS
MBH COMMODITY ADVISORS INC
P.O. BOX 353
WINNETKA, ILL. 60093
COMMODITY CHARTS
MONTHLY CASH AVG
COPYRIGHT 1985
THE DATA CONTAINED HEREIN IS TAKEN FROM SOURCES WHICH WE BELIEVE TO BE RELIABLE, BUT IS NOT GUARANTEED AS TO ACCURACY OR COMPLETENESS.
18.00
16.00
14.00
12.00
10.00
8.00
6.00
4.00
2.00
0.00
1900
Base Building
Stage #9

Figure 2-23. *Stage #9: base building in stock prices during economic lows of 1893–1898.*

different markets, focusing on Stage #9. Note that I've included markets not only from the last economic lows, but from previous economic lows as well. Observe the relative absence of a lengthy sideways period.

As previously indicated, Stage #9 has frequently ended with a war. It is both functional and symbolic that the final and lowest stage of the long-wave cycle should end with a war: functional since it stimulates the economy, symbolic in its destruction of the "old" order. The Revolutionary War ended the long-wave cycle that bottomed in the 1780s. The Mexican–American War came near the economic lows of 1843. The Spanish–American War came with the economic lows of 1896, and World War II came near the economic lows of the late 1930s.

Figure 2-24. *Stage #9: base building in copper prices during economic lows of 1843–1850.*

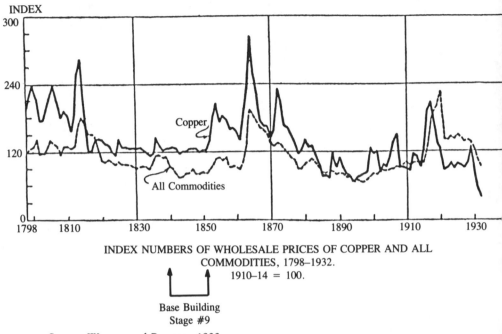

INDEX NUMBERS OF WHOLESALE PRICES OF COPPER AND ALL
COMMODITIES, 1798–1932.
1910–14 = 100.

Base Building
Stage #9

Source: Warren and Pearson, 1933.

Typically the bottom wars have been popular wars. In other words, they have been wars supported by the American public, whereas the top wars have not had a great deal of public support. Top wars are seen as ending prosperity, whereas bottom wars are seen as ending depression or recession. Bottom wars have come as a relief to the long period of depression or disinflation that preceded them. What's next?

Following the bottom war, there is a return to Stage #1. As in every one of the stages outlined in the preceding pages, there are no rigid starting and/or ending dates. At times the transition from one stage to another is rapid and easily discernible; at other times it is gradual and virtually imperceptible. I caution the reader not to form rigid generalizations about any of the stages. Every cycle is different, though it tends to follow the same basic patterns. Every cycle in every market is different from every previous cycle; however, there are sufficient similarities to allow forecasts, reasonable generalizations, and, most important, long-range investment planning.

As I have previously indicated, however, those who make an effort to examine current trends and economic events in the light of historical trends and economic events are those who will benefit from the application of long-wave economic theory. Although the controversy about whether long-wave economic cycles exist will continue indefinitely, those who employ long-wave theory in making important economic decisions are convinced that the long-wave cycles are as real as they could possibly be. Certainly, the late 1980s through the mid-1990s will serve as a strong statement in favor of the long-wave theory, or as further fuel to the fires of controversy that have enveloped long-wave economic theory since before the days of Kondratieff.

Now that I've given you a general picture of the long-wave cycle stages, structure, and correlates, we can examine the evidence supporting the long-wave cycles.

Chapter 3

Statistical Evidence
Supporting the Long-Wave Theory

Never before has American business been as firmly entrenched for prosperity as it is today. Steel's three biggest customers, the automobile, railroad and building industries, seem to me to justify a healthy outlook. . . . Stocks have crashed, but that means nothing to the welfare of business. . . . Wealth is founded on the industries of the nation, and while they are sound, stocks may go up and stocks may go down, but the nation will prosper.

—Charles M. Schwab
Chairman, Bethlehem Steel Corporation
December 10, 1929

Modern social science is a discipline that demands statistical evidence in support of theories and hypotheses. Psychology, sociology, and, in particular, economics have achieved the level of quasi-sciences partially as a result of numerous techniques designed to confirm or negate claims and theories. Wherever possible, such statistical procedures as Chi Square, F-Test, Bartels Test, Standard Deviation, Correlation, and others are applied to the collected data in order to arrive at a level of confidence or significance to support or reject the theory being tested. Statistical data will either support the hypothesis, negate it, lead researchers in another direction, or confirm part or parts of the theory. Where a host of variables is concerned, a family of procedures termed "factor analysis" can be applied to the data in order to weigh the numerous variables according to their individual or collective influence(s). Computer analysis of data is the contemporary standard. There are numerous statistical programs supplied by various programming concerns. They are designed specifically for objective analyses of data gathered by social scientists.

Given the state of "sophistication" in the fields of psychology, sociology, political science, and economics, one might certainly expect a concomitant increase or improvement in results and pragmatic applications. However, reality does not seem to justify the expense of conducting the voluminous research, nor does the research appear to have improved the lot of the average citizen. For all of its theories, sociology has not brought visible or lasting changes to the plight of the urban poor in America or other large urban centers of the so-called free world. Poverty in America is still shocking, embarrassing, and totally unacceptable. Crime in America continues to increase in spite of costly research conducted by criminologists and psychologists.

Political self-interest and irresponsibility continue to be the dominant attributes of bureaucracies throughout the world. Corruption in every level of government is now the standard; it is justified as an unavoidable byproduct of modern political institutions, regardless of ideology or political affiliation. Many of the advances in social science are not implemented by corrupt governments. Consider, for example, mental illness in America which is a chronic and growing problem; still, it goes essentially untreated in those who do not have the financial means to buy individual psychotherapy, and even then the prognosis for a lasting cure is poor.

World economies are in a state of upheaval that pales all previous economic trends and events. Currency relationships and fluctuations are at their highest level of volatility in economic history. Yet, in spite of the fact that world economies are in a state of turmoil, ivory-tower professors and "think tank" scholars sit in their padded cells, surrounded by expensive computers, reams of data, theories and hypotheses galore, and little to show in the way of pragmatic results.

But perhaps I am being too harsh. Perhaps I am judging academia too severely. It's not fair to condemn the achievements of an entire group without giving credit where credit is due. Is it not true that some social scientists have contributed meaningful research of a pragmatic nature? Yes, it is true. But they are few and far between. Perhaps only a handful of studies and a fewer number of academicians have earned my respect for meaningful contributions to American society. And even in these cases, the implementation of their well-documented and statisti-cally significant results is being hampered by political procrastination and self-interest–inspired foot-dragging.

Social science could come to its own defense by claiming that it cannot implement results without the cooperation of government, and this may very well be true. It is my contention that governments throughout the world, whether capitalistic, socialist, or communist, no longer represent the will of the people. Political machinery and bureaucracy have become cumbersome and lugubrious because of their sheer size and inefficiency.

The promises of self-interest, power, and vast financial gain have lured and side-tracked political figures in key positions throughout the world. Indolence, inefficiency, corruption, self-interest, political favoritism, dictatorship, nepotism, racial prejudice, ethnic favoritism, sexual intrigue, and blatant theft are more the rule than the exception. The juxtaposition and contrasts between government action and the will of the people are glaringly evident. On a one-to-one level, people with vast ideological differences can achieve and cooperate, producing results beneficial to all. But encumbered by the bumbling machinery of bureaucracy, otherwise peace-loving people are turned to hate one another. Statistical validation of theoretical constructs and/or volumi-nous data is meaningless and virtually impossible to implement in the face of a contemporary political structure.

But what is the purpose of my indictment of social science? Of what value are my criticisms, even if they are true? What can be done about this situation? What does it have to do with the long-wave cycles? Here are a few points to consider:

1. The statistical and scientific endeavors of social science are praise-worthy from an academic or pedagogical perspective, yet results do not, in most cases, support their dollor cost or human input.
2. Even those studies which have provided valuable and potentially applicable conclusions have either not been applied at the human level nor been corrupted by self-interest and political ambition.
3. The lot of humankind has not improved sufficiently to warrant a positive attitude toward social science. There exists a vast and uncharted expanse between theory, statistical validation of theory, and its pragmatic application. This casts doubt on the value of

research and, indeed, the wisdom of continued public support for such programs.

4. The handful of findings that have both highly relevant statistical significance and face validity are too controversial to implement.

5. Private industry has been more successful in its applications of social, economic, political, and psychological research than has government. This has not, however, been particularly beneficial to the average citizen, nor to the poor and starving throughout the world.

6. Theories that cannot be scientifically validated because of a lack of data are routinely criticized and rejected by social scientists.

7. Even theories that appear to be statistically valid are often embroiled in academic controversy and disagreement regarding techniques, data collection methodology, and/or relevance.

8. Results of studies are differentially applied because of social class, financial ability, and political orientation.

The situation seems hopeless. Solutions are not readily evident. Yet, I suggest that although there may not be an all-encompassing solution to this problem, the individual investor can be successful in spite of the pervasive disorder. Many of the answers that seem evident to me fly in the face of acceptable scientific procedures, political protocol, and established methodologies. I suggest the following:

1. Inasmuch as social science has not provided solutions that have been implemented to any meaningful extent, consider applying, where possible, results independent of traditional channels. If, for example, the research shows that there is a valid three- to four-year business cycle, take advantage of the cycle to further the safety and profits of your own business and personal financial situation. Don't wait for local, state, or federal governments to recognize or implement the findings of such research. It will never happen; and even if it does, it will be bumbled. If, for example, social science research suggests that there will be major shifts in population densities, don't wait for the government to implement plans that will prepare municipalities for such changes; rather, take action yourself. Buy or sell real estate to take advantage of such shifts. Plan ahead. Form political action groups or investment associations to make practical

use of the research. While the U.S. Environmental Protection Agency may spend millions of taxpayer dollars conducting research on the environmental impact of pollution on the condition of the Great Lakes, it takes an organization such as Greenpeace to prompt the EPA to release its results.

2. Don't be fooled into thinking that science, statistics, and technical methodology are the only approaches that can produce meaningful results or financially rewarding alternatives.

3. Observation, history, personal study, self-evaluation, and simple correlation of events, time, and patterns can be just as effective as the most sophisticated computerized procedures.

4. Don't believe, for even one moment, that a theory or claim unsupported by reams of statistical data cannot be right or valid. While it's true that totally preposterous claims without a shred of statistical or historical evidence in their favor should be rejected, it does not necessarily follow that theories with limited historical statistical significance are worthless as well.

REJECTING THE WAVE THEORIES

The perennial antagonism between academicians and those with limited academic credentials is well documented in every era of U.S. history. In the final analysis, however, innovation has not been the exclusive property of laboratory science or academia. Industrial processes and technological advances have emanated both from organized science and from private citizens. While theoretical scientists such as Albert Einstein have given us powerful concepts, it has taken pragmatic thinkers to put them into practice.

Economists have long disagreed on virtually everything that could be interpreted in more than one way. Consequently, the theories of Kondratieff have been rejected, ridiculed, and scorned by a generation of "modern" economists with a wealth of statistical data. There have been many criticisms of the Kondratieff Long Wave. If you are interested in studying the criticisms, I refer you to the reference list at the end of this book, which includes many of the criticisms. In fact, Kondratieff was criticized by his own peers and communist bosses. But their displeasure with his work was far more serious than mere dislike.

Kondratieff was banished to Siberia for his views because his conclusions about the cyclical nature of capitalist economies was in blatant disagreement with the party line. Rather than supporting the communist view that capitalism would self-destruct as a result of intensified social-class conflict resulting from its inequities in the distribution of wealth, Kondratieff's view was that capitalist economies would rise and fall at relatively regular intervals because of a natural cycle. He maintained that the cycle was more a function of age and process than of social-class discontent and conflict.

The road for followers of the Kondratieff Wave theory has not been any less difficult. A vast majority of professional economists still reject Kondratieff's work on the basis of theory alone. In addition, the following objections have been cited:

1. The statistical evidence in support of Kondratieff's work is limited. His original theory traced only several long-wave cycles in Europe and America. Statistically, this is clearly insufficient to support conclusions of the magnitude and importance reached by Kondratieff's theory. As I've indicated earlier in this chapter, modern social scientists demand vast amounts of statistics in support of theories and hypotheses. They require computer-validated tests, high levels of confidence, and intricate tests of significance in order to conclude that a given theory or hypothesis has real meaning. The original Kondratieff work cannot meet even the most limited tests of statistical significance unless it is appended, extrapolated, and expanded.

   Jay W. Forrester of the System Dynamics Group at M.I.T. has done just this. He has expanded the statistical base of Kondratieff's work to include a multitude of economic variables and data. In the words of Forrester:

   > The new economic pressures are mutually reinforcing. The emerging patterns are locked into one another like pieces of a jig-saw puzzle. Productivity is related to capital investment; environmental pressures arise from the growth of population and industrial activity; energy questions are connected to the falling value of our dollar. Symptoms appear in one economic sector from causes that arise in another. Each part changes through time and sets up new situations to which other parts respond. More and more, we realize that everything is connected to everything else. But the multiple interconnections are not easy to understand. Intuition and political debate are proving to be inadequate tools for managing economic change. . . .

For the last six years we have been constructing such a labora-tory representation of the economy in the form of the System Dy-namics National Model which is built up from policies followed in major sectors of an industrial economy. The Model connects sectors through flows of people, information, money, prices, and goods. It represents the details of economic activity at the level of the internal structure of corporations. It contains 15 industrial sectors, such as consumer durables, capital equipment, energy, agriculture, and building construction. Each industrial sector of the Model is con-structed to represent a typical business firm in that sector of the economy. The Model represents production processes in compre-hensive detail, adjusting changes in in-put factors for production on the basis of many aspects of the economic environment—including inventories, prices, costs, order backlogs, growth rate, marginal productivity, liquidity, profitability, return on investment, and reg-ulatory restraints. . . .

The market clearing function, which balances supply and demand, responds not only to price but also availability of the product; this availability, or delivery delay, simulates market be-havior in the real economy, where many prices change slowly and supply and demand are partially balanced by allocation and delays in filling order backlogs. . . .

In similar detail, the Model contains a labor mobility network for the movement of people between sectors, a banking system, the Federal Reserve, household-consumption sectors, a government sec-tor, and a demographic sector. The Model is a translation into computer language of the knowledge people have about organiza-tional structure and operating policies surrounding their daily activi-ties. [*The Futurist*, Vol. 12, #6, p. 379]

Forrester has concluded that

managing the balance between inflation and deflation will become part of the question of managing debt. Historically, it has never been possible to pay back all the debt after a peak in the long wave. Deflation leads to erasing debt by defaults, thereby paying back only a fraction of the amounts due. Alternatively, inflation erases debt by depreciating the currency, thereby paying back only a fraction of the purchasing power originally borrowed. As we move out of a long-wave peak, can debt be repaid?

If not, is there a better way to postpone repayment or write down debt than by using default or inflation? The balance between inflation and deflation and the question of how to extract ourselves from a heavy debt load are critical policy issues that need prompt resolution.

If we are now at a peak in the long wave, we face the possibility of another major depression in the future. Such a prospect is at first frightening and seems inevitably pessimistic until one pauses to examine the fundamental nature of an economic depression. [*The Futurist,* Vol. 12, #6, p. 383]

In spite of the voluminous research and statistically sound˙techniques employed by the Forrester group, his conclusions are still not accepted by many economists, government officials, investors, market analysts, and others. Why? I say that it is because of the nature of his findings and the clear unpopularity of disinflationary conclusions. The public wants candy, not cod liver oil. "Let them eat cake," says the government. But Kondratieff and Forrester won't go away. Reality won't change.

2. Kondratieff Wave theory has also been criticized because of flaws in the original research. Some claim that Kondratieff did not appropriately select his statistics and that he was biased in his interpretation of the results. This may well be true; however, recent evidence, to be discussed later in this chapter, has clearly and unequivocally supported the long-wave theory. Many analysts and economists claim that even if the statistics support Kondratieff's long-wave theory, government today is so far advanced that a repetition of long-wave phenomena won't occur. They claim that we have learned from our mistakes, that government has broader powers, and that regulatory agencies can expand and contract economic growth in order to smooth out the bumps, and in order to avert violent swings in the economy. Where were they when interest rates climbed to record highs in the 1980s? Where were they when farmer after farmer went bankrupt? Where were they when bank failures in the 1980s reached record levels?

3. Another criticism that has been lodged against long-wave theory is that it is deterministic. In other words, its structure is rigid and unresponsive to other inputs that clearly affect economic trends. It is claimed that no one economic trend is similar to any other and, furthermore, that one cannot predict social, political, psychological, or religious behavior on the basis of economic developments.

4. Still other economists and analysts claim that political factors are the major elements in economic trends and that new domestic and international political events will clearly affect the anticipated outcome of the current long-wave cycle.

5. Finally, there is a general lack of agreement by long-wave theorists regarding key dates of major economic tops and bottoms. In addition, long-wave theorists have disagreed about the types of data that should be used in analyzing the cycles, about where we now stand in the long-wave cycles, about where we are going, when we'll get there, how bad it will be, what to do about it, how to avoid it, how to prepare for it, what caused it, and so on. Obvious disagreement within the ranks has presented the outside world with a picture of disunity that detracts from the theory. Disunited long-wave analysts have been unable to mount a strong offensive. Long-wave theory has suffered from disrespect as a consequence of its disunity and multiplicity of opinions.

A FEW KEY STUDIES

This book was not written in order to offer retorts to the criticisms cited in the foregoing paragraphs. Such an effort would be totally fruitless, although meritorious. We are all getting older by the second. There is nothing more than ego gratification to be gained from heroics. I will not attempt to convince you or anyone else about the validity of the long-wave cycles. I can certainly direct you to a veritable gold mine of statistical studies, all of which clearly and without question in my mind support the existence of long waves and patterns in virtually every aspect of economic life.

Data validating the forty-five- to sixty-year cycles, eleven- to fourteen-year cycles, eight- to ten-year cycles, three- to four-year cycles, and nine- to eleven-month cycles in business and economics are voluminous. Refer to some of the studies cited in my reference list at the end of the book if you want to read these for yourself. This, by the way, is something I urge you to do. You will see for yourself, and you will benefit richly from the experience. Don't take my word for it—go see with your own eyes and analyze with your own mind.

The economic ideas I offer you do not originate in the teachings of an East Indian holy man or in the dreams of a Marxist revolutionary. They derive from the study of history, patterns, and statistical research (although, as I've indicated before, some would argue that the statistics are insufficient). They are based on the history of economics.

There have been numerous studies designed to ascertain the existence and role of many different economic cycles and patterns. Yet only a few key studies rank high on the list of "must" reading. Not only do these studies support the existence of long-wave cycles in economic data and trends, but they also support the most meaningful finding that long-wave cycles appear to exist in many apparently unrelated phenomena. What follows is a relatively brief discussion of several key studies. Again, I strongly suggest that you consult the references cited at the end of this book in order to expand your knowledge of cyclic studies and findings.

The Beveridge Wheat Cycle

Lord William Beveridge studied the long-wave history of European wheat prices from 1500 to 1869. In December 1921, Beveridge compiled his statistics in a study first published in the *Journal of the Royal Economic Society.*

Later analysis by Gertrude Shirk of the Foundation for the Study of Cycles confirmed the statistical significance of several cycles based upon the Beveridge wheat data. Figure 3.1, reprinted from *Cycles* January 1975, shows the record of wheat prices in Western and Central Europe from 1500 to 1869. Shirk reached the following conclusions about wheat data based upon a spectral analysis (*i.e.*, statistical procedure used to find repetitive patterns in a data series):

It must be mentioned that because of the upward trend in the figures, Beveridge conducted the analysis on departures from a 31-year moving average trend. In the work that I summarized . . . the moving average trends were close to the length of the period indicated. That is, there would in many cases be less distortion introduced because of the moving average. Nevertheless there are several points of agreement, or very near to exact agreement between the results I obtained, and the Beveridge results. At about 15 years and at about 19.9 to 20.35 years the agreement is close. At 35 years the agreement at this early stage is reasonable.

Figure 3-1. *A record of the price of wheat in Western and Central Europe, 1500–1869.*

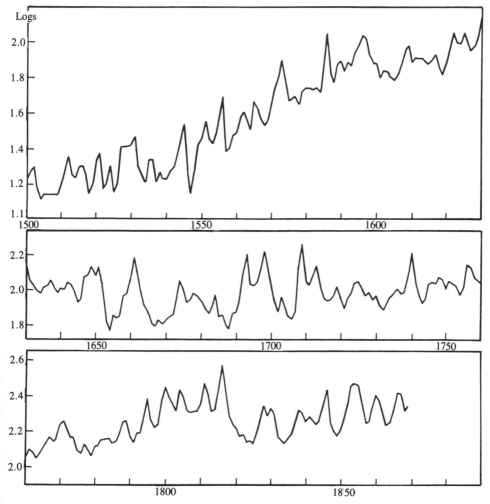

Source: Cycles, Vol. XXVI, #1, January 24, 1975 (Foundation for the Study of Cycles, 3333 Michelson Drive #210, Irvine, CA 92715).

With respect to what I list at 12.85, 9.72, 12.00, 8.08 and 7.42, it could be said fairly that the agreement between Beveridge's harmonic analysis and our spectral scan is exact.

The periods that Beveridge decided were reliable enough to use in his synthetic curve were 3.415, 4.415, 5.1, 5.67, 5.96, 8.05, 12.84, 19.9, 35.5, 54 and 68.

The discrepancy that exists between the lengths of 54 and 57 [years] is difficult to resolve. Some checking by array analysis has been made for both lengths, and the 57 period gives more satisfactory results. If the length of 54 is more accurate, the current crest would be at 1968. If the length of 57 is more accurate the current crest would be at 1983. One of the problems is that there are too few repetitions of these longer lengths, even in a series as long as the Beveridge wheat record. ["A Spectral Scan of Wheat Prices in Western and Central Europe, 1500–1869," *Cycles*, January 1975]

The data reveal a cycle of approximately 54 years as well as a cycle of approximately 68 years. Also found were cycles of 3.4215 years (the so-called "business cycle"); 12.84 years, which corresponds to the Juglar cycle previously mentioned; and a cycle of 8.05 years, corresponding closely to the 9-year average cycle in wheat prices that has been evident since the 1800s. Given the close relationship between movement in commodity prices and the general economic trends, it is reasonable to conclude that the 1500-to-1869 period witnessed approximately similar periods of economic expansion and contraction.

European Grain and Cereal Prices, 1392–1490

The Cambridge Economic History of Europe offers a most scholarly and thorough accounting of virtually every phase of European economic history. Unfortunately, it would take many hours of reading to assimilate the wealth of information contained in these volumes. Those who have the time should most certainly read all of the volumes for a complete historical perspective of economic history in Europe. Chapter VIII of Volume 1 contains an excellent study of crises from the Middle Ages through modern times written by Professor Leopold Genicot of the University of Louvain, France. The article contains important statistical data on the price of spelt during the period 1392 through 1490. Figure 3.2 shows the price of spelt (a cereal) as compiled by Genicot. You can see that there are two definite peaks and troughs in price. One trough is noted in approximately 1394. Fifty-one years later, in 1445, prices reached another trough. Thereafter prices moved higher again, only to reach another trough in approximately 1503 (see Figure 3.1). The cycle ran approximately fifty-eight years, trough to trough. Another study in the Cambridge work showed essentially similar cycles were noted in the price of wheat, beans, oats, and beef (Figure 3.3).

Here, from an entirely different source than the Beveridge wheat data, is further evidence that wheat, grain, meat, and cereal prices have moved in approximate fifty-four-year cycles. This evidence dates back to 1392. Figure 3.4 updates the cash wheat cycle through 1988 and projects its future course.

Robert DeGersdorff

Robert DeGersdorff studied economic trends in England for the period from 1200 through 1932. He concluded the following:

1. A major cycle with an average length of approximately 54 years appears to have existed in consumer and wholesale prices for the last 700 years.

Figure 3-2. *The price of spelt at Namur, 1392–1490.*

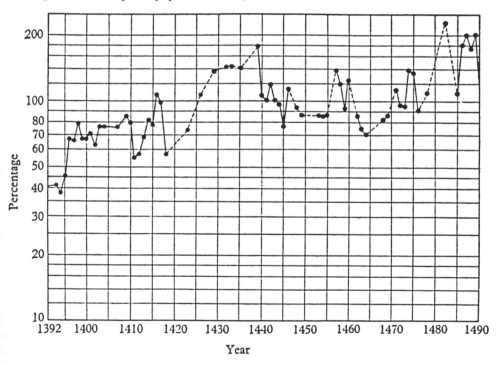

Source: The Cambridge Economic History of Europe, Vol. I, Cambridge University Press, Cambridge, MA, 1966, p. 685.

Figure 3-3. *Prices of some farm products in England, 1300–1500, in deniers.*

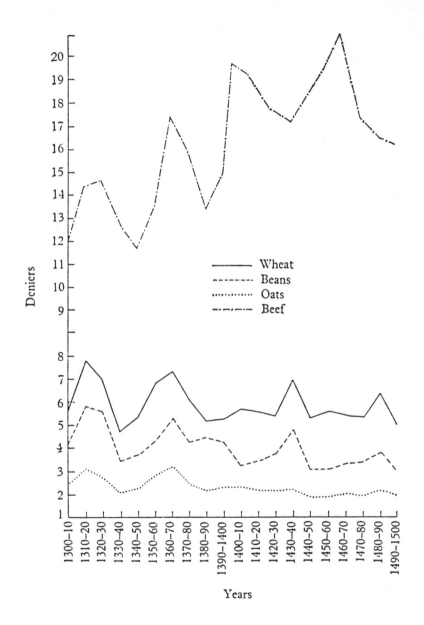

Source: The Cambridge Economic History of Europe, Vols. II and III, Cambridge University Press, Cambridge, MA, 1963.

Figure 3-4. *Update of the approximate fifty-four-year wheat cycle (A = last 54-year low, B = current 54-year-cycle low). Also shown are 8.9-year cycles and 26-year-cycle highs (arrows).*

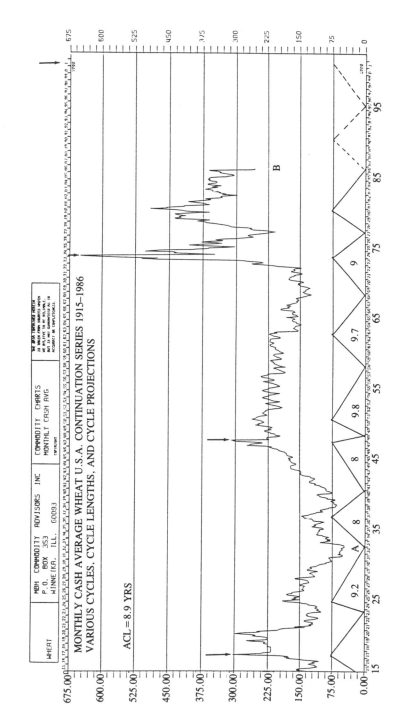

2. These cycles are usually divided into three major subcycles with an average length of 18 years. Because it is a whole fraction of "harmonic," each subcycle has the same long-term timing as the major cycle.
3. These subcycles show some consistency in their percentage of rise and decline.
4. Adjacent 54 cycles seem to be paired with two cycles of relative inflation followed by two cycles of little or no inflation. The possibility of a 108-year cycle is suggested.
5. The pattern of cycle timing shown in the CPI data is replicated in both our one-hundred and fifty year history of U.S. wholesale prices and our current sixty-six year history of U.S. CPI. [*Cycles*, Vol. 30, 1979, p. 153]

Based on his work, DeGersdorff listed the following long-wave cycles (p. 153):

Cycle
High Inflation Trend 1288–1339
High Inflation Trend 1339–1393
Low Inflation Trend 1395–1437
Low Inflation Trend 1437–1509
High Inflation Trend 1509–1571
High Inflation Trend 1571–1621
Low Inflation Trend 1621–1672
Low Inflation Trend 1672–1723
High Inflation Trend 1723–1780
High Inflation Trend 1780–1834
Low Inflation Trend 1834–1886
Low Inflation Trend 1886–1932

Although DeGersdorff confirms the existence of a long-wave cycle lasting from fifty to sixty years, low to low, his conclusion that a low was due in 1986 does not correspond with either my timing, or with the events accompanying the 1986 economy. Figure 3.5 shows the price index used by DeGersdorff in his analysis. This study is among the most viable of all studies conducted heretofore. It confirms the long-wave cycle both in the United States and England.

While there may be some inherent limitations in the DeGersdorff analysis, there is, nevertheless, clear-cut evidence that an approximate 50- to 60-year economic pattern has characterized the data for more

Figure 3-5. *DeGersdorff's long-term price index and the fifty- to sixty-year cycles.*

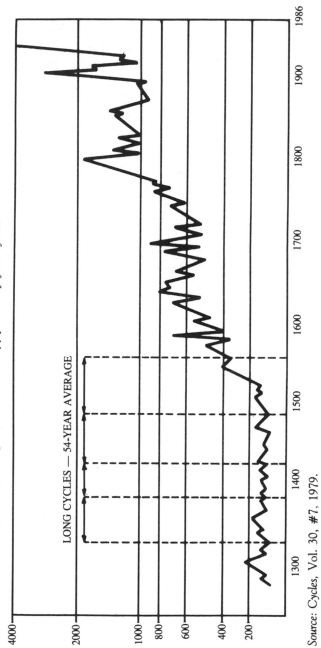

LONG CYCLES — 54-YEAR AVERAGE

Source: Cycles, Vol. 30, #7, 1979.

than 700 years. Whether you accept the DeGersdorff findings in total or in part only, there is considerable food for thought in this landmark study. Unfortunately, most contemporary economists have not heard of DeGersdorff, nor have they studied his results.

"The Cyclical Analysis of Global Economy"

Dr. Norman Z. Alcock, director of the Canadian Peace Research Institute, published in the June 1977 edition of *Cycles* an article entitled "The Cyclical Analysis of Global Economy." This study is must reading for all who are interested in the long-wave cycles and their past, present, and future. Using a measure of average energy consumption in the "twelve largest rich nations of the world," Alcock statistically determined the presence of the following cycles:

1. The 3.3-3.4-year Kitchin cycle
2. The 3-7-year business cycles
3. The 8-11-year Juglar cycles
4. and 12-25-year Kuznets cycles, and
5. The 50-60-year Kondratieff cycles

The study was a most detailed one with attention given not only to the cycles selected for study but also to the procedures. Alcock concluded the following:

> Multiple regression analyses were performed for the world economy, with rate of change of energy consumption per capita for 12 rich nations as the dependent variable and five precise sinusoidal cycles (having 3.33, 5.6, 9.4, 20.5, and 54 year periods) as the independent variables, for one pre-war interval (1922–38) and one post-war interval (1950–66). As a result of the analyses, a composite cyclical index was made up and used to project the world economy for the next 25 years. A period of no-growth or stagnation is indicated, the average annual growth rate of energy consumption per capita, from 1977 to 2001, being 0.6 ± 0.1 percent. Tables and graphs for both average rate of change of energy consumption per capita and average energy consumption per capita and average energy consumption per capita versus time are included. Fifty-one percent of the variance of the rate of change in energy consumption per capita and ninety-seven percent of the variance of

energy consumption per capita were accounted for by the composite cyclical index. A "resonance" model is proposed, reconciling this analysis with previous cyclical analyses based on various feed-back processes. [*Cycles*, Vol. 28, #4, June 1977]

In addition, Alcock's work produced the results shown in Figure 3.6, which project energy consumption through 2001. What does the future hold in store based on the Alcock study? Here are the words of Alcock:

> What then of the future?
>
> According to our projection, based on a trend line (the constant of equation 4) and the sum of five cyclical variations, the next twenty-five years will be a period of slow growth—close to stagnation. The analysis upon which it is based has, over 32 years, accounted for 97 percent of the variance. Yet our hypothesis is that freedoms remain. If so, we can limit the fluctuations about the trend line by suitable economic policies. We may even be able to alter the trend line. The extent to which either of these acts of volition is possible, however, still remains a matter for speculation.
>
> Our analysis of the "global" economy, of course, has been based on just 12 nations, though these 12 rich nations do account for approximately 75 percent of world GNP. A period of slow growth or stagnation for these rich countries, though it does introduce difficult problems, does not result in massive hardship or starvation. A period of slow growth or stagnation for the poorer nations of the world, however, does result in just that, in my opinion. If the prediction of this paper is correct, then, and to the extent that it is correct, the satisfaction of third world needs cannot be met simply by an increase in world GNP. [*Cycles*, Vol. 28, #4, June 1977]

Consumables in Southern England, 1271–1954

A most compelling study was conducted by Gertrude Shirk of the Foundation for the Study of Cycles (*Cycles*, Vol. 24, #3, 1975). Based on statistics originally developed by Brown & Hopkins,[1] Shirk examined the price index of a basket of consumables in southern England for the period 1271–1954. The study isolated four significant cycles, all of which were present at high levels of statistical significance as determined by both an F-ratio and the Bartels test of significance. Shirk's

[1]See: *Cycles*, Vol. 24, #3, 1975.

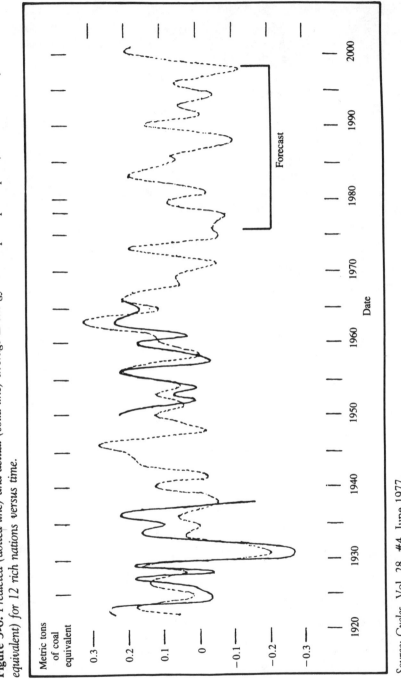

Figure 3-6. Predicted (dotted line) and actual (solid line) average Δ energy consumption per capita (in metric tons of coal equivalent) for 12 rich nations versus time.

Source: Cycles, Vol. 28, #4, June 1977.

results are shown in Figure 3.7. The chart of the raw data is shown in Figure 3.8. Taking the data one step further, Shirk compared the four significant cycles combined with an ideal trend, only to find that the four cycles explained a great percentage of the variation in trend. Figure 3.9 shows her combined cycles chart. What is one to conclude from this powerful piece of research? Here are Shirk's conclusions:

> The index in its original form certainly gives no hint of a cycle in the area of 54 years. The data were detrended and a systematic period reconnaissance was performed. An important peak at 55.5 years was revealed by this process. In addition, five other periods were suggested as possible cycles. Of these, three lengths were found to be statistically significant. They are 50.6, 40.3, and 60.4 years.
>
> Summary: A long price record (1271–1954) shows a statistically significant cycle that measures 55.5 years on the average and that has an ideal crest in 1981. Other cycles (50.6, years, 40.3, and 60.4 years) may also be present, and together they materially alter the appearance of the 5.55-year cycle. When the models for all four cycles are combined, a peak occurs in 1969, but this is followed by a succession of years at a high level until 1982, when the curve turns down. The overall trend of the figures, and other cycles that might be present are not included in the analysis. . . . [*Cycles*, Vol. 24, #3, 1975]

But most important of all is the cycle synthesis and projection through the year 2000, shown in Figure 3-10. Examine the figure closely. Note

Figure 3-7. *Results of the Shirk study.*

Characteristics of Four Cycles and Their Combination			
Period	55.5	50.6[a]	40.3[a]	60.4[a]
Current Crest	1981.9	1968.89	1965.8	1982.44
Amplitude (in logs)	.0499	.0327	.0325	.0278
F-ratio	4.05	2.90	5.10	2.50
Bartels Test	.0089	.0110	.002	.008
Cumulative Reduction in Variance	27.9%	43.2%	57.2%	65.4%
Successive Correlation with Departures	0.52	0.65	0.75	0.81

[a]After removal of other cycles.

Note: The higher the F-ratio and the lower the Bartels, the more significant the result.

Source: Cycles, Vol. 24, #3, 1975.

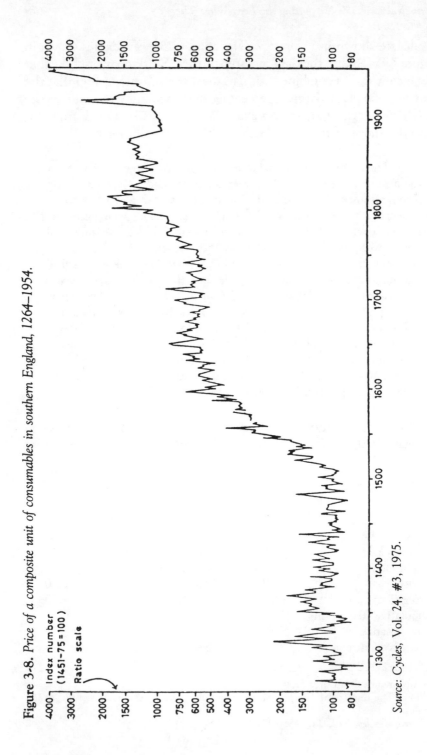

Figure 3-8. *Price of a composite unit of consumables in southern England, 1264–1954.*

Index number
(1451–75 = 100)

Ratio scale

Source: Cycles, Vol. 24, #3, 1975.

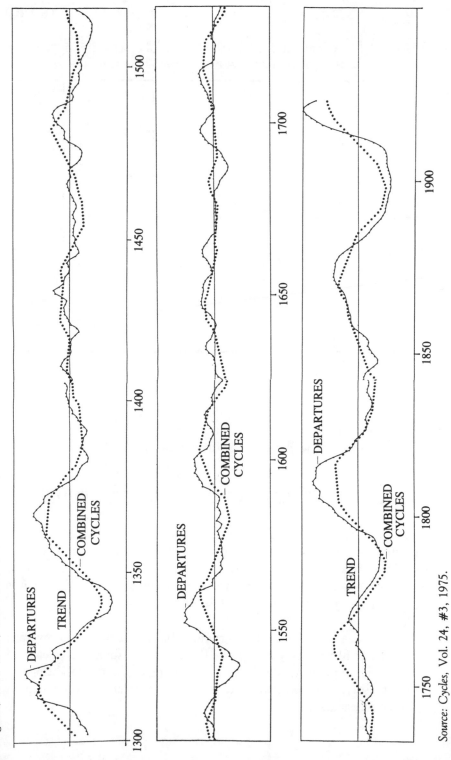

Figure 5.9. A comparison of the combination of four cycles (idealized) found in the index of the price of consumables in southern England, 1300–1925, with the detrended and smoothed data.

Source: *Cycles*, Vol. 24, #3, 1975.

81

Figure 3-10. *A synthesis, 1900–2000, of four ideal cycles (55.5, 50.6, 40.3, and 60.4 years) as found in the price of consumables in southern England.*

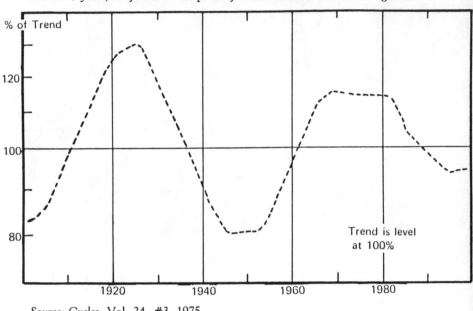

the projected trend. Remember that the chart and projection were prepared in 1975, well before the turmoil of the late 1970s and 1980s.

WHAT CAN WE LEARN FROM THE KEY STUDIES?

In spite of the fact that the key studies I've cited can be criticized on the basis of statistical procedures, it is true that virtually any study or analysis of data could be similarly criticized. Yet, in spite of limitations on the data series, data history, and continuity of the data, I think it is safe to reach the following conclusions:

1. The price of wheat and other grains has fluctuated in an average cycle of fifty to sixty years since the 1300s. Inasmuch as wheat and feed grain prices tend to reflect underlying economic conditions, it is reasonable to extrapolate to the economic trend as well based on the wheat data.

2. The work of DeGersdorff supports the long-term cyclic theory of Kondratieff, as well as the fifty- to sixty-year cycle is wheat prices.

3. The findings of Alcock support both of the above and project a period of stagnation through the year 2001.

4. The findings of Shirk are most compelling. They clearly suggest that the late 1980s and 1990s should be marked by disinflation and/or deflation.

Based on the above, it is also reasonable to assume that the 1970–1980 decade marked the time period of a long-wave cycle peak in the U.S. economy. Though other capitalist nations of the world may not have had similar economic peaks as yet, these could develop in the very near future inasmuch as economic conditions throughout the world are significantly affected by the economic condition of their trading partners. Even the Soviet Union and China are likely to be affected because their reliance upon trade with the West and Europe has increased steadily over the years.

The work of Kondratieff has been given only minor attention in this chapter. I have done this intentionally in order to demonstrate that Kondratieff is not the only researcher who has claimed the existence of long-wave economic cycles. In fact, the classic Kondratieff theory will not be examined in great detail. You can certainly read his works on your own. I have merely drawn from his ideas and extrapolated from the timetable given in his original works.

Regardless of how much statistical evidence is presented in support of long-wave cycles, there will still be those who doubt their existence. Some of the more statistically advanced studies have not been mentioned herein. You can consult these on your own.

As I close this chapter, consider the words of Jay W. Forrester, remembering that his conclusions are the result of advanced, in-depth statistical research on the long wave and its many economic components:

> Long-wave behaviour, as revealed in the National Model, seems to explain many things now happening around the world. Current economic conditions are much like those that the National Model exhibits at a peak of the long wave. At such a peak one should expect a decline in new capital investment, rising unemployment, a levelling out in labour productivity, high interest rates, rising prices, falling return on

investment, increasing amplitude of business cycles, and reduced innovation from maturing of the current wave of technological advance. Such conditions fit today's situation. Similar conditions last occurred in the 1920s at the previous long-wave peak. . . .

The life cycle of growth describes the processes of youth, growth, and maturity. There can be a life cycle of population growing to fill geographical capacity. Might there not be a life cycle of technological innovation? Past growth in technology may be a transient that could reach a reasonable maturity. Some recent technical innovations seem to be little more than for the sake of innovation, rather than for a lasting contribution to human well-being. Supersonic air transport seems to have overreached human need and economic justification. Atomic power is beset by growing difficulties. Space flight can scarcely solve the problems on earth. Perhaps the next innovation is not to rely on technology but to look at ourselves. It would be a true innovation to discover enough about the behaviour of social and economic systems to allow humanity to live in a happy and sustained balance with the capacity of the planet. . . . ["Innovation and Economic Change," *Futures*, August 1981]

What can we conclude about the statistical evidence in support of the long wave? Here is a summary of my observations:

1. It is clear that the amount of evidence supporting the long-wave cycles is insufficient from a strict statistical standpoint.
2. Existence of the long wave could be questioned, and rightfully so, if statistical validation is the only yardstick used for evaluation.
3. Historical evidence, however, as well as several key studies (cited in this chapter) suggest that long-wave cycles are real and that they must be reckoned with by all investors, businesspeople, and governments the world over.
4. Even if the statistical evidence does not clearly support the existence of long waves, the coincidences and correlates of presumed long-wave activity are too compelling and numerous to ignore.
5. At the very least, evidence—both statistical and historical—is sufficient to stimulate further thought, further research, and various degrees of preparation for the next long-wave decline, which, if theory is correct, is now in process.

Of course, the long-wave theory is not without its critics. An excellent article entitled "A Spectral Analysis of the Kondratieff-Cycle" by Casper van Ewijk[2] statistically evaluated the long-wave theory reaching the conclusion that "the long wave seems to be confirmed as far as price-series are concerned." Furthermore, Ewijk concluded that "if a long-wave cycle exists at all, it would seem to be restricted to the price and possibly to the monetary sphere." Interestingly enough, this study, in its effort to disprove the long-wave cycle, actually confirms my conclusion that the long-wave price cycles do, indeed, exist. Specifically, the author concluded that his studies contradicted the existence of a long-wave cycle in "real variables." As far as I'm concerned prices, price fluctuations, and monetary fluctuations are about as "real" as real can be.

---

[2]van Ewijk, C., "A Spectral Analysis of the Kondratieff-Cycle," *Kyklos*, Vol. 35, Fasc. 3, 1982, pp. 468–499.

Chapter 4

Patterns and Cycles
in Interest Rates

*All knowledge is from the past. No gain or success is possible unless one is willing
to study and learn from the past. The past is prologue to the future.
The future is but a repetition of the past. There is nothing that is new.*

—W. D. Gann

Capitalism is built upon the concept of money making money. Hence,
the availability of capital at low rates of interest tends to result in
economic growth, whereas the burden of high interest rates tends to
stifle economic growth. With high interest rates and the concomitant
disincentives to expansion comes a decline in employment. The net
result of lower employment is decreased earnings, greater government
expense on social welfare programs, and decreased national productivity. This highly oversimplified explanation will likely clot the blood of
economists and rattle the bones of politicians. In reality, interest rates
are both a cause and an effect at the same time. At different times in the
cycle they are more a cause than they are an effect, whereas at other
times they are more an effect than a cause.

Although there are many explanations of how interest rates and
money supply affect economies, my approach is a most simple one.
When the economy has been in a long-term decline, demand for goods
and services has also been on the decline. During this period money is

hard to come by. Concern on the part of consumers and business results in decreased levels of spending. Consumer goods that are not essential to survival are not purchased aggressively. Consumption, therefore, decreases markedly. There is usually a chain-reaction effect of decreased consumer activity; this results in lower employment because of the decreased consumer activity's negative impact on business and sales. During declining economic trends, concern is reflected in high levels of saving and low levels of spending and consumption. This results in a relatively high level of cash and, therefore, lower interest rates. A further downward stimulus on interest rates is the usual decrease in government borrowing. The end result is, therefore, a ready supply of money. Inasmuch as supply and demand are ingredients of price, the high relative supply of money and/or the low demand for money combine to force interest rates down.

All cycles eventually reach a point of equilibrium or, perhaps, a point at which prices are so low that demand is eventually stimulated. At economic lows the cost of money becomes sufficiently low to foster an increase in demand that might not otherwise exist. The low cost of money has now become a cause. It has caused the consumer to act in response to a perceived opportunity. In other words, interest rates are so low that even the most skittish of investors or businesspersons are prompted to take action. Even at low profit margins and low consumer demand that accompany long-wave cyclic lows, demand will increase if the cost of doing business is low enough.

Concomitant with low interest rates, the low cost of raw goods and that of land are also stimuli for increased money demand. In other words, the equilibrium of price, cost of doing business, and potential return have reached a level at which they stimulate increased business activity. This process often takes many years. All but the most astute investors stand aside during times of economic lows and deflation. Yet the best long-term business opportunities exist at the economic lows. When the overwhelming majority is unwilling to initiate or expand business, the shrewd investor is accumulating land, real estate, businesses, and money at absurdly low prices. It's a buyer's market. You can just about name your price and get it. Figure 4.1 shows a cycle trend chart of real estate activity from 1790 projected through 2000. Note that the chart does not show actual highs and lows but rather trend highs and lows in percentage deviation from trend.

Figure 4-1. *Cycle trend chart of real estate activity (1790–projected through 2000).*

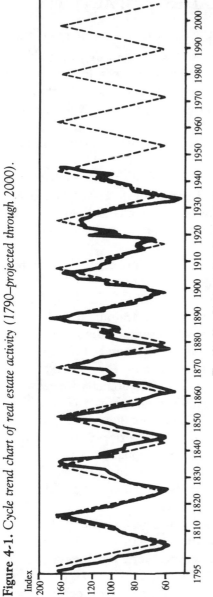

The 18⅓-Year Rhythm in Real Estate Activity

Real estate activity in the United States, 1796–1946 (after Roy Wenzlick in the *Real Estate Analyst*). Data are for January of each year. A regular 18⅓-year cycle has been added and projected to 2000, to show in a general way what will happen if this rhythm continues. *Ratio scale.* Ideal tops fall 1888.6, 1907.0 (i.e. June 30, 1907), 1925.3, 1943.6, and 1962.0; lows 1897.8, 1916.2, 1934.5, 1952.8, 1971.2. Dashed line = Projected trends.

Source: Cycles, 1970, p. 343.

INTEREST RATES AND REAL ESTATE ACTIVITY

Long-wave cycle #10 [see Chapter 2] bottomed in 1843. Real estate activity started to increase several years thereafter as investors took advantage of low interest rates and low land prices. In fact, the low interest rates prompted by the debt repudiation depression of the early 1840s witnessed commercial paper rates at approximately 4½ percent down from the late 1830s top in the 18½ percent range. This stimulated an economic recovery that, with only several recessions, lasted through the 1864 peak.

Long-wave cycle #11 bottomed in 1896 with the silver campaign depression. In 1893–94 commercial paper rates were slightly above 3 percent. Again, real estate activity began to increase several years thereafter as low interest rates and low land prices prompted increased participation.

Long-wave cycle #12 began in approximately 1932. Interest rates, however, did not make their major lows until the late 1930s, yet they were so absurdly low that, when combined with the exceptionally low prices of land and real estate, activity once again increased, bringing real estate prices and interest rates higher through the 1970s. Figure 4.2 shows commercial paper rates from approximately 1830 to 1930. Figure 4.3 shows long-term interest rates from 1857 to 1987 and long-term bond yields and various significant phenomena at peaks and troughs. Figure 4.4 shows short-term interest rates from 1890 to 1987.

However, low interest rates alone are not sufficient to prompt increased buying activity. Land and real estate prices must be low as well. Commodity prices must also be low enough to stimulate the businessperson and the consumer into action. In other words, low interest rates or "easy money" must also be accompanied by low prices across the board.

In spite of the fact that the economic peak of the 1920s was a period of great recklessness and fiscal irresponsibility in America, some clear thinkers realized that low interest rates alone were not enough to stimulate an economy. Writing for *The Magazine of Business* in October 1927, when commercial paper rates were in the low 4 percent area, Samuel Crowther, author of *Common Sense and Labor, Why Men Strike*, and others, observed the following in his article entitled "Can We Plan on Easy Money?":

Figure 4-2. *Commercial paper rates (short-term interest rates), 1830–1930.*

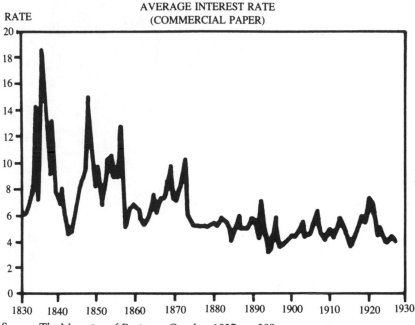

AVERAGE INTEREST RATE
(COMMERCIAL PAPER)

Source: *The Magazine of Business,* October 1927, p. 389.

What advantage should a man in business take of easy money?

The present banking policy is to keep money rates low. Since the Federal Reserve has really been functioning, rates have tended toward stabilization, but many men still continue to think in the old money terms and do not realize the complete change in the credit position.

The new position is that, unless some changes of great moment occurs, a low rate can be considered normal.

The practical business question is this: What advantage should a man in business take of easy money?

The best answer I found was from a banker of long experience. He said:

In the old days, a period of low money was a good time to make commitments, but I am inclined to believe that the man in business need not today pay much attention to rates unless they should go high. It is not reasonable to imagine that they will go high.

For a long while we can take easy money as normal, and my advice would be to act according to plans without respect to money. By this I mean that the

Figure 4-3. *Long-term interest rates, 1857–1987.*

| RRBONDS | MBH COMMODITY ADVISORS INC
P.O. BOX 353
WINNETKA. ILL. 60093 | COMMODITY CHARTS
MONTHLY CASH AVG
COPYRIGHT 1987 | THE DATA CONTAINED HEREIN
IS TAKEN FROM SOURCES WHICH
WE BELIEVE TO BE RELIABLE.
BUT IS NOT GUARANTEED AS TO
ACCURACY OR COMPLETENESS. |

LONG TERM INTEREST RATE YIELDS MONTHLY AVERAGE
1857-1988

Post-War Recovery

Secession Depression

Railroad Prosperity

Recession

After Effects
of 1893 Panic

War Prosperity

Post-War
Depression

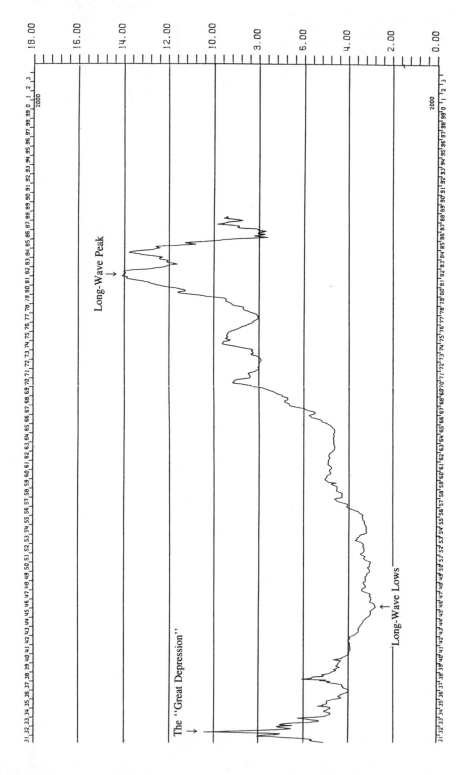

Figure 4-4. *Short-term interest rates, 1890–1987.*

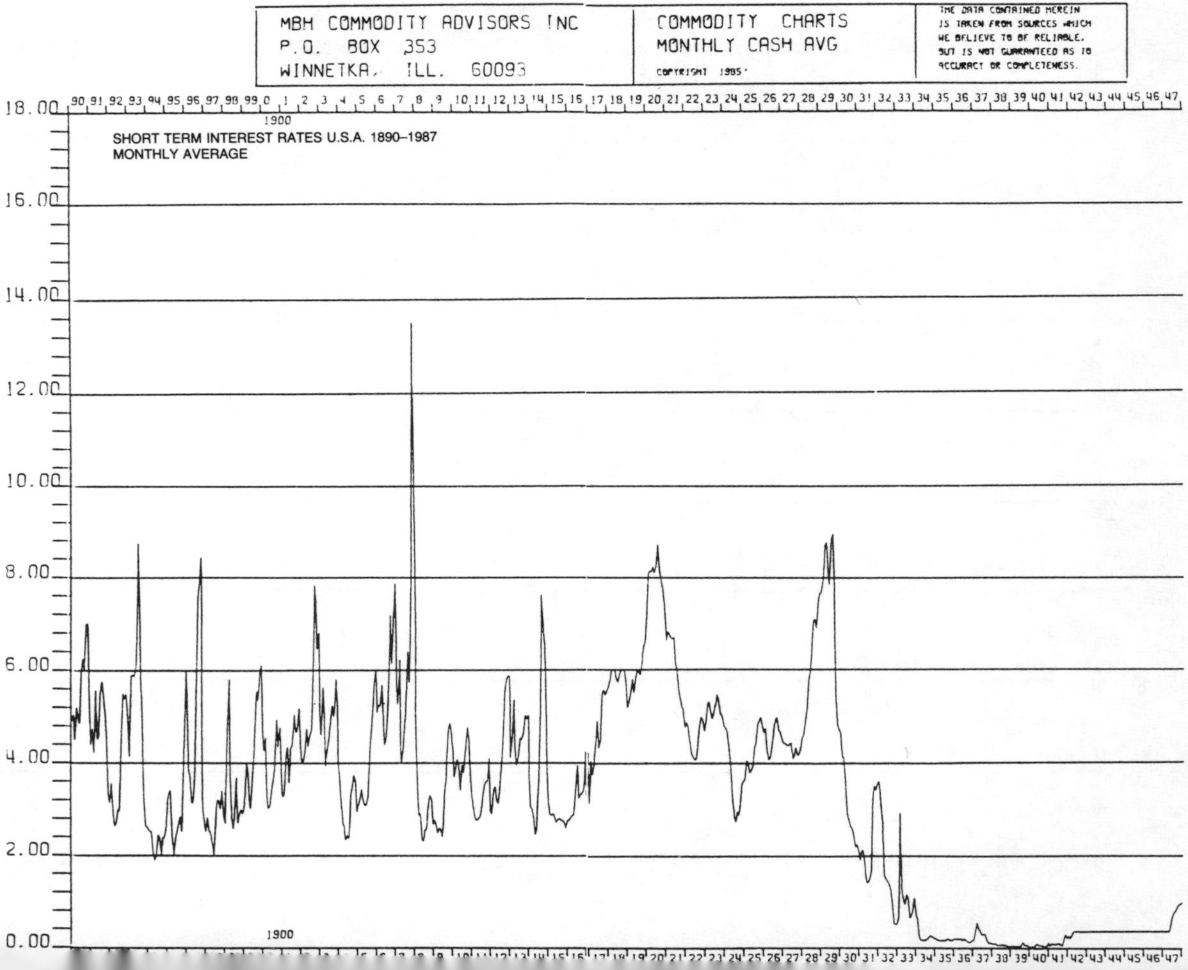
MBH COMMODITY ADVISORS INC
P.O. BOX 353
WINNETKA, ILL. 60093
COMMODITY CHARTS
MONTHLY CASH AVG
COPYRIGHT 1985
THE DATA CONTAINED HEREIN IS TAKEN FROM SOURCES WHICH WE BELIEVE TO BE RELIABLE, BUT IS NOT GUARANTEED AS TO ACCURACY OR COMPLETENESS.
SHORT TERM INTEREST RATES U.S.A. 1890–1987
MONTHLY AVERAGE
1900
18.00
16.00
14.00
12.00
10.00
8.00
6.00
4.00
2.00
0.00
90 91 92 93 94 95 96 97 98 99 0 1 2 3 4 5 6 7 8 9 10 11 12 13 14 15 16 17 18 19 20 21 22 23 24 25 26 27 28 29 30 31 32 33 34 35 36 37 38 39 40 41 42 43 44 45 46 47

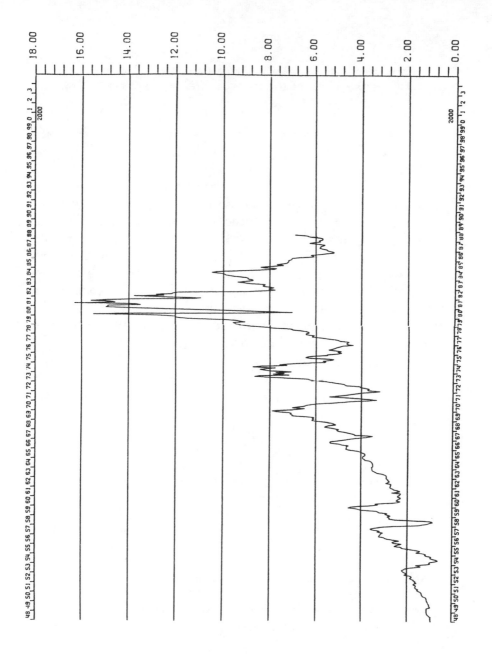

price of credit ought not to be the determining influence. For a man playing to
the money market is apt to forget that credit is credit and has to be repaid whether
it be borrowed dearly or cheaply.

In fact, easy money was not enough to avert the crisis that was to follow
over the next few years. It was not until the 1932–34 time frame, when
prices bottomed virtually across the board, that low interest rates began
to stimulate increased business activity and higher real estate prices.
Interest rates started higher and continued higher for many years to
come. In spite of the fact that leading business publications, economists, and market analysts continued to warn that interest rates would go
higher and higher, that inflation was likely to become uncontrollable,
the long-term interest rate cycle, once set in motion by low interest
rates and low commodity prices, had taken hold and could not be
stopped. The long-term cycles were almost exactly on schedule. The
persistently higher trend of interest rates through the 1950s, 1960s, and
1970s could not be halted for more than relatively brief periods, regardless of forecasts and warnings from business, economists, and analysts.
(See Figures 4.3 and 4.4.) Note the following chronology of magazine
reports from 1940 to 1965, with an approximation of interest rates.

FINANCE
Bank Loans Up

Commercial institutions far exceed normal autumn business, with
full impact of defense program yet to be measured.

One of the significant financial trends as 1940 goes into its final
month is the sustained rise in loans to industry contributed by the
country's commercial banks. By Nov. 13 the commercial, industrial,
and agricultural loans of weekly-reporting Federal Reserve member
banks in 101 cities had set a new post-depression record (BW—Nov. 23
'40, p. 58); now the total has crossed $4,900,000,000 with the velocity
of the November gain the greatest witnessed during that month in many
years. [*Business Week*, November 30, 1940] *Long-term bond yields about 4
percent.*

THE MARKETS
Bond Prices Turn Down Again

You aren't going to be able to borrow money any cheaper for the
next few months. It might even cost you a little more. The whole

structure of interest rates has firmed up distinctly since the start of the year. [*Business Week*, March 18, 1950] *Long-term bond yields about 3 percent.*

FINANCE WEEK
Money to Cost More—or Same
Tighter Credit Likely

Out of the confusion over anti-inflation measures, only a mild squeeze on money and credit is to be expected. The argument revolves around only a small increase in short-term rates. Interest may rise a bit on ordinary bank loans. Applications for loans may be screened a little more closely. Real estate and installment loans probably will be tightened. But, for most purposes, businessmen and individuals with good credit records probably will be able to get bank loans. Federal Reserve's action does not mean any freeze on credit. [*U.S. News & World Report*, September 1, 1950] *Long-term bond yields about 3 percent.*

The Credit Reins Stay Tight

Fed's Open Market Committee, seeing only a pause in boom, plumps for continued restraint; but with a subtle shift to "watchful waiting" before action. This tightening culminated when the banks raised the prime loan rate to a 25-year high of 3½% (BW—Oct. 22, '55, p. 29). But last week conditions eased somewhat. The Treasury bill rate, which had soared to 2.33%, dropped back to 2.23%. And federal funds—temporary loans between banks—were more readily available than they had been for weeks. This looked like the beginning of the expected turn away from restraint towards ease. But it is now evident that the Fed will not continue to ease the squeeze on credit. On the contrary, it intends to keep pressure on the money market . . . [*Business Week*, October 29, 1955] *Long-term bond yields about 3.7 percent.*

Long-Range Trend:
Interest Rates Up

Study indicates what borrowed money will cost you [more] in years ahead. [*Nation's Business*, February 1960] *Long-term bond yields about 4.6 percent.*

It Looks Like a Lenders' Market

Any businessman who is counting on the cost of money going down substantially next year seems likely to be disappointed. From all

indications, 1961 shapes up as another year of tight—and expensive—
money for most borrowers. The one situation that could produce a
dramatic reduction in interest rates is a full-fledged depression, which
neither lenders or borrowers expect. [*Business Week*, December 24,
1960] *Long-term bond yields about 4.7 percent.*

It Will Cost More to Borrow—
Here's the Word from Bankers

The White House is unhappy about it, but—
Interest rates are up, and lenders say they will keep rising. Banks,
paying more for money, insist they must charge more for it. This report is
based on talks with many bankers. [*U.S. News & World Report*, October
18, 1965] *Long-term bond yields about 4.9 percent.*

Pressure Goes on Fed
Not to Tighten Credit

Administration hopes by keeping the heat on prices to avert a need
to restrain demand. But bankers are less confident that interest rates can
be held as they are.
Upward pressures: For all this, market forces are pushing toward
higher interest rates.
Credit demand remains very strong, though it is still hard to say
whether it's more than seasonal. A *Business Week* roundup of bankers
reveals that loan-to-deposit ratios are rising, with a lot of the borrowing
attributable to corporate borrowers' anticipation of higher rates. [*Business Week*, November 13, 1965]

The upward pressure of the long-wave economic cycle, and of the
approximate fifty- to sixty-year cycle in interest rates, kept pushing
rates higher in spite of government action, political promises to keep
rates low, and brief periods of recession. The long-wave trend, once
initiated, is difficult (or impossible) to stop. It is at this point that
interest rates become a symptom as opposed to a cause. When rates are
low, at the long-wave bottoms, they are a stimulus or cause. They
prompt action. When the economy starts back up and interest rates get
higher, they are the effect or symptom of increasing levels of demand for
credit. Should rates go even higher they shut off buying, once again
becoming a cause. When too high, interest rates become one of the
causes of declining demand.

Not all economists feel that economic cycles are here to stay. The British economist John Maynard Keynes, whose theories are well known, proposed that the downward portion of economic cycles could be eliminated by government spending and the concomitant stimulation of consumer demand. This theory was espoused as a seemingly painless answer to the problems of business cycles. After all, if government spending increased during times of economic downturn, the result should be lower interest rates, or at least the availability of credit. Keynesian economic theory was attractive to many countries with its implied promise to put an end to the negative portion of business cycles. Imagine that! Breathing in without having to breathe out. What a wonderful idea it was. Good times could go on forever. If Keynesian ideas were valid, then interest rates would not fluctuate a great deal, and even if they did, their changes would not have a significant impact on their underlying economies.

But time has clearly shown us that this is not the case. Unlimited government spending has debased the U.S. dollar, creating immense currency fluctuations and wreaking havoc in the financial markets, all resulting in a living hell for businesspeople dealing in foreign trade. Since deficit spending has become the stock and trade in the United States, we have seen everything but stability. Interest rates have fluctuated wildly, reaching record heights and hastening the financial ruin of many individuals and corporations, the most significant among these being U.S. farmers. Ironically, Keynes himself observed that interest rates and wholesale prices tend to move together. In his *Treatise on Money*, Keynes cited the work of A. H. Gibson, who stated that from 1791 through 1928 interest rates and wholesale prices moved together. Keynes noted that Gibson's observation is "the most completely established fact within the whole field of quantitative economics, though theoretical economists have mostly ignored it. . . . Paradoxically, Keynes supported the long-wave theories of Kondratieff, without knowing it!

WHY UNDERSTAND INTEREST RATES?

The ability to understand interest rates, especially their dual function (*i.e.*, as a stimulus and as a response), and the ability to forecast their movement with reasonable accuracy are quintessential tools for investment success, business profits, and effective fiscal policy. Yet interest rates are very much like the weather. Weather trends are cyclical. They can, to a given extent, be predicted, yet it is difficult if not impossible to substantially alter their course. There are some things we can do to affect weather by acting directly on its causes; however, they are minimal. Our best hope is:

1. to know how to predict the weather
2. to know the severity of future weather changes
3. to know how various weather conditions combine to produce serious consequences, and,
4. to be prepared for drastic weather changes by seeking shelter well in advance.

This is also how we should treat interest rate fluctuations. Armed with the right information, an investor, businessperson, economist, speculator, agricultural producer, banker, and government agency will know how best to prepare. Here is what we all need to know:

1. What is the current trend in interest rates?
2. Is it a long-term trend, a short-term trend, or an intermediate-term trend?
3. When is the trend likely to change?
4. How high or low could interest rates go before they change?
5. Are there predictable patterns and/or cycles in interest rates that will make the above tasks more successful?
6. What are the relationships between interest rates, prices, and the economy?

REPETITIVE TENDENCIES IN INTEREST RATES

Interest rates can be a cause or they can be symptomatic of an underlying cause. They can be both at once. This is why it is so difficult to understand the behavior of interest rates. This is why interest rates do not always respond to similar influences in the same way. And this is also why low or high interest rates do not always have the same economic effect. Yet the ability to answer questions 1 through 6 just posed can help solve much of the interest rate mystery. I am convinced that if interest rates were understood, if their patterns, history, and cycles were generally known, humankind as a whole would be in a much better state. I offer the following observations derived from my studies of interest rates. They will help solve some of the mysteries.

The Approximate Fifty-four-Year Cycle

Evidence of an approximate fifty-four-year cycle in interest rates was published by Edward R. Dewey and the Foundation for the Study of Cycles. As far back as 1957 and earlier, Dewey had researched the approximate fifty-four-year cycle in interest rates using a combination of interest rate measures derived from English consols (*i.e.*, interest rates) and U.S. interest rates. Figure 4.5 shows Dewey's 1957 chart and his interest rate trend projection. The evidence was quite clear, in 1957, that U.S. interest rates should maintain a fairly steady rise through the late 1970s or early 1980s (given the margin of error in cyclic forecasting). The cyclic forecast was very specific. In addition, there was little doubt in the minds of many business analysts that interest rates would move higher for a period of years. The signs were unmistakable. Demand for money was high. Money supply was not keeping up with demand. Then in 1969 interest rates began to fall sharply. The long-term-cycles forecast, however, did not change. *U.S. News & World Report* ran the following headline in its September 21, 1970, issue: LOWER INTEREST RATES AHEAD: AS EXPERTS SEE IT NOW. Few analysts, however, knew that short-term rates were near their lows. In fact, short-term and long-term interest rates were within several years of their largest and most dynamic upmove in history. While the cyclic forecasts based on the fifty-four-year cycle expected still higher interest rates, economists, government, and the public reacted more to the heat of battle and to the events of the moment. The *U.S. News & World Report* article cited earlier went on to report:

> Borrowing money is becoming easier in many communities and, in some cases, cheaper. A cross-country survey of lenders shows what to expect. From George W. McKinney, Jr., vice president, Irving Trust Company:

Figure 4-5. Dewey's 54-year cycle in interest rates (1820–projected to 1980).

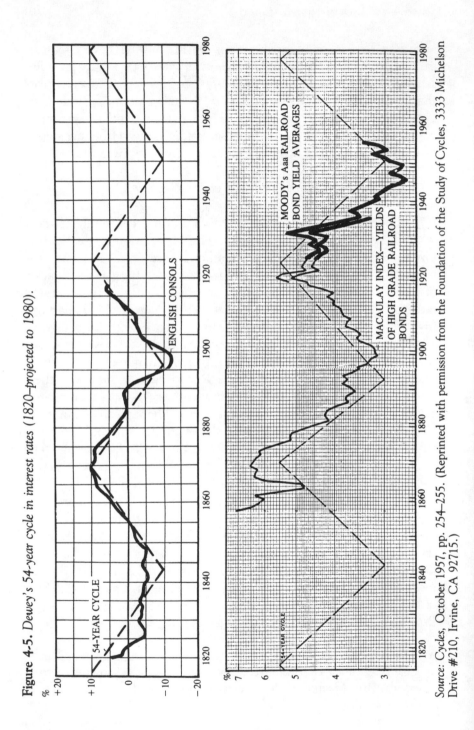

Source: Cycles, October 1957, pp. 254–255. (Reprinted with permission from the Foundation of the Study of Cycles, 3333 Michelson Drive #210, Irvine, CA 92715.)

I think the general trend we ought to expect in interest rates is mildly downward . . . and that mild downward drift is going to take place over a long period . . . years, not just months. In the meantime, I'd look for a good deal of volatility. The downward movement will have a saw-tooth pattern, with interim rises and declines.

Albert H. Cox, Jr., chief economist for the management-consulting firm of Lionel D. Edie & Company, Inc., is optimistic for borrowers. He said:

My feeling is that the basic forces are working toward rather sharply lower interest rates. What is holding back an interest-rate decline is the economy's need to catch up on liquidity. Also the heavy volume of bond offerings. But these will taper off by the end of the year.

[*U.S. News & World Report*, September 21, 1970]

While economists expressed varied opinions regarding interest rate expectations and causes, the cyclic forecast continued to project a lengthy rise. I do not suggest that economists were generally incorrect in their forecasts. *Business Week*, in its March 31, 1975, issue did an excellent job of forecasting the rise in rates through the end of the decade. Note the following:

The Fed is bound to respond to the avalanche of criticism of its tight money policy, and turn on the tap. But as the economy recovers in 1976, relatively rapid monetary growth will start to look intolerable and the Fed will cut back, adding upward pressure to short-term interest rates.

Economists are in far less agreement about the dimensions of the 1976 rise in interest rates than they are about the 1975 decline. Optimists foresee no more than a cyclical rise in rates, while some pessimists like Kaufman and Ture worry about another credit crunch. All agree, however, that the interest rates levels that will prevail between now and midsummer may not be seen again in this decade. Accordingly, borrowers with vital projects to finance should cast their credit nets wide and cast them now.

Yet for all of the jawboning and theorizing, professional opinions were split on the long-term trend in interest rates, the magnitude of expected moves, and the time frame of the coming move. The Dewey Forecast, made in 1957, was still the same. In addition, long-wave theory clearly suggested that interest rates should make all-time highs, that the highs should be made in a dramatic fashion (*i.e.*, an upsurge of unprecedented magnitude), and that they should then decline for an extended period of time thereafter. The Dewey cyclic work supported this theory.

In 1981, long-term and short-term rates peaked after six years of unprecedented volatility. Record highs were established. The cyclic forecast was validated. What then? Interest rates began to drop precipitously, again validating the long-term cyclic forecasts of both the long wave and of the fifty-four-year cycle. In the mid-1980s, short-term interest rates dropped to their lowest levels since 1976. (See Figures 4.3 and 4.4.)

Events in the interest rate markets are entirely consistent with long-wave theory. Still, economists, analysts, and government cannot agree on the future direction of interest rates. Yet, if long-wave cyclic theory is correct, interest rates will continue an extended decline until the next ideal approximate fifty-four-year cycle low, which is projected to occur during the 1990s for short-term interest rates and toward the end of the century for long-term interest rates. Naturally, the predicted long-term declines in interest rates will not be without interruption, inasmuch as there are several other highly reliable and predictable patterns in interest rates that have, with considerable success, predicted most major turns in interest rate trends since the mid-1850s. Specifically, I am referring to the patterns that will be discussed momentarily.

In closing my comments regarding the approximate fifty-four-year cycle in interest rates, I hasten to add that the long-wave scenario does not rule out the opposite alternative. The possibility of a hyperinflationary, German-style reaction is indeed real. By the 1990s, if not sooner, the outcome should be more clear as the United States, in a "checkmate" situation, is forced to make a major decision regarding the U.S. dollar. Either the dollar will be permitted to lose value to foreign currencies, or U.S. interest rates will be raised to mercilessly high levels in order to defend the dollar. The die is cast. The hour of decision is surely coming.

The Approximate Ten-Year Cycle in Interest Rates

Figure 4.6 shows long-term U.S. bond yields, monthly average price, from 1857 through 1987. Long-term interest rates have shown a long-term cycle of approximately nine to eleven years, from low to low. When combined with earlier historical data (not shown in Figure 4.6) the approximate nine- to eleven-year cycles exhibited in Figure 4.7 are found.

The relative regularity of the approximate nine- to eleven-year long-term interest rate cycle leads to the inevitable question: "Has Federal Reserve policy been an effective tool in controlling interest rates?" I'd say that if I knew nothing about the Federal Reserve and its actions, then I certainly couldn't tell from the charts that any agency with significant power was attempting to control or regulate interest rates. Perhaps things might have been worse without the "Fed," yet the cycle lows and highs have most certainly not been significantly affected. My work with the long-term interest rate chart and monthly averages (Figures 4.6 and 4.8) suggests other relationships as well.

The Mid-Decade-Low Pattern

Another noteworthy feature of the long-term interest rate trend is the tendency for low points in long-term rates to be made during the approximate mid-point of the decade. Although this pattern did not exist in similar form prior to 1916, it followed a most remarkable course from 1916 through 1986, the last mid-decade low. An examination of the cycle low listings 10 through 17 and/or a study of Figures 4.6 and 4.7 will show that a long-term low interest rate was established very near the 1976 low in rates. Whether this pattern is sufficiently significant to be repeated will be known only with the passage of time. Yet, still another pattern should be examined.

The Late-Decade-High Pattern

Figures 4.6 and 4.7 also reveal a tendency for highs in long-term interest rates to be established late in each decade, or early in the next decade. Examining the long-term interest rate chart, we find the following pattern of highs, or points from which interest rates moved significantly lower for a period of several years:

1. a high in 1848–49, followed by a decline lasting 2 to 3 years
2. a top in 1860–61, followed by a decline lasting approximately 3½ years
3. a top in 1869, followed by a decline lasting approximately 3 years

Figure 4-6. *Monthly long-term interest rate cycle turns U.S.A., 1857–1987. (Note arrows.)*

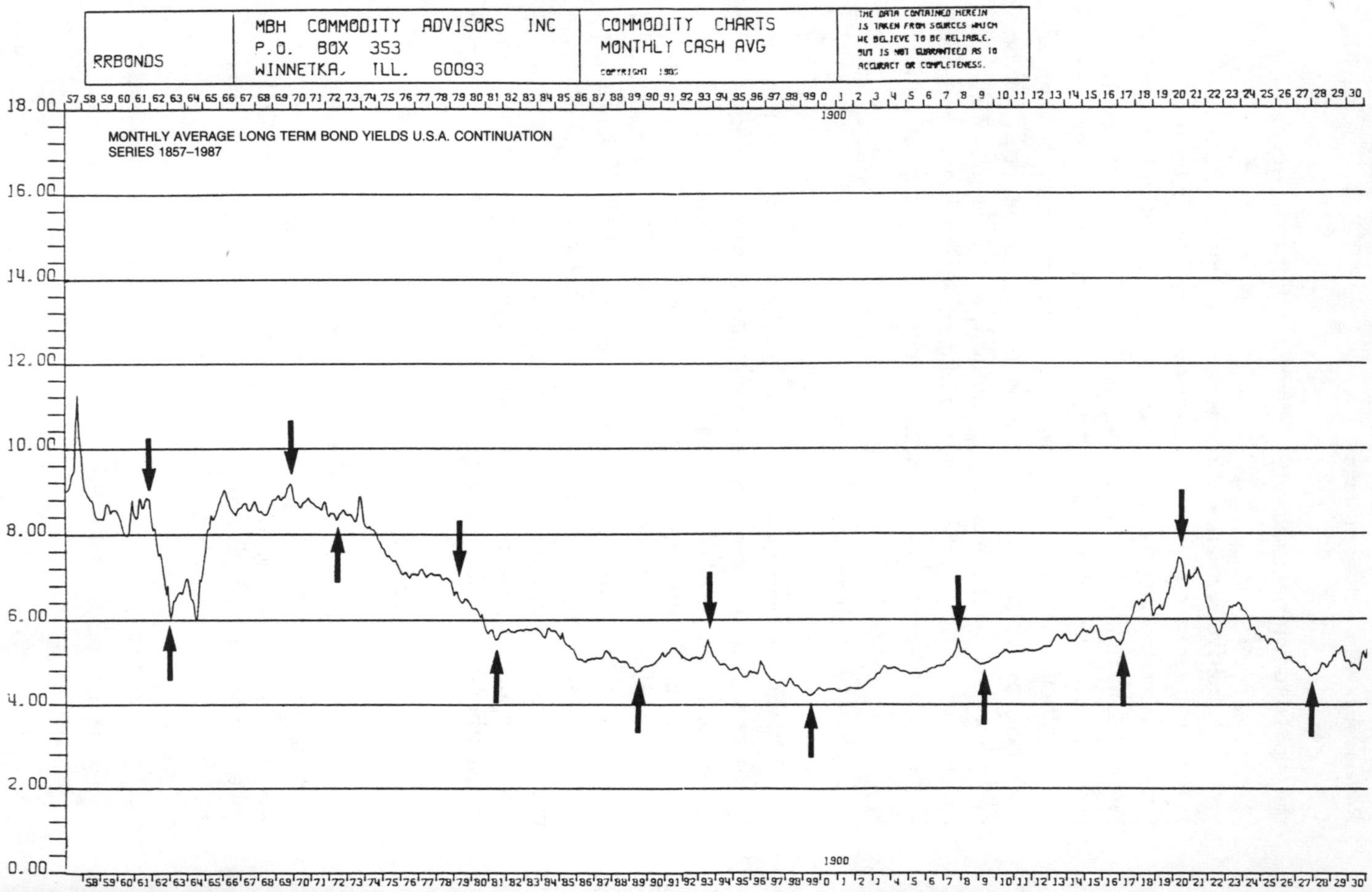

106

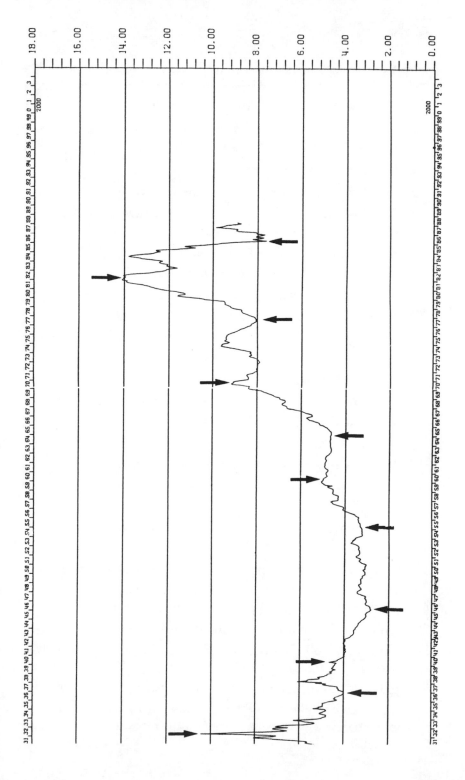

Figure 4-7. *Monthly analysis of interest rate cycles, 1831 through 1987.*

---

1. 1831 low through 1842 low = eleven years
2. 1842 low through 1852 low = ten years
3. 1852 low through 1863 low = eleven years
4. 1863 low to 1872 low = nine years
5. 1872 low through 1881 low = nine years
6. 1881 low through 1889 low = eight years (actually closer to nine years because of early-1881 low)
7. 1889 low through 1898 low = ten years
8. 1898 low through 1908 low = nine years
9. 1908 low through 1916 low = eight years
10. 1916 low through 1927 low = eleven years
11. 1927 low through 1936 low = nine years
12. 1936 low through 1946 low = ten years
13. 1946 low through 1954 low = eight years
14. 1954 low through 1965 low = eleven years
15. 1965 low through 1977 low = twelve years
16. 1977 low through 1986 low = nine years
17. 1986 low through projected 1996 low = ten years

---

4. a top in 1891–92, followed by a drop lasting approximately 6 to 7 years
5. a top in 1919–20, resulting in a decline lasting approximately 2½ years
6. a top in 1931, followed by a bottom about 5 years later
7. a top in 1940, followed by a drop through 1946
8. a top in 1959–60, followed by a decline lasting approximately 4 years
9. a top in 1969–70, followed by a decline lasting 2 to 3 years
10. a top in the 1980–81 time frame, followed by a decline lasting approximately 2 years before a significant recovery to the area of the highs.

The importance of the top pattern should not be underestimated. Though it might reasonably be argued that there are insufficient observations here from which to form a statistically significant conclusion, there does appear to be a trend that can be forecast with a reasonable degree of confidence. When subjected to further mathematical analysis and market timing, the probability of accurate forecasting is enhanced. The simple application of a moving average indicator,* as shown in Figure 4.8, can measurably improve accuracy of timing, adjusting substantially for the degree of error inherent in using patterns and/or cycles for the purpose of long-range forecasting.

THE COMBINED CYCLE AND PATTERN INDICATIONS FOR LONG-TERM INTEREST RATES

Based on my studies, the following conclusions appear warranted:

1. Long-term interest rates have exhibited a long-wave cycle of from 50 to 60 years' duration, low to low. The next low point of this cycle is due in the mid-1990s.

2. Long-term interest rates since 1916 have exhibited a mid-decade-low tendency.

3. Long-term interest rates since 1830 have exhibited a late decade to early next decade top or high pattern (*i. e.*, a point in time and price from which lower levels usually develop for a period of several years).

4. Each approximate 54-year cycle in long-term interest rates consists of approximately five 9- to 11-year cycles.

5. Long-term interest rates made lows in 1843, 1899, and 1945. In each case the lows were made at or close to the time frame of long-wave economic cycle lows.

6. Long-term interest rates made highs in approximately 1815, 1857,

---

*A moving average is computed by taking the sum of the last N number of prices and then dividing the total by N. The next item in the data series is computed by removing the oldest data point from the series of N points, adding the most recent point into the total, and then dividing again by N to get the next data point. This procedure is more thoroughly described in any elementary book on technical market analysis. Its function is to smooth a data series for the purpose of making market entry/exit more accurate and less responsive to random or unexpected price swings.

Figure 4-8. *Long-term bond yields and sixteen-month moving average.*

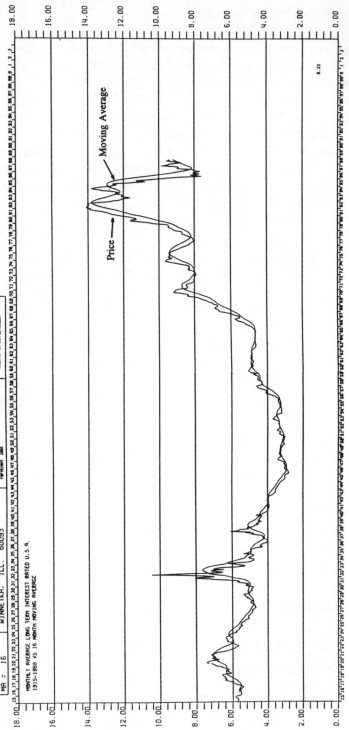

110

1919, 1931, and 1981. Each top was in the same time frame as the long-wave economic peak or while the decline was in process.

7. Long-term interest rates since 1916 have shown a tendency to bottom toward the mid-portion of each decade and to peak late in the decade or early in the next decade.

8. Long-term interest rates since the early 1800s have shown a highly predictable and fairly symmetrical cycle of approximately 9 to 11 years from one low point to the next, with the shortest cycle being 8 years and the longest being 12 years. On average, the approximate 9½-year time span has been fairly reliable and dependable.

Based on the above analysis, I conclude the following:

1. The approximate fifty-four-year cycle lows in long-term interest rates are not due until well into the 1990s (or later).

2. The approximate nine- to eleven-year lows in long-term interest rates are due to a fall in the 1995–96 time frame. These lows could fall concomitant with the approximate fifty-four-year cycle lows.

3. A rise in long-term interest rates through 1989 or into 1990 is likely. It is entirely possible that the rise in interest rates could last until 1991.

4. If the long-wave economic cycle has peaked, then long-term interest rates should not make record highs during the next few years. Rather, they should rise moderately, eventually yielding to the pressures of disinflation and deflation rather than to the forces of inflation.

5. The possibility of a hyperinflationary type "blowoff" top is certainly real; however, no definitive statement can be made at this time. Much depends on government policy, reaction, overreaction, and/ or error.

SHORT-TERM INTEREST RATE CYCLES AND PATTERNS

Short-term interest rates have also shown several important cyclic tendencies and patterns since the early 1800s. While it is highly likely that the approximate fifty-four-year cycle is also identifiable in short-term interest rates, several other patterns are more important to the investor and businessperson from the standpoint of planning and investing. An examination of these tendencies follows.

The Approximate Ten-Year Cycle

Figure 4.9 shows monthly average short-term interest rates in the United States from 1890 to 1987. Examination of the chart and of short-term interest rates data not included on this chart reveals the following:

1. A low in 1830 was followed by another low in 1841 for a cycle length of about eleven years.
2. The 1841 low was followed by a low approximately ten years later, in 1851.
3. The 1851 low was followed by another low in 1862, for a cycle length of approximately eleven years.
4. The 1862 low was followed by a low in 1871, for a cycle length of about nine years, low to low.
5. The 1871 low was followed by another bottom in 1883, for a cycle length of approximately twelve years. This cycle was clearly longer than the average expectation; however, the approximate short-term interest rate low about one year earlier (which would have been more in keeping with the cycle length) was about 1½ percent higher than the 1883 low. No great loss other than time would have resulted if commitments had been made a year earlier, when the cycle was theoretically due to make its low.
6. From the 1883 low to the 1894 low was about eleven years. Note that the 1894 low was also the lowest short-term interest rate until 1930.
7. The 1894 low brought higher levels and then another low in approximately 1904, ten years later.
8. The 1904 low was followed by a low approximately ten years later, in 1914. Note that from the 1914 low, interest rates rallied for well over four years to the next cyclic top. This further underscores the historical importance of the approximate ten-year cycle.
9. The 1914 low was then followed by another bottom in 1924, ten

years later. After the 1924 low, short-term interest rates moved higher again, and with considerable persistence, through the 1929 peak.

10. The 1924 low was followed by another low approximately ten years later, in 1934. In actuality, the final lows of the long-wave cycle in short-term interest rates did not come until the late 1939/early 1940 time frame. An investor or businessperson who took action in 1934 based on an approximate ten-year cycle low would have been somewhat early in terms of time but very close to the long-term low in terms of interest rates.

11. Another low of sorts was made during 1944. Ten years later, in 1954, lows were made again. This suggests that the confluence of World War II and an approximate fifty-four-year cycle low in the 1939–40 time frame may have distorted the cycle, yet it appears to have gotten back on track by 1954.

12. Another ten-year cycle was due in approximately 1964. The low did not develop until 1967, three years later than expected. Yet it is interesting to note that the 1967 low and the 1964 low were about the same and, furthermore, that interest rates moved considerably higher after 1964. Though the ten-year cycle was clearly late, the market acted as had been anticipated (*i.e.*, with higher interest rates).

13. Measuring from the actual low in 1967, which is consistent with accepted cyclic technique, another low came fairly close to schedule in 1977, about ten years later. Though it was not as low as the 1971 bottom, it was an important low inasmuch as rates then started a major rise.

14. The most recent low in the series was projected to fall in 1986, and it did.

15. Based on the approximate ten-year cycle, we are likely to see several more years of higher short-term interest rates, followed by a cyclic low in approximately 1996.

The Early-Decade-Low Pattern

Another reasonably consistent historical feature of short-term interest rates has been the tendency for lows to be made early in the

Figure 4-9. Short-term interest rates, 1890–1987.

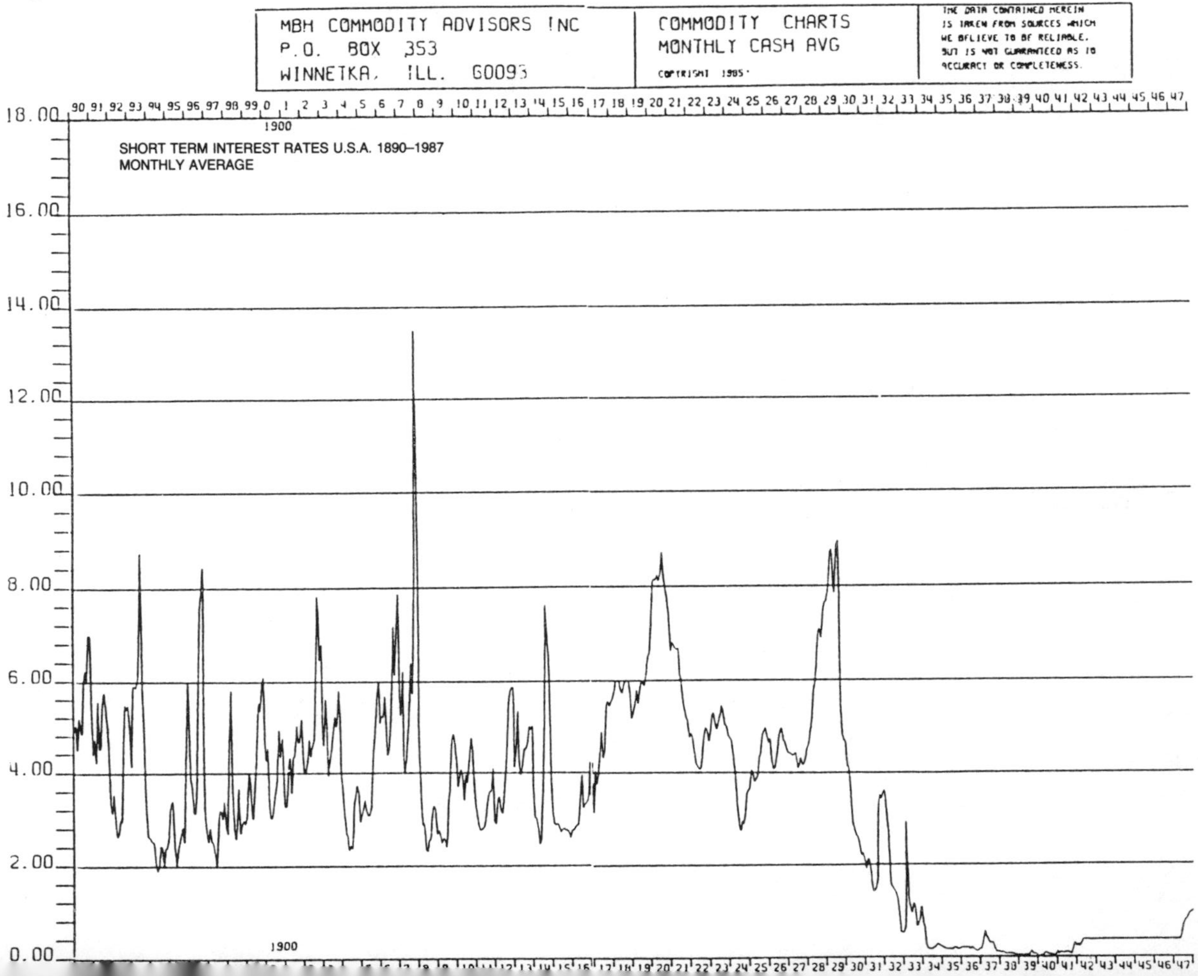

SHORT TERM INTEREST RATES U.S.A. 1890-1987
MONTHLY AVERAGE

MBH COMMODITY ADVISORS INC
P.O. BOX 353
WINNETKA, ILL. 60093

COMMODITY CHARTS
MONTHLY CASH AVG
COPYRIGHT 1985

THE DATA CONTAINED HEREIN
IS TAKEN FROM SOURCES WHICH
WE BELIEVE TO BE RELIABLE,
BUT IS NOT GUARANTEED AS TO
ACCURACY OR COMPLETENESS.

114

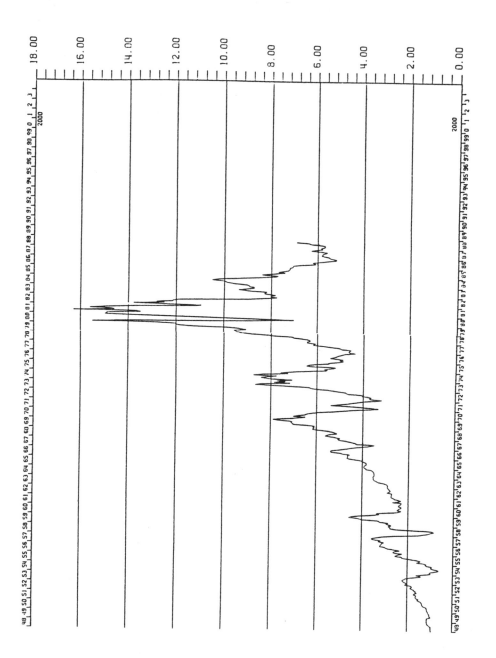

115

decade, or for interest rates to begin a significant rise early in each decade whether or not actual lows are made early in the decade. Consider the following analyses:

1. A low was made in 1930, consistent with the early-decade-low pattern. This was followed by an upswing that brought commercial paper rates from a low of 6 percent to a high of more than 18 percent during the next five years. In this case, the early-decade low coincided with the approximate ten-year cycle low.

2. Another low was made in 1841, again coinciding with the approximate ten-year cycle low.

3. Another low was made in 1851. It brought commercial paper rates from a low in the 6½ percent area to a high in the 12¾ percent area. Once again the importance of early-decade lows is plain to see.

4. A low was made in approximately 1862—again, early in the decade. This low marked the start of a slow but certain rise in rates from approximately 5½ percent to a high of 9¾ percent.

5. This was followed by a low in the 1871 time frame. Although rates moved higher, they stopped their ascent about one year after their bottom.

6. A low was made in 1883, again relatively early in the new decade; however, it was not a significant low in terms of appreciation inasmuch as interest rates climbed only briefly before turning lower again.

7. Another low was made in the 1883–84 time frame, still in the early part of the decade but later than had been the case since the 1831 bottom. It appeared as if the early-decade-low pattern was beginning to fail.

8. Another low was made in early 1894, still in the first half of the decade but not as early as had been the case in the 1830–71 time frame.

9. The next low came in the late 1903/early 1904 time frame. It appeared as if the early-decade-low pattern was beginning to take hold again.

10. Then from late 1930 to early 1931, interest rates made a low that failed to last. Another attempt at a low was made in 1932. From 1932 through 1940 a sideways-to-lower pattern developed that

eventually brought prices down to their early-decade low in 1940. Now the pattern was back on schedule.

11. The next low was actually made in 1954; however, the 1950–51 time frame was a level from which rates moved higher for several years. In fact, the 1954 low was not much lower than the 1950 low. The validity of early-decade lows in short-term interest rates was maintained.

12. There could not have been a more perfect validation of this pattern than the bottoming phase in short-term interest rates that developed from 1960 to 1961. Again, the validity of short-term interest rate lows early in the decade was confirmed.

13. Short-term interest rates "took off" only to peak in the late 1960s. This was followed by another early-decade low. This time the bottom came in the 1970–72 time frame. Thereafter, short-term interest rates jumped sharply for several years, peaking in the 1974 time frame.

14. Then, in early 1980, interest rates bottomed again, consistent with the early-decade-low pattern, and skyrocketed to all-time highs in 1981, only to begin a steady and fairly persistent decline to the approximate ten-year cycle low in 1986.

The validity of the early-decade-low pattern in short-term interest rates is most impressive. It has certainly captured my attention. Yet, in my many conversations with bankers, economists, and even cyclic market analysts, I have met few people who are either aware of or employ this most significant pattern in their trading, forecasting, and/ or investing. The greatest economic truths are there for the taking. They are simple and obvious. But they must still be found and, most important of all, employed.

Late-Decade-High Pattern in Short-Term Interest Rates

In addition to the early-decade-low pattern, the history of short-term interest rates from approximately 1830 to 1987 suggests that there has also been a pattern of late-decade highs. Note the following:

1. After the early-decade low in the 1830 time frame, short-term interest rates rose from approximately 6 percent to a high of near 19

percent in the 1837–38 period. A top was made in the second half of the decade.

2. The next low, early in the subsequent decade, was followed by a rise in short-term interest rates from approximately 4½ percent to a top in late 1848 to early 1849. Again, the late-decade pattern was confirmed as rates peaked at about 15¼ percent.

3. The next low came in 1851. It was followed by a top in the 1857 time frame, again in the latter part of the decade.

4. The next low, in approximately 1862 at about 5¼ percent, was followed by a move to near 10 percent and a late-decade top in 1869. Once again the late-decade-top pattern was confirmed.

5. The ten-year period from 1870 to 1880 was clearly atypical. It failed to fit the pattern that had been established for several decades in succession. In fact, the deviation continued into the next decade; however, it was not as pronounced. Although interest rates made a peak in 1893, they were followed by a second peak in 1896 that nearly matched the first top.

6. The pattern then got back on track with a significant peak in short-term interest rates in late 1907.

7. From the 1907 high, interest rates fell to their low in 1914 and peaked again in the 1919–20 time frame.

8. Following the 1919–20 high, interest rates moved lower to bottom in mid-decade and then to top again in the 1928–29 time frame. Once again the late-decade-high pattern was validated.

9. The era of the Great Depression witnessed generally lower interest rates for the entire 1930–40 decade; however, a brief spurt and top were made in 1937.

10. The next top was made late in the following decade as interest rates peaked in 1949. Only a minor decline developed before rates moved considerably higher in the 1950s. Still, there were two tops in this decade, one in 1957 and one in 1959.

11. Then came the large increase in interest rates that ran from approximately 1961 through the late-decade top in 1969. This was followed by a precipitous drop and another major peak in 1979. The 1979 peak was followed by one of the most severe declines in short-term interest rates ever seen. Again, the decline began late in the decade.

What can we learn from the patterns and cycles in short-term interest rates? Consider the following conclusions:

1. Short-term interest rates have shown a historical tendency to bottom prior to mid-decade, usually in the first few years of the decade. Tops have come in the latter part of the decade, usually in the last few years.

2. The pattern has significant implications for the businessperson. It suggests that borrowing should be initiated early in the decade for several years forward at fixed rates.

3. Given the late-decade-high pattern, it would also be reasonable to avoid borrowing late in the decade; however, if borrowing must be done, then loans should be taken at an adjustable rate as opposed to a fixed rate.

4. Short-term interest rates can also be used as an index of inflation/deflation. This suggests that the ideal time to begin a business that is inflation-sensitive is early in each decade, and that the best time to sell a business that is inflation-sensitive has been late in the decade.

5. There are other important economic and investment implications of the patterns and cycles in short-term interest rates. I will expound on these in a later chapter.

WHAT'S AHEAD?

Provided that the cycles in short-term and long-term interest rates remain valid, then the following scenario should be expected:

1. A peak in short-term interest rates during the late 1980s. It is not likely that the peak will match the record highs; however, the increase could be significant.

2. This suggests a period of inflationary economic recovery.

3. This in turn suggests that increases should be seen in most commodity prices, including petroleum and precious metals.

4. Thereafter, most likely in the late 1980s, a significant decline in interest rates and the economy should begin. Long-term interest rate lows and economic lows are due in the mid- to late 1990s.

These are the forecasts based on interest rate cycles and patterns; however, forecasts are one thing, and preparation is another. The coming economic turmoil will made an effective and comprehensive investment strategy more important than ever before. The collapse that surely awaits us cannot be avoided other than by sensible application of patterns and cycles such as the ones discussed in this chapter and throughout the course of this book. But sensible management by government is not something we can expect. History has shown us that mismanagement and reaction rather than logical preparatory action are the stock and trade of many governments.

Chapter 5

Precious Metals
and the Long Wave

The constancy of human nature has led me to conclude that economists may be no different than alchemists: both are charlatans . . . economists denigrated gold and asserted that they could more accurately measure value with an elastic paper money system . . . both groups have their tools, formulas, dogmas, and rituals . . . but the computer term most aptly describes the results: garbage in, garbage out. . . .

—Robert A. Ellison
Cycles, November 1987

The history of gold and silver prices has been marked by lengthy periods of stability interspersed with relatively brief periods of violent fluctuation. The glitter of precious metals has been a stimulus for war and betrayal, as well as the expression of love and thanks. Their historical value has made them a vehicle for speculation as well as a haven for safety in times of economic turmoil. Those interested in learning more about the history of precious metals can consult any number of excellent books on the subject. One of the better sources is *The Golden Constant.*[1]

It is only through an understanding of gold history that we can achieve a thorough awareness of its value during all types of economic climates. Yet, to merely understand the importance of gold is not, in and of itself, an asset to the investor. To understand is one thing; to act

[1]Jastram, Roy W., *The Golden Constant*, John Wiley & Sons, Inc., NY, 1977.

is yet another. To know what should happen and to prepare for what should happen are two distinctively different things. To know what one must do and to actually do it are both necessary ingredients for success. The investment world is abundant in "should have dones" and "would have dones." For every one investor who did what he or she was supposed to do when it should have been done there are hundreds who did not act appropriately. Many of us know the rules; few of us follow them. And for the few who do manage to know and follow the rules, timing becomes a major problem. We get into or out of investments too early or too late, we allow ourselves to be talked into or out of investments at the wrong time, and then we must find someone to blame for our errors. What does this have to do with the precious metals? Virtually everything! Why? Because investing in precious metals is an emotionally charged issue. Whether you're an investor who accumulates precious metals slowly in expectation of economic uncertainty or a speculator who buys and sells precious metals in anticipation of, or in reaction to, news and events, emotion often reigns supreme.

When the Hunt brothers attempted their corner on the silver market in 1979–1980, prices shot up almost vertically. Investors and speculators clamored to get on board. When silver was at $10 per ounce, the forecasts were for $15. When they reached $15, the forecasts were for $25, and when they were at $25, there were forecasts of $100 an ounce. Figure 5.1 shows the daily price chart of silver futures during the time of the last bull market peak. There is no doubt whatsoever but that the peak was an emotional one. For those who acted late in the game, the result was a significant loss, unless they were fast enough to get off the roller coaster before it turned lower. For those, however, who were shrewd enough to gradually accumulate silver during the late 1960s and early 1970s, consistent with the price cycles in silver, the ride was a profitable one indeed. When the emotional explosion in prices was at its apex, the wise and early buyers were slowly and surely selling out most of their holdings.

The gold and platinum futures markets were also dominated by emotion and wild trading during this period. Figures 5.2 and 5.3 show the daily price charts of platinum and gold futures during their major peaks. Those who were familiar with the long-term gold and platinum cycles were buyers well in advance of the bull markets. If these same visionary investors maintained their discipline during the emotion-laden days accompanying the top, they acted consistent with the price cycles and liquidated their gold and platinum holdings.

Figure 5-1. *Daily silver futures prices during last bull market peak.*

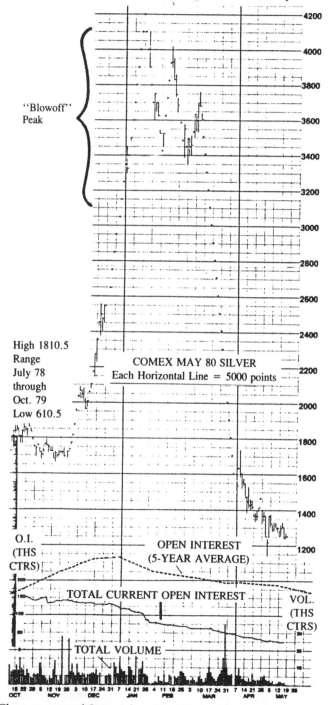

Source: Chart courtesy of Commodity Price Charts.

Figure 5-2. *Daily prices of platinum futures during the last long-wave peak.*

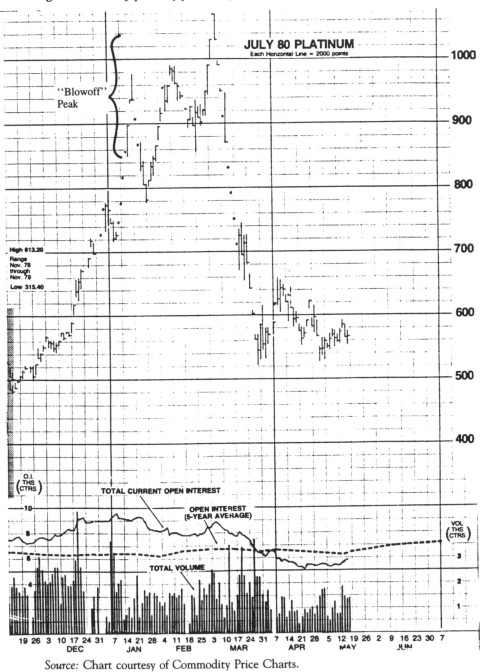

Source: Chart courtesy of Commodity Price Charts.

Figure 5-3. *Daily price futures of gold during the last long-wave peak.*

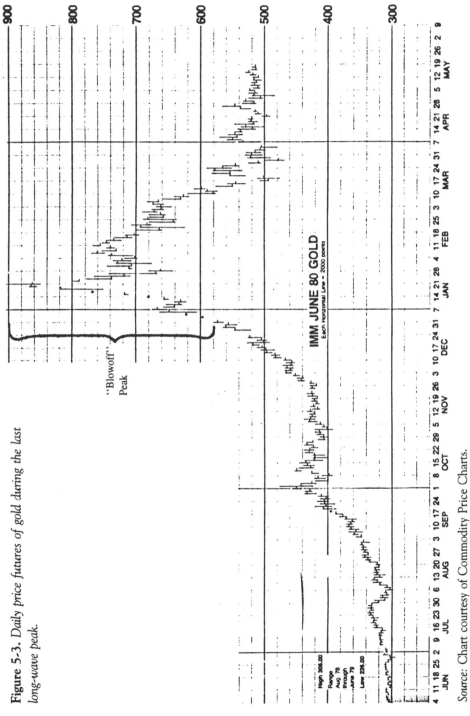

"Blowoff" Peak

IMM JUNE 80 GOLD
Each Horizontal Line = 2000 points

High 306.00

Range
Aug. 78
through
June 79

Low 226.00

Source: Chart courtesy of Commodity Price Charts.

Precious metals were not the only markets to explode during the 1970s. Virtually all markets reached their peaks during the same general time frame. To a large extent precious metals are commodities just like the grains, meat, foods, and financials. However, history clearly supports the dual purpose of precious metals. In oversimplified terms, the precious metals have always been seen as a hedge against uncertainty. But uncertainty can take many different forms. *What is uncertain in one era is not uncertain in another.* If, for example, Iran had fired on oil tankers in the Persian Gulf during the mid-1970s, the result would have been a massive rally in precious metals prices. In 1987, however, tankers were fired upon or sunk almost weekly with virtually no reaction in the price of precious metals. Why? Because precious metals, although valuable in varying degrees, do not always respond to crisis. One must also give consideration to other variables. Precious metals prices do not move up and down in a vacuum. They are not worthwhile possessions at all times. While it is true that they glitter and have numerous applications in industry, they are not always favored investments. There are, in fact, times when precious metals should be sold—even sold short by more aggressive investors or traders who are familiar with and able to accept the attendant risks. The ownership of precious metals is not a panacea. Yet those who understand the role of precious metals will also understand when to own them and when to avoid them, when to love them and when to hate them, when they are likely to rise in value and when they are likely to fall in value.

THE BASIC RELATIONSHIPS

There are many different viewpoints on precious metals. Some analysts and investment advisors suggest that precious metals should be held only during times of inflation, whereas others suggest that precious metals should be held during times of disinflation and deflation. During the last disinflationary period, when U.S. gold prices were fixed by government decree and could not go lower, the purchasing power of gold increased substantially. This can be seen from Figures 5.4 and 5.5, which are reprinted from *Prices,* the excellent reference work by Warren and Pearson.[2]

[2]Warren, George F. and Pearson, Frank A., *Prices,* John Wiley & Sons, Inc., NY, 1933.

Figure 5-4. *Pounds of commodities required to buy an ounce of gold in June 1929 and June 1931.*

Commodity	Prices		Pounds Required to Buy an Ounce of Gold		Percent Increase
	June 1929	June 1931	June 1929	June 1931	
Corn, contract grade, Chicago, per bushel..................................	$ 0.92	$ 0.57	1260	2033	61
Wheat, No. 2 red, Chicago, per bushel..................................	1.22	0.75	1016	1656	63
Hogs, fair to choice heavy butchers, Chicago, per 100 pounds.....	10.66	6.50	194	318	64
Cotton, middling, New York, pound..................................	0.188	0.084	110	246	124
Pig iron, basic valley furnace, per ton	18.50	15.50	2235	2667	19
Copper ingot electrolytic, refinery, per pound.............................	0.178	0.0825	116	251	116
Lead, pig, New York, per pound....	0.070	0.0375	295	551	87
Tin, pig, New York, per pound	0.443	0.225	47	92	96
Zinc, slab, New York, per pound ...	0.070	0.0355	295	582	97
Sulfate of ammonia, New York, per 100 pounds	2.22	1.85	931	1117	20
Average increase..................	....	....	....	....	75

Source: Warren, G. F. and Pearson, F. A., "The Price Series" in *Prices*, Book 1, John Wiley & Sons, Inc., NY, 1933.

Yet the last experience does not necessarily forecast accurately what is likely to happen again. In fact, while gold was holding its value during the last disinflation, silver and platinum prices were falling sharply with all other commodity prices (see Figures 5.6 and 5.7). Today, gold prices are free to float with virtually all other commodity prices. Gold in many respects is merely another commodity. It will respond to the ups and downs of inflation and disinflation as do most other markets. However, it is very likely that in the event of a full-scale banking crisis or a full-scale monetary crisis, precious metals will once again be held in high regard as a stable store of wealth. This is, in fact, the role that they have had for thousands of years. What to do? Here are a few general guidelines regarding precious metals ownership and the long-wave cycles:

Figure 5-5. *Index numbers of wholesale prices of all commodities and the value of gold, 1814–1932 (1910–14 = 100).*

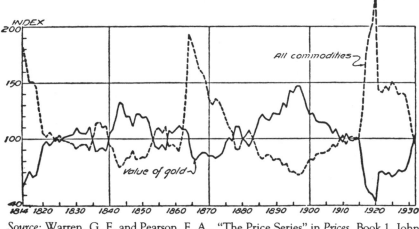

Source: Warren, G. F. and Pearson, F. A., "The Price Series" in *Prices*, Book 1, John Wiley & Sons, Inc., NY, 1933.

1. When the long cycle is in its initial stages, precious metals are likely to be relatively low priced with low volatility. The long-term investor can slowly and methodically accumulate precious metals on a steady investment program using dollar cost averaging methods (*i.e.*, regular purchase program regardless of prices). As an alternative, purchases can be made only on significant price declines.

2. As inflation begins to accelerate, the accumulation program continues, perhaps at a faster pace, in expectation of higher prices in line with increased inflation.

3. As the long-wave economic cycle approaches its peak and precious metals prices explode, moving violently and dramatically higher, the long-term investor should slowly but deliberately begin to liquidate positions. Since prices tend to drop faster than they rise, selling would need to be done more quickly and over a comparatively short period of time.

4. Platinum prices tend to gain more ground than gold prices during the upward swing, reaching a very large premium at the top. As the markets decline, platinum prices tend to come more closely into line with gold prices. Figure 5.8 shows the typical platinum gold spread at the last market top and at the last market bottom. It may,

Figure 5-6. *The decline in platinum prices during the last long-wave deflation (1923–32).*

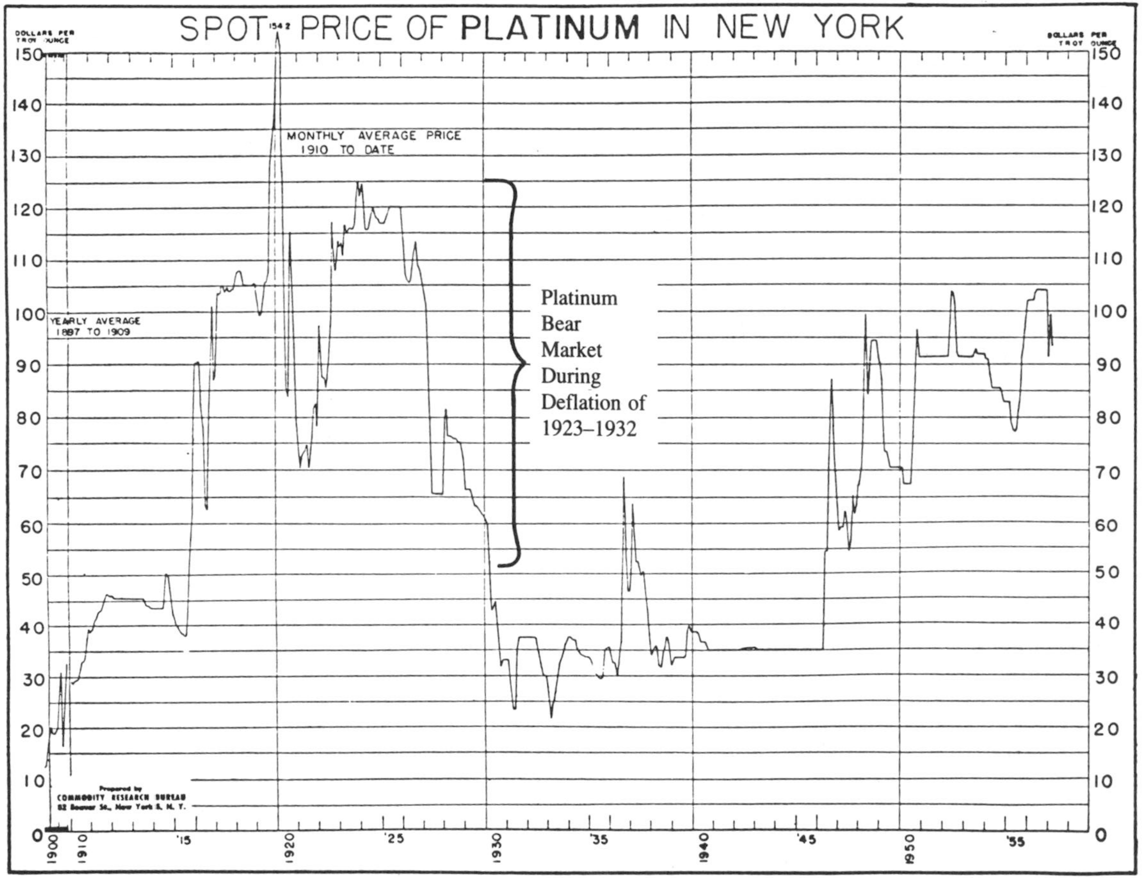

SPOT PRICE OF PLATINUM IN NEW YORK

Platinum
Bear
Market
During
Deflation of
1923–1932

MONTHLY AVERAGE PRICE
1910 TO DATE

YEARLY AVERAGE
1887 TO 1909

Prepared by
COMMODITY RESEARCH BUREAU
82 Beaver St., New York 5, N. Y.

Source: Courtesy of Commodity Research Bureau.

129

Figure 5-7. *The decline in cash silver prices during the last long-wave deflation (1923–32).*

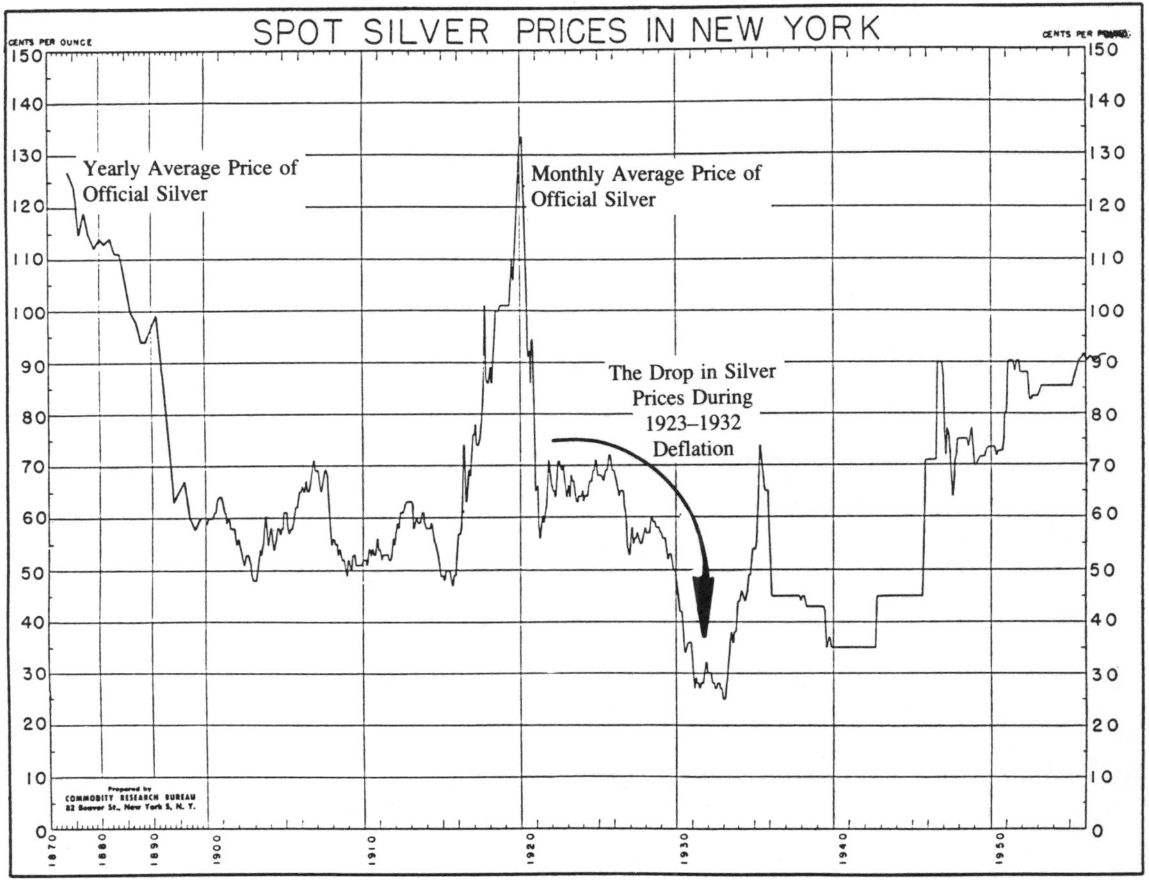

SPOT SILVER PRICES IN NEW YORK

Monthly Average Price of
Official Silver

Yearly Average Price of
Official Silver

The Drop in Silver
Prices During
1923–1932
Deflation

Source: Courtesy of Commodity Research Bureau.

Figure 5-8. *The platinum/gold spread at the 1980 and 1986 market tops and at the 1982 and 1985 market bottoms.*

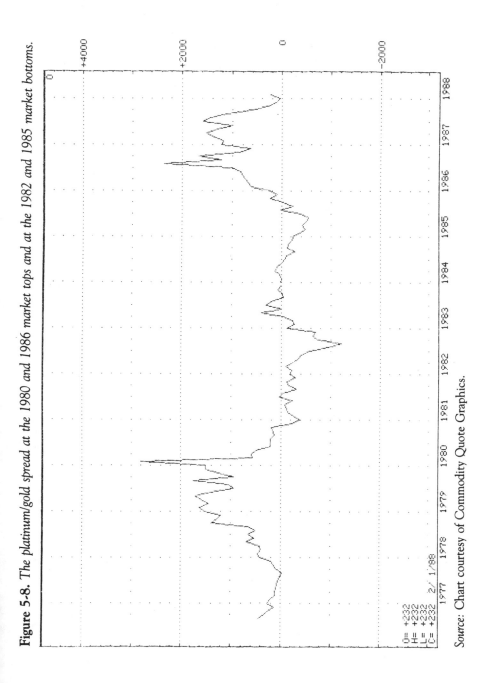

Source: Chart courtesy of Commodity Quote Graphics.

therefore, be better from a dollar profit standpoint to own platinum in a larger proportion than gold. This point of view is distinctly different from that voiced by those who constantly tout gold in preference to all other precious metals investments.

5. Serious investors should not discount palladium as a reasonable investment alternative in preparation for inflation. Palladium prices are lower than are those of platinum or gold, but they are higher than that of silver. The single most important fundamental in palladium is the fact that well over 95 percent of the world's palladium comes from one country, the Soviet Union. The Soviets can cut off supplies at whim. And one day they will.

6. Silver is the most speculative of the precious metals because it is the lowest in price. Yet silver prices can increase many more times than can gold, platinum, or palladium prices. But silver tends to make its largest moves toward the end of an inflationary period. Therefore, do not enter silver too heavily in the early stages of an economic upswing.

7. Precious metals should be sold out prior to or during the time frame of the economic peak. In fact, a good majority of the holdings should be sold off just prior to or during the "blowoff" phase. It is, of course, not always possible to tell when the blowoff is in process. One good way to know is by listening to the news. When the news becomes incredibly bullish, when the experts are making wild forecasts about how prices will go, and when good sense appears to have left the market, it is time for you to begin selling some of your holdings. Remember that timing will not always be perfect, but if you are close enough to tops and bottoms your percentage gain will be fantastic, and you will have had the protection you needed.

8. During the disinflationary phase, when the prospect for financial panics and bank failures is high, the metals may again have value for the long-term investor. However, during a disinflationary period precious metals are likely to decline in price with other commodities. Cash will likely be a better investment, unless the dollar is backed by gold, in which case dollars will be as good as gold. It is likely, but not guaranteed, that in the event of a severe disinflationary plunge, precious metals will become attractive to investors as they flee *en masse* from virtually all other types of investments.

SUGGESTED PRECIOUS METALS PORTFOLIO

Many market analysts overestimated the role and value of precious metals in the 1970s. They erred in thinking that the upswing in precious metals would last forever. The cast of characters in the "Gold Follies of the 1970s" included some of the best-known names in the investment business. Some forecasts published in the 1970s were outrageously bullish. A good majority of analysts were most bullish at the top. Fortunately, the more sensible and well-established advisors retained their good sense and advised caution or liquidation when prices were rocketing skyward, with seemingly no end in sight. Yet a few actors in this tragic comedy were unabashedly bullish and remained bullish as the roller coaster plummeted earthward. These characters will go unnamed, as they have suffered enough. Yet they seem to resurface with every brief upturn in the precious metals, once again ready to peddle their undying bullish forecasts to the public. Their failure, in addition to not exercising good sense, was in closing their eyes and ears to the economic realities of precious metals as commodities that would move up and down in response to inflation and disinflation. A more rational point of view on the precious metals is proposed herein. Donald J. Hoppe, whose work I hold in the highest esteem, notes:

> But when gold is undervalued, as it was in the 1920s, before the devaluation of 1934, and again in the 1960s, before the abandonment of the fixed $35 per ounce gold parity for the dollar, gold mines were going out of business. There is little profit in mining gold when operating costs are high and the price of the metal (that is, its purchasing power) is low. On the other hand, in the late 1970s and thus far into the '80s, gold has not only increased in price, but has become overvalued (again in terms of its purchasing power). I agree it is not as overvalued as it was at its all-time high of $850 per ounce. . . .
>
> In any case, could it be that the price of gold has become inflated along with everything else? Remember, for the first time in the history of money, gold, since 1973, has been freely traded, and its price has been set by the market rather than by government fiat. And if the market has now overvalued gold, will the market not ultimately correct this error—or even make the contrary error of undervaluing it in the future? [1988, p. 24]

What follows is a listing of precious metals portfolio suggestions, subject to modification as a function of actual events.

1. The profit potential of precious metals during a deflating or disinflating economy will be limited unless prices are fixed by government mandate or decree. If the U.S. government moves to increase gold reserves or otherwise acts to buy gold, bolstering U.S. dollar strength, then precious metals will increase in value regardless of underlying economic trend, particularly if purchases are heavy. This is not considered a particularly realistic possibility at the present time.

2. If the U.S. government decides to print its way out of debt, then inflation will explode and with it the price of all commodity items, whether foods, metals, livestock, or fibers. All markets are then likely to move higher, and precious metals will be favored.

3. In the event of a serious banking crisis, precious metals may increase in value; however, the need to own precious metals well in advance of such a crisis is mitigated by their probable disinflationary decline. Therefore, it may be best to buy precious metals at the inception of such a crisis, but not until then.

4. In the event of a serious military confrontation, precious metals could increase in value.

5. During the disinflationary stage of the long wave, I recommend that no more than 20 percent of one's portfolio be in precious metals.

6. I recommend a mix of the 20 percent distribution as follows: approximately 30 percent gold, 40 percent platinum, 20 percent palladium, and the balance in silver.

7. This distribution will change as the long wave begins its upswing and as the upswing approaches its latter stages.

ALTERNATIVES TO PRECIOUS METALS

This book is not intended to serve as a step-by-step investment guide to the precious metals. There are, however, several suggestions I can give you, all drawn from my personal experience and observations in the areas cited:

1. Mining stocks have long been a favorite of investors. Whether Canadian, U.S., South African, or Australian mining shares, this

aspect of the precious metals market has always fascinated speculators and investors. As you know, there are investment-grade mining
stocks and there are speculative mining stocks. There will always be
the potential to make and/or lose fortunes in speculative stocks. But
I consider them too risky for most investors.

Those who favor stocks over bullion point to the most incredible rise in Homestake Mining during the Depression era of the 1930s.
This was, of course, due to a special situation. Namely, the price of
gold was fixed, and investors flocked into the shares market as an
alternative, since gold ownership was not legal in the United States.
Will this happen again? If it does, then gold shares will be a
worthwhile investment.[3]

2. Bullion coins are probably the most sensible way for the investor to
   participate. They are readily bought and sold, they need not be
   assayed or verified as to content, and they are well known throughout the world. There are gold, silver, platinum, and palladium
   bullion coins. Remember to do business with a reputable and established dealer!

3. Bullion in the form of bars or ingots is not recommended for the
   average investor. It takes time to sell bullion, it must be reassayed,
   and it is generally not as popular or liquid a medium as are bullion
   coins.

4. Futures and options are for the most speculative of investors, those
   with large amounts of risk capital. In the proper economic environment, inflating or deflating, the disciplined trader can acquire a vast
   fortune speculating in futures; however, there is also the distinct
   possibility of loss. The fact is that more than 90 percent of all futures
   speculators lose. The odds are clearly against you. But if you have
   some risk capital, if the time is right, and if your timing is on target,
   you stand to make it big.

5. Precious metals mutual funds may be the best way to go if you're
   interested in stocks but if you haven't the time or the inclination to
   follow all of the stocks.

---

[3]It should be noted that there may be problems associated with the ownership of South
African gold shares.

CONCLUSION

I conclude that there will be a time and a place for precious metals. Metals make up only part of your investment portfolio; however, during times of disinflation such as those that are likely to be seen in 1989 and in the mid-1990s, it is likely that the role of metals will be one of minimal importance. It should be noted, as mentioned earlier, that several cycles in precious metals are likely to bottom in 1989. This could bring a new round of strength in precious metals. The precise economic stimulus for the expected upswing is uncertain; however, it could very well be the results of banking problems. If this is the case, then investors should prepare for upswing by taking a more aggressive stance when the cycles begin to turn higher. Refer to the gold, silver, and platinum cycles charts for specifics. Above all, don't allow yourself to become a precious metals fanatic. Take a commonsense viewpoint, put only a portion of your assets into precious metals, and do so at or near the proper time(s).

Chapter 6

Is War Inevitable?

The iron and steel industry . . . roused itself for the only quarry it had now the vigor to pursue—man eating. It had long ceased to dream of new liners and bridges or railways or steel-framed houses. But it could still make guns and kill. . . .

—H. G. Wells, 1933

Whether you believe it or not, it's a fact that virtually every long-wave top and every long-wave bottom has been accompanied by a war. The top and bottom war phenomenon, although well documented, is a matter of continuing debate. Why? Again, the arguments are primarily statistical. Opponents of this theory claim that there have not been sufficient repetitions of war and the long-wave cycles to allow for a statistically valid test of the war/long-wave top and bottom hypothesis. At this time the issue remains one of conjecture. Nevertheless, there are other indicators and theories which support concerns that the current long-wave cyclic bottom is likely to end with a war. What are some of the studies? How valid are they? What are some of the theories? Are they reasonable or merely idle speculation? This chapter will review some of the cyclic and theoretical evidence pointing to the possibility of a war at or near the bottom of the current long wave.

IS WAR A CONSEQUENCE OF AFFLUENCE?

There has been considerable debate about the role of war in the long-wave scenario. Joseph A. Schumpeter, in his many writings about the long-wave cycles, advanced the notion that war was an inextricable part of the long wave. While some economists and historians have claimed that war is a byproduct of economic growth, others claim that war is not necessary and, furthermore, that there is no cause-and-effect relationship between economics and war. Statistically speaking, the relationship is a tenuous one at best. Yet even this is a subject for debate.

Ciriacy Wantrup, according to Professor A. H. Hansen (1941), proposed the theory that war is the leading cause of long waves. This point of view was also supported by Rose in his "Wars, Innovations, and the Long Cycle: A Brief Comment," which was published in *American Economic Review* (March 1941). Rose stated:

> Modern war may be the innovation par excellence . . . and as such, the dominant cause of long waves in economic activity. [p. 105]

This point of view was echoed by Silberling in Chapter 4 of *The Dynamics of Business.* Yet, Clemence and Doody in their scholarly review of the Schumpeterian System noted the following:

> According to this view, the prosperities preceding wars are to be accounted for in terms of increasing armament expenditures, while the succeeding depressions are attributable to the dislocations ensuing on the curtailment of war expenditures. This is by no means an adequate account of the theory. . . . [p. 90]

The authors cited Hansen's work, which concluded that war was not correlated closely with long-wave cyclic bottoms:

> On balance, it may perhaps be said that, in the "upswing" phase of the first so-called long wave, wars occupied a position of major importance, perhaps equal to that of the innovations introduced by the Industrial Revolution. Each reinforced the other, and it is difficult to disentangle the relative potency of each factor. For the second "Aufschwungsspanne" it appears reasonable to conclude that the major factor was the railroadization of the world, and that wars played a relatively minor part, with respect to both the good times and the

ensuing period of chronic hard times which followed. For the third period the most reasonable conclusion appears to be that the electrification and motorization of the Western world played by far the dominant role, reinforced toward the end of the period by the first World War, and that for the succeeding period of economic difficulties postwar readjustments played an important role, though it may well be that the adaptation of the economic structure to the innovational developments of the preceding period was of equal significance. [Hansen, 1941, p. 35]

Also at issue is the question of whether war is a cause or an effect. Upon closer examination, it may ultimately be found that war is neither a cause nor an effect. But in reality, there is no issue here at all—unless, of course, we want to get bogged down in academic exercises. The fact is that there appears to be a correlation. Correlation itself does not imply cause or effect. Eventually it may be found that war is influenced by a host of factors—social, political, economic, and psychological. Each of these variables may influence one another. Inasmuch as we will probably never know the answer for certain, I suggest that we stop thinking about causes and begin looking at correlations. Once we know that correlation is high, we can know what to look for and when to look for it without digging ourselves into the hole of causation (since it tends to ruffle the feathers of social scientists). We will know when the probability of war is high and when it is low. We will then know that we must prepare for it. This, of course, begs the question of whether it is possible to prepare for war. In particular, it presupposes that if there is to be another world war there will be an escape.

Paul P. Craig and Kenneth E. F. Watt, in a study entitled "The Kondratieff Cycle and War: How Close is the Connection?," analyzed the subject at hand. The authors carefully studied data previously compiled by Richardson in 1980. They concluded the following from their studies:

There is a clear correlation between the economic long wave and deaths in wars. This data base, using data from Lewis Richardson's *Statistics of Deadly Quarrels*, published in 1960, includes 315 wars and is averaged over 11 years. . . .

These calculations imply that, if the historical experience of the industrial nations is extrapolated into the future, we are now close to an economic low, after which there will be improvement until early in the next century. They also suggest that the next decades may be a time of low war casualties but that the beginning of the next century will be dangerous. . . . [1985]

Figures 6.1 and 6.2 are taken from Craig and Watt's analysis. Clearly, their findings suggest that as we approach the time frame of a long-term economic low, the probability of war will be increased. Particularly frightening is their forecast (which is given in an almost perfunctory and detached fashion):

> The extrapolation suggests that the death toll in the next major war period will be about 1 billion individuals, for an average of 100 million war deaths per year over a decade. Death tolls in this range are readily within the capabilities of modern technology and could be much larger if "nuclear winter" effects were triggered. [1985]

Figure 6-1. *A schematic summary of long-wave highs and lows and war deaths. The correlation is apparent. The chart extrapolates historical experience into the future, forecasting a surge of war deaths in the early part of the twenty-first century.*

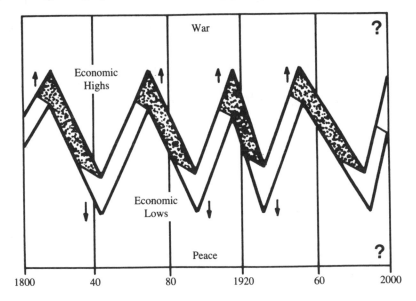

Source: Craig and Watt, *The Futurist*, April 1985.

Figure 6-2. *War deaths. There is a clear correlation between the economic long wave and deaths in wars. This data base, using data from Lewis Richardson's* Statistics of Deadly Quarrels, *published in 1960, includes 315 wars and is averaged over 11 years.*

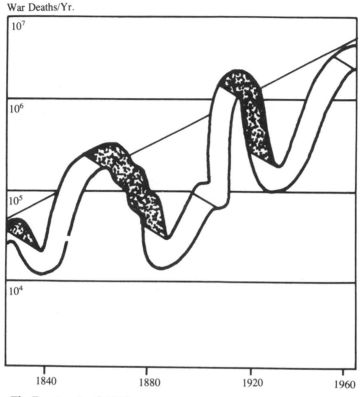

Source: The Futurist, April 1985.

CYCLES IN INTERNATIONAL CONFLICT

The cycle studies on international conflict are based on a massive amount of historical data and analyses. Their conclusions are equally significant in pointing to the high probability of a war late in the 1980-to-mid-1990 time frame. Here is some background on the cyclical studies:

1. The 17.7-year cycle 600 B.C.–A.D. 1957 was studied by Edward R. Dewey. His findings were published by The Foundation for the Study of Cycles in its *Research Bulletin #2*, 1964. The following summary of the 17.7-year cycle is reprinted verbatim from Dewey's report:

Significance of the 17.7-Year Cycle

The nature of this rhythmic phenomenon (a quasi-periodicity in contrast to a true periodicity) makes it difficult to determine statistically the probability of the observed behavior arising by chance. Since the behavior from wave to wave may be *inherently* irregular with respect to both amplitude and timing, classical tests for periodicity are likely to be negative. Nevertheless, there is a pattern in the observed behavior but it is not the sort of pattern postulated by ordinary mathematical models. The pattern is evolutive rather than stationary.

Since the observed pattern is present only on the average, it could be the result of auto-regressive characteristics. Such patterns, however, tend to diminish in amplitude as more and more waves are included in the average.

It is quite unlikely that the observed behavior in this study is a result of the autoregressive characteristics since the data for each half of the series were used separately and the observed pattern continues to appear in both halves with no significant change of average amplitude, period, phase, or shape. Moreover, the amplitude of the cycle computed from all 140 sections does not differ materially from the amplitude of the halves, each computed from 70 sections.

Although adequate mathematical tests for statistical significance of this cycle are not available, empirical tests can be made.

The general procedure for one such test would involve: (1) using randomized deviations to construct a large number of 17.71-year periodic tables of 140 lines each; (2) averaging each of these tables, *in toto*, and by quarters in order to obtain average waves; and (3) calculating how often the average waves derived from the tables of the randomized deviations would attain (a) the strength, (b) the symmetry, (c) the regularity, and (d) the close calendar datings achieved by the deviations in their actual order.

In particular, one must determine the probability that calculations from a periodic table of randomized deviations yield: (1) an average wave of overall range equal to or exceeding 26.61%; (2) an average of nine consecutive column averages (centering on the column average of maximum value) with an amplitude of 3.82% or larger; and (3) a timing of sinusoids (fitted to each quarter of the table) falling within 0.73 years of the timing of the cycle as a whole.

Although the above empirical tests were not conducted in detail, preliminary calculations indicated an extremely low probability that the observed cyclic behavior could have occurred by chance. A future report is planned to study in depth the statistical significance of this cycle and others reported upon by the Foundation.

In addition to the above study, Dewey has documented war cycles of 510 years, 170 years, 84 years, 61.4 years, 57 years, 54.9 years, 50 years, 33 years, 22 years, and so on. Figure 6.3 shows Dewey's combined index of International and Civil War Battles (p. 630). Figure 6.4 shows Dewey's statistical reconnaissance of the cycles in International Battles. Note the large amplitude of an approximate 54-year cycle.

2. "The Cycle Synthesis: Index of International Conflict," also published by Dewey, is reprinted in Figure 6.5. It clearly suggests a peak in international conflict during the present time frame. In fact, the index forecast remains high into the early 1990s and begins to decline sharply thereafter. Remember that the forecast and reality do not always go precisely hand in hand. The forecast merely tells us when the probability of an event is higher than usual.

AN UNPLEASANT TOPIC

There's no doubt that this is a most unpleasant topic, particularly when we consider the possibility that the next war, if and when it happens, could very well be the last war. But we must be prepared for tomorrow. If, in fact, the bottom war turns out to be much less serious than expected, you will be prepared for it, and in being prepared you will improve your probability of personal and financial survival. Here are a few of my conclusions and comments derived from my readings and analyses:

1. The likelihood of a bottom war by the mid- to late 1990s is very high.

2. This conclusion is supported by statistical data on the long-wave economic cycles and by studies on cycles in international conflict.

Figure 6-3. *Possible cycles in war, battles, military activity, and human excitability.* [a]

Alleged Period in Years	Interval	Type of Phenomena
510	600 B.C.–A.D. 1943	Civil Wars
170	600 B.C.–A.D. 1943	Civil Wars
142	1–1950	International Battles
84	b	Political and Social Unrest
61.4	b	International Battles
57	1751–1950	International Battles
54.9	b	International Battles
50	b	Wars and Commodity Prices
33	1760–c	Wars and Peace
22½	1400–1943	International Battles
21.95	600 B.C.–A.D. 1943	International Battles
17¾ (or 17.728)	600 B.C.–A.D. 1950	Combined International and Civil Wars
12.1	1532–1910	International Battles
11.2 (or 11.245)	600 B.C.–A.D. 1950	International Wars
11 + [d]	b	Human Reactions in Wars
11 + [d]	500 B.C.–A.D. 1900	Military and Political Activity
9.6 and 12.3 pattern	560–1957	International Battles

[a]Research on work performed by others has been limited to material available in the library of the Foundation and to otherwise conveniently available sources.
[b]No dates given.
[c]Date not given.
[d]Length stated as approximately one sunspot cycle.

Source: Dewey, 1964.

3. If the bottom war does occur, it is likely to be a war supported by the American people, or by the so-called free world if it proves to be international in scope.

4. The bottom war is likely to bring with it a marked improvement in the U.S. economy.

5. The bottom war is more likely to stem from economic causes than have any of the previous wars. Regardless of precipitating event or

Figure 6-4. *Systematic period reconnaissance, index of international battles, 1700–1913.*

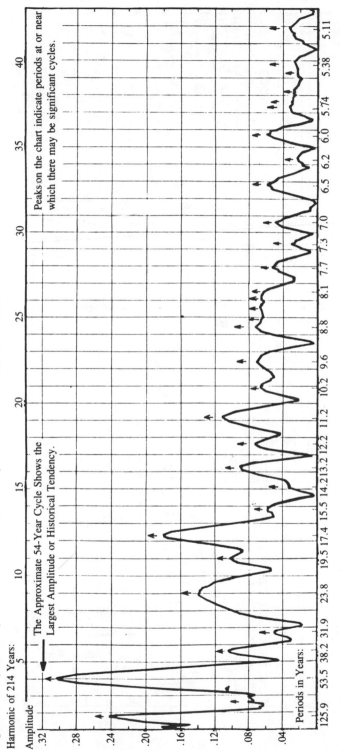

Source: Cycles, January 1967.

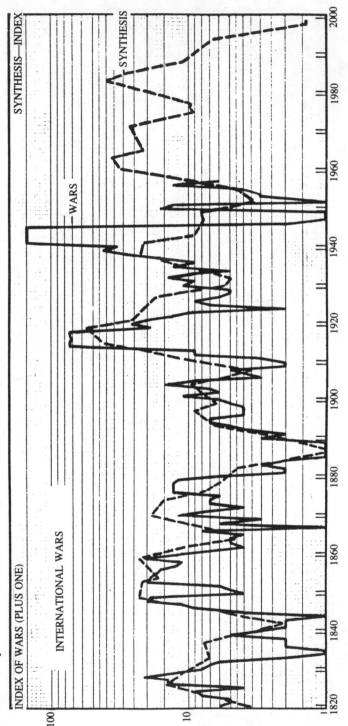

Figure 6-5. *The Index of International Conflict (plus one). The broken line shows a synthesis or combination of the 11.2-, 22.14-, 57-, and 142-year cycles, projected to the year 2000. An important increase in the number and intensity of international battles was due in the period 1959–1965, and an upturn is expected in the late 1990s.*

Source: Cycles, 1967.

events, the actual stimulus is likely to be economic in origin. Whether this takes the form of war over petroleum routes, mineral rights in outer space, territorial rights in outer space, or economic struggles between classes in a third-world country, the net result is likely to be a more pervasive and internationally emcompassing conflict.

6. Technology will likely make rapid advancements just prior to the bottom war. The bottom is apt to end with the military application of a technological breakthrough, as did World War II.

7. The bottom war, should it develop, will be a signal to investors that the current long wave has drawn to an end and that a new era of economic progress awaits.

8. Prior to the bottom war there is likely to be significant disruption of trade routes, and a possible imposition of price controls, trading suspensions in stocks and futures, and other wartime government intervention.

9. A bottom war is not a necessity; however, its probability is high. The war could prove to be a series of successive conflicts on different fronts throughout the world and even in outer space. A marked increase in international conflict, such as is now clearly in process, could indicate that the bottom war this time will not focus on just one issue or in one area, but rather an intense series of confrontations by different participants in diverse geographic locations, because of a variety of purported causes.

10. It is hoped that this coming long-wave low will prove to be the exception to the rule; however, the probability of this long wave ending with a "breakout of peace" is slim indeed.

Be prepared for the worst. Study past wars, their effects, results, and economic consequences. Determine how you can best prepare for the "unexpected." Remember that you have specific and unique economic needs mediated by your financial assets and liabilities, and by your personal situation. Hence, there is no single answer for all investors. You must do some thinking about your own situation, and you must plan ahead. Sun Tzu in *The Art of War* noted:

> just as water retains no constant shape, so in warfare there are no constant conditions . . . he who can modify his tactics in relation to his

opponent, and thereby succeed in winning, may be called a heaven-born captain. . . . [Clavell, 1983, p. 29]

In order for you to be the captain of your own destiny you will need to be prepared for the unexpected. This can be achieved only through an understanding of historical conditions preceding each war, particularly those that developed at or near long-wave cyclical lows.

CAN YOU TAKE THE CHANCE?

Still, there are those who say that another war is unlikely. There are those who claim that today's ultimate weapons, nuclear and biological, will dissuade humankind from war. But the probability of war by accident increases with each passing moment. Proliferation of weapons to irresponsible terrorist groups is increasing at an alarming rate. Conflict throughout the world is escalating daily. With each increase in conflict, no matter how minor, comes an increase in the probability of an accidental war, which will likely drag the superpowers into conflict as well.

Even if the cycles are incorrect, can you afford to be unprepared? My work has convinced me that there will most definitely be another war, that it will be a major war, and that it will begin sooner than most of us expect. Don't let another day pass without preparation. Even if your preparation consists of studying and reading, it is, nevertheless, preparation. After you've done some reading, you can act. Unfortunately, I cannot as yet offer any concrete suggestions on how to prepare, but we still have time. We cannot afford to risk being unprepared.

Adding a note of mysticism to the question of a major war in the offing are the words of the sixteenth-century seer Nostradamus. Those who are unfamiliar with the works of Nostradamus should know that many of his specific forecasts have become realities in spite of the fact that they were made hundreds of years ago. Rene Noorbergen, in *Invitation to a Holocaust: Nostradamus Forecasts World War III*, interprets Nostradamus's forecasts as translated from the sixteenth-century French:

> Soleil levant un grand feu l'on verra,
> Bruit et clarté vers Aquilon tendants:
> Dedans le rond mort et cris l'on ouira,
> Par glaive, feu, faim, mort les attendants. [II, 91]

At sunrise one will see a great fire,
The noise and light will be aimed toward Acuilon [nations of the far north]
Within the lands of the Arctic Circle one will hear cries of death
Through instruments of steel, death with come through fire and famine. [1981, p. 45]

Noorbergen concludes the following from the prophecies:

In the light of international developments, it is extremely interesting that Nostradamus—as far back as the 1500s—gives the Middle Eastern nations a major fighting role in the war. This might seem somewhat implausible in the light Israel's repeated military victories over her Arab neighbours in recent years, but while the Middle Eastern nations may not appear to be strong enough now, the next five years will undoubtedly witness a radical change. Already they are wielding tremendous economic power because of their oil reserves. The Russian influence in the region has been declining for a number of years, and the USA's insistence on support for Israel is rapidly undermining her influence in that part of the world. By exchanging their American and Russian "benefactors" for Peking, the Arabs may find an ally who will have no qualms about supplying them with nuclear bombs as well as bacteriological/chemical and other more conventional weapons. Once their arsenal has been rebuilt along these lines, they will strike west; China will strike south and World War III will be upon us. [1981, p. 19]

Fortunately, Noorbergen's forecasts have not yet come to pass, however, the record of Nostradamus's forecasts and their coincidence with findings and theories presented in this chapter are far too compelling to ignore. It is food for thought, and one hopes, for preventive action!

In closing, let us not forget that cyclical analysis is by no means precise. The probability of a major war, although likely based on the studies cited in this chapter and upon the ideal manifestation of the long wave, does not necessarily guarantee its occurrence. We would do well, however, to admit to its possibility and to prepare accordingly. The ideal situation, of course, would be to take appropriate remedial action. Unfortunately it could very well be true that war is a necessary economic "purgative" that functions to cleanse capitalist economies of their excesses, inefficiencies, and fallow resources, in a sense rejuvenating and restructuring the industrial machinery. It is this aspect of war and the economic cycle that concerns me most.

Chapter 7

Saved from the Brink: Preparing for the Future

Anyone taken as an individual, is tolerably sensible and reasonable—as a member of a crowd, he at once becomes a blockhead.

—*Schiller*

The economic future as I've presented in this book does not hold positive promise. The prospects for economic well-being are poor. The global economic outlook is also in jeopardy. It would be a simple matter indeed to allow the seeming hopelessness of the situation to be used as an excuse for indolence. Excuses are not hard to come by. Constructive action, however, takes effort, study, concentration, planning, persistence, perseverance, and follow-through. If there are any constructive actions that may be taken in preparation for the inevitable economic collapse, then we must implement them well in advance or we will be no better than the bureaucratic procrastinators whose failings have driven us to the brink.

Not too many years ago I watched the noted economist Milton Friedman on a television program that addressed the history, causes of, and cures for inflation. As the chronicle drew to a close, Dr. Friedman, positioned near a U.S. government printing press that was producing paper currency at breakneck speed, quipped in a calm and confident voice, "The way to stop inflation is as simple as this." He turned to the large switch at the press and turned it off. The machine came to an instant halt. The presses fell silent.

Wouldn't it be wonderful if the answer to our economic woes was as simple as turning a switch on or off? Wouldn't it be simple to institute such a solution? Perhaps there are many switches as opposed to one. But is the fantasy realistic? Even if there were a grain of reality in the dream, we, as skeptical human beings, wouldn't believe it. Were the answer such a simple one, we would most likely not employ it. Years of schooling and higher education have imbued us with a host of erroneous beliefs that, unfortunately, stay with us until we go to the grave. Worst among these is the belief that what is simple and understandable cannot also be valuable. Rather, we place value on the worthless obfuscations of aloof academicians who cannot see reality for the complexity of their theories. Instead of dealing with the obvious, we confuse issues with theory, hypotheses, and pedagogy. Sadly, even simple ideas could become hopelessly complex and dysfunctional in the hands of modern bureaucrats.

In order to survive and prosper during the collapse that lurks just ahead, we will need to change our attitudes, beliefs, behaviors, expectations, and strategies. We will need to change our perceptions, and we will need to radically alter our understanding of economic reality. Those who are old enough and fortunate enough to have survived the last economic collapse may be better prepared than the "baby boomers." Their changes will not need to be as radical, their adjustments not as extreme; but change will be necessary in every walk of life and in every social class.

The intent of this book is to elucidate, forewarn, and help you prepare for the coming events, whatever they may be. Though I cannot be as specific as I would like regarding the many cataclysmic events that are still in the offing, I can assure that most of tomorrow will be like most of yesterday and today. While the names and places may be changed (to protect the innocent, as they say), the theme or common threads will be similar. As events unfold, you will find that they fall conveniently into many of the general categories that have been analyzed in this book. I am convinced that you will find virtually every national and international event—political, social, economic, religious, medical, and scientific—consistent with the long-wave structure provided herein. This will facilitate your understanding of the fundamentals, and, furthermore, it will allow you to evaluate each event regarding its relative importance, meaning, and the action(s) or response(s) you should take.

If history is a guide to the future, then the most volatile days are yet to come. I hasten to add that I am not proposing a theory of historical or economic determinism. I am merely drawing from the teachings of history and economics to illustrate the patterns and similarities between economies of the past, economies of the present, and economies of the future. You must remember, above all, that *not every event, action, reaction, trend, indicator, or government policy will be precisely the same as it has been during previous economic cycles!* However, this does not mean that the fabric of each event will be totally different from that which has gone before. The lessons of history will serve us well— but only if we use them to our advantage. In order to do so, we must know and understand economic history, but above all, we must employ it.

So that we may effectively prepare for the ultimate collapse, no matter how bad it will be, I suggest you consider taking the following general and specific actions (though not necessarily in the order given):

1. *Study the history of economics* and learn about how economies have fared in response to events and how events have been precipitated by economic realities. Learn how governments have responded to shifts in economic trends and how they have either willfully or inadvertently created economic crises. Understand why, how, and when fiscal mismanagement has been promulgated by political self-interest and greed. Learn how various investments have fared during good times and bad, during economic expansion and contraction. Some answers have been provided in this book, yet there is so very much to learn that I cannot possibly recount it all in one work. I refer you to the list of articles and book references I've provided.

2. *Understand the social, political, religious, and scientific correlates* of inflation, disinflation, and deflation. In order to do so, you will need to be well versed in the various events of different long-wave cycle phases. This book has provided you with an overview of the different cycles, their phases, patterns, and approximate time spans. The rest is up to you.

3. *Think for yourself!* There will always be friends, relatives, brokers, investment advisors, counselors, accountants, financial planners, and others who claim to know the right answers for you. Don't

listen to any of them! Don't listen even to me! Instead, learn the concepts and apply them yourself. You know your situation better than anyone else could possibly know it. You care more about your economic well-being than anyone else does. You must think for yourself and act accordingly.

4. *Take a realistic look at your current financial condition.* Take stock of all assets, liabilities, resources, and commitments. Determine how much you owe, whom you owe it to, and how long it will take you to pay it back. If you have lent money to others, then determine how long it will take to get it all back. What's your "bottom line," net worth, balance of payments? Do you own more than you're worth? Are you worth more than you think you are?

5. *Reduce debt* as quickly as possible. Pay off debts when interest rates are low. Refinance debts taken on at high rates when rates are low, if you cannot pay them back. Do all you can do to improve your liquidity. During the coming economic collapse, debt will be your worst enemy and cash will be your greatest asset and ally.

6. *Dispose of bad investments* when economic trends are on the up-swing. If the long-wave cycle is on schedule, or close to schedule, then the upswings will be relatively brief in comparison to the downswings. Take advantage of economic strength (or improve-ment) to increase liquidity and to dispose of non-income-producing or unprofitable investments.

7. *Return to basics.* If the lessons of history and the mistakes of the past are to be of value in the present and future, then the coming economic collapse will require a return to basics. Life will become less complex. Material wants and needs will not be fulfilled as readily as they were during times of inflation and/or economic growth. Become accustomed to living without credit, credit cards, high debt, and impulse spending. Those who are in a good, solid cash position when the decline hits will be more able to afford some of the luxuries of the time; however, those who have not planned ahead will suffer terribly, so be prepared by slowly returning to basics now.

8. *Develop a balanced and diversified investment portfolio.* There are those who would have you believe that in order to avoid the dangers of economic contraction, you will need to have all of your funds in precious metals. Still other extremists will suggest that you

retreat to the hinterlands with several years' supply of food, ammunition, and medical necessities. In actuality, any extreme position is likely to prove too one-sided. What's needed are balance, good sense, and the proper perspective. Each of these can readily be acquired through your study of historical patterns and economic tendencies of previous long-wave economic cycles. Make use of the information and resources I've provided in this book. Consider the various aspects of my long-term investment strategy as previous discussed. An investment portfolio that is too heavily skewed to one side will not serve you well in a variety of economic environments; however, a balanced and well-planned investment portfolio will help you survive and prosper in virtually all economic climates.

9. *Be prepared for declines of as much as 85 percent or more from previous high values* in the many different inflation-sensitive items. These include land, real estate, collectibles, stock and commodity prices, and so on. When this happens, there will be many opportunities. But will you have the cash to take advantage of these incredible bargains? If you've planned ahead, you will. If, however, you have not accumulated a large and unencumbered cash reserve, you will not be financially able to capitalize on the many unbelievable opportunities that will surely come when the decline grips the free-world economies the world over.

10. *Don't count on the government to help matters.* While it may be true that governments today have broader powers to regulate economies, they are still unable to effectively deal with crisis situations. In their day-to-day workings, government machinery and regulatory agencies are capable of dealing with flash fires and isolated crises; however, in the face of a full-blown crisis it is likely that controls will not work, or that the wrong controls will be implemented. Either could easily exacerbate the situation. Therefore, I suggest you not expect any meaningful assistance from the government. In fact, I wouldn't be surprised to see government measures during a true economic crisis prove to be counterproductive.

    Nor should you count on the government to help bail you out of any personal financial crisis. Government has established a pro–large business policy in recent years. Government is willing to bail out large banks and corporations, but it is unwilling to come to the direct aid of the small businessperson, the farmer, or the average consumer. Perhaps, in the final stages of the long-wave bottoming phase, government may step in to stimulate the economy with federal employment programs and work projects, as it did in the 1930s. For the near future, however, I do not see assistance from government as a meaningful or particularly likely possibility.

11. *Expect the worst* and you may be pleasantly surprised. It has been typical for the downward phase of the long-wave cycle to bring with it numerous panics and sharp, severe declines. Whether the next few years will bring panics in the banking sector, stocks, futures, and/or the bond market, it is best to be prepared for the worst. Stock prices have witnessed a record increase. There is an old saying in the market. It warns investors and traders that "new highs beget new lows." Since we've already seen the best in many markets, we must now prepare ourselves for the worst.

12. *Expect innovation and prepare to take advantage of it.* I have previously mentioned the various theories of innovation and the long wave. If it is indeed true that innovations tend to cluster in the latter stages of the long-wave down leg, then we should soon expect major technological advancements. Based on current trends in scientific research, I expect these advancements to come in the areas of communications and genetic engineering. These two aspects of technological innovation will likely provide the initial fuel for the next long-wave up cycle. In addition, they are likely to be the best long-term investments during the next long-wave cycle upswing. Keep in touch with the news and, in particular, with new trends in scientific research. They will alert you to some of the best long-term investments and businesses in the next long-wave cycle upswing.

13. *What about war?* Another strong correlate of long-wave cyclic tops and bottoms is, as I have earlier mentioned, war. The top war and the bottom war have been well documented. Naturally, the question many of us are asking is: "Will there be a bottom war?" Based strictly upon the history of cycles in war and international conflict, primarily resulting from studies by the Foundation for the Study of Cycles, I have to conclude that there will be another war, and furthermore, that the war is likely to come by the mid- to late

1990s. It is entirely possible that one will develop in the mid-1990s, particularly if the long-wave cycle bottoms earlier than expected.

The next question is: "How severe will the war be?" This is a difficult question to answer. On the one hand, we are confronted with the clear and undeniable threat of full-scale nuclear warfare and the ensuing holocaust. This would, of course, put an end to civilization as we know it. It would destroy virtually everyone and everything. It would set "civilization" back hundreds of years. It would bring with it many decades, perhaps centuries, of nuclear contamination and disease. If Darwin is correct, then only the fittest will survive, and they will, eventually, parent a distant generation of superhumans. The war would probably throw all economic cycles off course.

The other alternative is for a relatively nuclear-free conflict, whether global or circumscribed. We'll let the futurists and military strategists advise us on what they think will happen. My work suggests a global type of conflict, one that could be conventional (*i.e.*, nuclear free), or partially nuclear. I am not ruling out the possibility of biological and/or chemical warfare.

What nations will be involved? Today's knee-jerk reactions to events, complete with their domino effect on virtually all international superpowers, suggests that no nation will be immune from one type of military involvement or another. There are so many "hot spots" the world over that any guess is likely to be as good as another. I suspect, however, that the conflict may be close to home (*i.e.*, the United States). The trend toward increased isolationism that typically develops in the long-wave down phase tends to result in a "pulling back" by America. Only that which directly threatens American shores will have a sufficient impact to prompt declaration of war. Hence, the most logical geographic location for conflict are South America, Central America, and/or Cuba. I wouldn't rule out Mexico as a possible area of military confrontation. Finally, it is very possible that several superpowers could be dragged into a Mideast conflict, perhaps unwillingly.

As you can see, the question of war and its many ramifications is not a simple one to answer. Nor is it particularly easy to think about. But think about it you must. And plan for it you must. Surely there will come a day of reckoning—a day of confrontation—even if by accident or as a result of irresponsibility. With so many third-world countries and terrorist groups acquiring nuclear weaponry, the likelihood for accidental conflict increases daily. It would be foolish not to expect a war. It would be even more foolish to expect one later rather than sooner.

It has been difficult for me to write the immediately preceding words. I have family and children, just as many of you do. It is painful to think about the folly of humankind. It is only the dreamer, however, who cannot see that the history of humankind is the history of conflict. There are things we can do, but they will require the most immense effort and the greatest cooperation of like-thinking human beings ever assembled on the face of the Earth. Where is there a leader equal to such a task?

14. *Don't expect timing to be precise!* I've said this before. Please don't forget it. The cycles are not perfect. There is a given degree of error. Because many different cycles are at work, the bottoms, tops, downswings, upswings, and phases aren't as predictable as we'd like them to be. Because cycles are not regular, because their amplitude (magnitude) is not as predictable as we'd like it to be, and because government action can retard or accelerate cyclic tops and bottoms, timing *will be affected!* However, it is impossible to determine by how much or to what extent timing will vary. This is why *you must become a student of current events, and this is why you must learn to recognize the signs of the times!*

15. *Don't hide from the inevitable.* Many people will either hide from what is clearly visible, and still others will know that the worst is about to happen, yet they'll be afraid to take action. While the coming economic crises will not all happen at once, they will seem irreconcilable and unavoidable when they do come. By the time they happen, it may be too late to take action. Therefore, *don't* react, but rather take *preparatory action* in advance of the crisis. While many of those around will be affected, the crises need not affect you at all or as severely. Preparation will be the key to survival and profit. The lessons of history are more definitive in this aspect then they are in any other aspect of the long wave. Be prepared and you will prosper; fail to prepare and you will be a victim to fate and the whim of government mismanagement. Prepare and you will float atop the waves of despair; procrastinate and you will sink in the economic tidal waves.

16. *What do I mean by "plan ahead"?* Clearly, those who plan far ahead will be better off than those who wait too long. Yet, to plan too far ahead may also be inadvisable. My experience and readings suggest that planning ahead by about one or two years should be sufficient. Because events change so rapidly and because government response may be somewhat different from what is anticipated, it is best not to plan *too* far ahead.

17. *What types of business ventures should do best* during the long-wave decline phase? Again, we turn to the lessons of history for an answer. Economic precedent suggests that during the declining phase, the so-called "vice-industries" tend to do well. Liquor and tobacco businesses are likely to prosper. Home entertainment may be better than outside entertainment, as it is less costly to watch shows, plays, and concerts at home on television than it is to go out. The real estate business, on the other hand, may slump, other than perhaps the rental aspect. The teaching profession is likely to remain stable.

    There will be continued demand for educators; however, their salaries may not grow or may, in fact, be cut as federal and local government programs are cut. Education, however, will remain mandatory, and, as a consequence, teachers will remain in demand.

    The medical profession may suffer as elective and cosmetic treatments decline because of lower disposable income. It is possible, however, that programs connected with AIDS and AIDS-related afflictions may increase given the current and projected epidemic of this deadly disease.

    Engineering and computer-related job prospects may very well decline, yet the clustering of technical innovations may also bring an increase in demand for professionals in these fields after the worst of the declining phase is over.

18. *Do I advise retreating to the hinterlands?* No. While there are those who feel that the United States may soon enter a period of social strife and class conflict, I do not envision the coming economic crises as sufficiently serious to prompt refuge in the backwoods. While it is true that there may be labor unrest and civil disobedience prompted by government ineptitude, I don't see the conflict as escalating into a class war.

19. *Will the banks fail?* In all probability, there will be numerous bank

failures, and many depositors will not get their money back. The rate of bank failures in the 1980s has reached record levels. This is just a sign of things to come. In spite of the U.S. Federal Reserve System, the current condition of U.S. banks is abysmal. The ratio of ready relative to demand deposits is frightfully low, perhaps the lowest in history. The number and dollar amount of loans to foreign countries that are in virtual default is at a record level. Odds are that many of these loans will never be repaid.

I conclude, therefore, that a serious banking crisis is both inevitable and unavoidable. Had there been a substantive change in the direction of significantly increasing bank reserve requirements, there might have been a chance of avoiding the crisis, but with conditions as they are, a chain reaction of bank failures is reasonably certain. Given this situation, the next item (#20) becomes important.

20. *How to avoid being hurt by the banking collapse.* The most simple answer is to keep a large amount of funds out of banks. Savings and loan institutions will likely be the most severely affected, as will the farm banks. The alternative is not your pillow or mattress, but government-backed or -guaranteed bonds or bills. Direct obligations of the U.S. government are likely to be a safe haven. It may also be possible to avoid the collapse by having funds in gold or platinum bullion or bullion coins. If obligations of the banking system are not met, then this is likely to increase the value of gold and other precious metals as investors flock to their relative safety. It is likely that gold-mining stocks will increase in value, although this is not a 100 percent certainty. Experts like to point to the fact that during the last depression in the United States, Homestake Mining, a U.S. gold-mining concern, increased in value by more than 1,000 percent during the disinflationary crisis. Furthermore, I have already pointed out that gold tends to keep its value in a disinflation relative to other commodity items. Therefore, gold is likely (but not guaranteed) to be a safe haven along with funds in direct obligations of the U.S. government in the event of a banking collapse. Of these, T bills would be the safest.

21. *Which precious metals will fare best?* Historical precedent can guide us, but it cannot answer the question completely. There have been many changes in the use and monetary role of precious metals. For example, silver once played an important role in photographic

processing. This role has gradually diminished with the development of alternative techniques of photographic processing. Platinum, which was used heavily in the manufacture of catalytic
converters during the 1970s and 1980s, has been replaced by
palladium to a given extent.

There are political factors to consider as well. The turmoil in
South Africa was not a factor during the last disinflation. The
possible disruption of gold mining in South Africa could dramatically affect the price of gold. Platinum production could also be
curtailed. Whereas gold is mined throughout the world, platinum
is not. A large percentage of the world's platinum is mined by the
Soviet Union and South Africa.

Palladium, which is now being used more heavily than ever
before as a substitute for platinum, is produced almost exclusively
by the Soviet Union. An intentional cutoff or decrease in supply by
the Soviet Union could trigger an explosion of palladium prices. It
is, therefore, important to maintain a balanced portfolio of precious
metals. Gold alone may not be the ultimate answer. See my earlier
suggestions regarding a reasonable mix of precious metals in your
long-term investment portfolio.

22. *Should you sell your home?* Like it or not, this is a valid and rational
consideration. If disinflation becomes a reality, then home prices
will decline from their presently inflated levels. In spite of the fact
that interest rates should be relatively low, too few people will have
funds to purchase a home. Higher-priced homes may not suffer to
the same extent. In fact, they may not be affected too severely
since buyers of these homes tend to be more affluent and have
probably made adequate plans prior to the deflation.

Yet for the individual who is convinced that the coming
collapse is inevitable and that it will be severe, there is no alternative but to sell out at what should be the top or close to it. The most
rational thing to do would be to rent. Still, many of us cherish our
homes, and we don't want to move. What's the alternative? If you
owe no money on your home, you may wish to keep it. If you owe a
great deal on your mortgage, however, you may wish to sell, pay off
the mortgage, and buy another, smaller home for all cash (*i.e.*, no
mortgage). This will keep your debts low and your cash outflow
low.

23. *Businesspersons should avoid inventory buildup.* Since the price of

most goods is likely to decline, it would be reasonable to avoid building up inventories with items that could decline in price over the months ahead. The best strategy would be to reduce inventories and to use a hand-to-mouth or "as needed" strategy. In a disinflation, the price of goods and services is likely to be lower tomorrow than it is today. Therefore, the strategy is *not to buy and hold*, but to *hold cash* and to *buy supplies as needed*.

24. *If you're on a fixed income or a pension*, then you are likely to suffer more than most. Since interest rates are likely to decline, your yield on funds will decline accordingly. Whereas the cost of living is also likely to decline, the amount of money you earn in interest may drop more rapidly. What's the solution? When interest rates rise again, as the cycles suggest they should, lock in the high yields. This will guarantee a good return.

25. *Consider selling collectibles, valuable* objets d'art *and so on.* While such things as rare paintings and other inflation-type investments may fare well when inflation is running wild, they tend to reverse course when inflation ends and disinflation begins. They could generate quite a bit of cash if sold near the top.

There are many more things I could tell you. But if you do a little reading and studying of the ideas in this book, and of the ideas presented in the references I've cited, you will learn more than what I can teach you. You will see clearly that there is validity to the warnings I've sounded. Deep in my heart I hope I'm wrong about most of what I've written. Yet I have long had strong and unyielding feelings that my warnings will most surely become facts. Since the early 1970s I've predicted the economic and price trend changes with a fairly high degree of accuracy for my clients. The forecasts have been made public, well before the facts, and they've been specific. To present a chronology of what I've said and how accurate it has been would be immodest.

The confidence I have in my forecasts and analyses is a direct result of my personal experiences with cycles, long term, short term, intermediate term and seasonal. I have invested with and speculated on these cycles. When I have, for reasons of pride, emotion, hope, fear, or greed, acted contrarily to my cyclic studies and timing indicators, I have wound up on the losing end.

Time alone will either vindicate my forecasts or invalidate them. Though my timing may not be perfect, there is no doubt in my mind that my analyses and forecasts will be right in terms of trends and events. Donald J. Hoppe, a man who has devoted years of study to economic cycles, history, and the markets, warned repeatedly about the coming collapse in stock prices. For several years prior to the Crash of 1987, Hoppe issued warning after warning, alert after alert, and forecast after forecast. Month after month his thought-provoking reports contained historical examples, economic analyses, technical analyses, and market patterns that pointed to the inevitable collapse of stock prices.

If one is to fault Hoppe, perhaps the only negative thing which could be said is that he was too early. If we were to fault the thousands, perhaps millions, who were caught in the avalanche of prices during the Crash of 1987, we could blame them for being too late. Shortly after the crash, Hoppe wrote the following in his newsletter, *The Kondratieff Wave Analyst:*

". . . Well, it has finally happened. The Great Crash I have been predicting for the past three years is now a terrible reality. . . ." [*The Kondratieff Wave Analyst,* Vol. II, #11, November 1987, p. 12]

Roger Babson was also too early. But he was also right. The many analysts who are now warning about the coming economic collapse will also be vindicated. One day, most likely sooner rather than later, my analyses, forecasts, and warnings will also be seen as having been prophetic. But those who have read my words will know that nothing in this book was achieved with tricks, mirrors, psychic energy, special effects, 20:20 hindsight, a profound understanding of micro or macro economics, or complex statistical analyses. It was all made possible by the simple application of study and visualization; by the development of historical perspective, and, most importantly, by the courage to come forward with my thoughts, no matter whom they may offend and no matter how much they may be rejected by traditional economists.

If the reader can be spared even 10 percent of the financial and economic anguish that will most assuredly come with the inevitable collapse, then my job will have been well done. Though world economies may be on the brink of collapse, we, as investors, need not go down with the ship. Though world economies are in a quagmire of upheaval that is certain to become even more obvious and severe in the years ahead, we, the people, need not sink in the quicksand . . . we need merely to see the life preserver, and to grasp it lest we fall into the abyss of financial ruin.

Chapter 8

How to Prepare for Each Stage of the Long Wave

Ten million more persons are now at work than were employed in 1921. . . . The shock of the deflation in security prices has largely been absorbed in three months. The danger of a long depression appears fairly over, with every evidence of an early renewal of the onward march [of prosperity].

—Julian H. Barnes, Chairman
U.S. Chamber of Commerce
February 18, 1930

Some of us avoid visiting doctors for routine checkups. We're afraid of getting bad news. In our superstitious little way, we think that avoiding bad news will make it go away. We all want to live in a utopia. We want to avoid problems. When problems arise, we want to solve them quickly and with as little pain as possible. On the other hand, we pride ourselves on being intelligent and educated. We know that it is in our best interest to admit to problems, to discover them early, and to deal with them before they become chronic. At times, however, what we know intellectually, we cannot do emotionally. Fear, greed, hope, desire, and anxiety stand in our way. Many of us avoid facing our mortality. We refuse to admit to illness just as we refuse to accept the possibility that economic trends may change or "die." In short, anything that threatens stability has no place in our thoughts or lives. While I may be exaggerating about the scope of such denial, it is, nevertheless, true that a great majority of people deny reality for most of their lives. Smokers, drink-

165

ers, and those who are overweight know that their addictions are injurious to life and health. Yet they persist in feeding their habits.

When required to accept the realities of economic life, many of us are apt to hide from the obvious as well. Although it is true that economic events and trends are not predictable with 100 percent accuracy, we can, with effective and sensible planning, be prepared for virtually any serious consequences if we know the lessons of history. In the past, those who have written books such as this one have been ridiculed and discredited as "gloom and doom sayers." The doctor who tells you that you must stop smoking is no more of a "doom sayer" than is the market analyst or the student of cycles who warns about what will come. But to be forewarned is by no means a guarantee that the person so advised will be prompted to action. Indolence and denial, fear and disorganization, procrastination and ignorance will take their toll regardless of warnings, advice, and/or directions, no matter how specific or logical. The facts clearly show that preparation, planning, and, above all, action are the ingredients to survival and profit in all types of economic climates.

The purpose of this chapter is to provide some investment guidelines, based on historical precedent, that will allow for protection of assets as well as capital appreciation. In order to achieve this end, I will examine the performance of various investment vehicles during the different long-wave phases. In addition, historically valid actions during each stage will be presented and discussed in detail.

STAGE #1: INITIAL GROWTH

During the initial growth stage, prices are relatively low in virtually all sectors. Land and real estate are still recovering from the disinflationary effect of the recent long-wave bottom. Commodity prices tend to be up from their recent low levels; however, they are still not too far from their long-wave lows. Interest rates are characteristically low. It would appear, therefore, that several key ingredients are present for optimum investment in virtually any vehicle that is likely to respond to the anticipated growth stage. The investor will have many choices. Few of them will, in the long run, be incorrect inasmuch as virtually all sectors are at or near their bottoms. There are two key considerations, however. First, a great majority of investors and businesspeople will have little or no cash reserve. The recent disinflation will have virtually depleted the cash reserves of those who had accumulated large debt during the previous long-wave cycle. Those who did not suffer bankruptcy are the fortunate ones. Yet, for those who have the capital to invest, this stage offers golden opportunities. This does not mean, however, that all caution should be thrown to the wind. Selectivity is still of the utmost importance. A balanced investment program must be developed, one that is likely to do well whether there is economic growth or not. In spite of the fact that the economy usually begins a long period of upswing at this time, there is still risk of extended recession or very slow initial growth. Therefore, selectivity is vital. Here are some general guidelines for investment directions during the initial growth stage:

1. Because interest rates are low and because money is the fuel that will run the machinery of capital growth and profits, it is advisable to borrow money at low interest rates, and for the longest possible period of time. In other words, such things as long-term loans or mortgages are desirable.

2. The monies borrowed should be used to provide a return sufficient to help defray the cost of the loan while bringing in income as well. Funds placed in real estate investments such as rental properties could achieve this goal. Although vacant land will also increase in value over the coming years, it will not give an immediate return. Such purchases can be delayed until there is more operating capital. Certainly, those who are in a position to buy vacant land can do so with the understanding that it will need to be held for the longer term. Included in this category is farm land. Although it, too, will take many years to reach its peak, history teaches that increases of well over 1,000 percent could be realized over the course of a twenty-year economic upswing.

3. Gold investments are generally not worthwhile at this time. Gold has its place, but not necessarily during this stage.

4. Stocks are likely to be at relatively low levels compared with prices at their peak. Figures 8.1 and 8.2 illustrate the level of stock prices (stock market average) during previous long-wave cycle lows in the United States.

Figure 8-1. *Stock average at long-wave low in the 1836–46 time frame.*

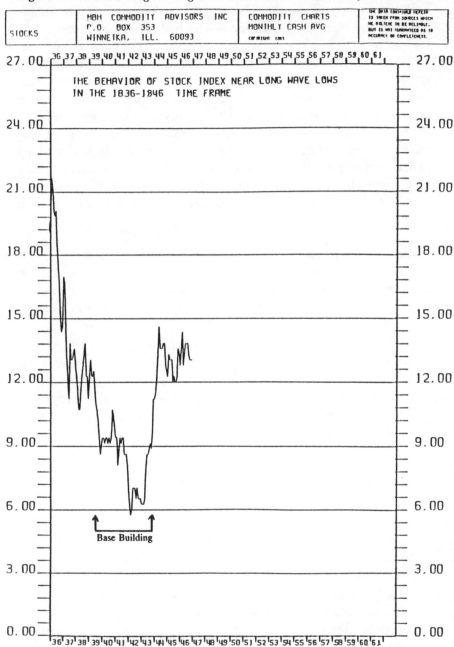

Figure 8-2. *Stock average at long-wave low in the 1890–1900 time frame.*

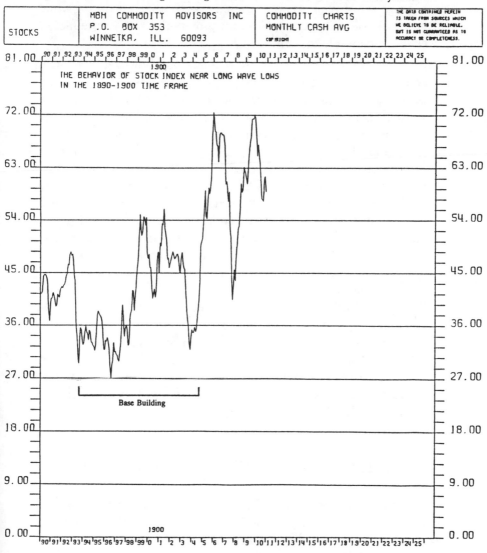

5. Technology stocks, however, may be a different matter, inasmuch as Stage #1 of the long-wave cycle is likely to be one during which new technology begins to blossom, providing much of the fuel for coming economic growth.

6. Business prospects for Stage #1 are numerous; however, my studies and research suggest that one must be selective here as well. Businesses dealing in new technology, real estate development, services to industry, energy, and transportation appear to be the most promising, whereas business in such things as leisure, recreation, entertainment, medicine, and other areas that rely on retail consumerism are not yet favored. Remember that the long-wave cycle upswing typically lasts for many years. There is always the possibility that recessions will occur along the way and, furthermore, that economic growth will not be as swift or as persistent as one might want. Consequently, it is best not to get too heavily involved in debt at the outset. There are, nevertheless, many "ground floor" opportunities at this. Historically, those who have expanded businesses during this stage or during the latter part of the long-wave decline have fared well over the long run, because the cost of money and expansion of production facilities have been very low. Stage #1 is a prime time to take advantage of low interest rates, relatively low prices for raw goods and land, and the relatively low cost of labor. Furthermore, this is also a time during which to take advantage of new technology that has developed in the long-wave downcycle that has just come to a close.

STAGE #2: EXPANSION AND SECONDARY GROWTH

During Stage #2, that of expansion and secondary growth, it becomes evident that the economy has clearly turned the corner, that economic growth is a reality. This stage is not without its economic ups and downs, yet, typically, growth tends to become more rapid, and, for the first time in many years, there is concern that inflation may become a problem. Indeed, the slowly rising rate of inflation suggests that inflation-sensitive investments may fare best. This stage is a continuation of Stage #1, but there is generally more certainty, more security, and more immediate return on investments. A number of important investment-related events are particularly important during this stage. They are as follows:

1. Interest rates are still relatively low during Stage #2. In fact, they may be lower than or equal to rates in Stage #1. However, there appears to be more promise of economic growth by the time Stage #2 has been reached. The importance of borrowing at low rates cannot be overemphasized. If substantial capital appreciation is to be realized in the coming years, then low-priced credit is the quintessential ingredient. Without cheap credit, maximum expansion will not be possible. Growth will be achieved, but credit is the vehicle to the super growth possible only in capitalist economies. The long-term investor will fare well if the low cost of money is used to its maximum. To borrow heavily, at low rates, and for the longest period of time possible is the single best strategy during Stage #2.

2. It is profitable to assume long-term and short-term debt, provided you take some precautions and provided you make proper use of the funds. Based on what we have learned earlier in this book about the tendencies and cycles in interest rates, you would do well to borrow for the short term early in the decade and to borrow for the long term at about the mid-decade point. Historically, this combination of timing and borrowing would have resulted in the least amount of risk exposure. Furthermore, the monies so acquired must be used to provide a return that will pay for the cost of the money while reducing the outstanding liability and increasing profits. Rental properties and businesses that provide a rate of return well above costs are best entered at this time in the long-wave cycle. The value of such properties is most likely to increase in the years ahead.

    Investments in well-established industrial concerns can yield the type of profits that meet the requirements. Whether this is done in the form of stock purchases or in the form of outright commercial enterprise is a matter of individual choice. It appears that there may be more leverage at this stage in actual industrial involvement rather than in stock purchases.

3. Inflation tends to begin its rise during this stage, but very slowly at first. Since inflation is still in its infancy, the fixed costs of production and business are not prohibitive. Inasmuch as the cost of

inputs is not rising substantially, there is no pressing need to inventory raw goods. This frees up funds for expansion of production facilities.

4. Profits rise rapidly more than do wages or taxes. This is very, very important. Low taxes and reasonable wages are the key ingredients of economic growth. They form the fixed costs to which I referred earlier. It is most productive to generate profits while they are rising more rapidly than are taxes and the cost of labor. Eventually there will come a time when profits are not keeping pace with the cost of wages and with the toll taken by taxes. At this point in the long-term cycle, however, profits are rising at a more rapid pace, and they are likely to continue in their heightened trend for a fairly long period of time. The efficient businessperson will be able to take advantage of the many vehicles for hedging costs that a capitalist economy offers. Such techniques as forward contracting, future hedges, and inventory of goods will further add to the profit margin.

5. Labor unions are likely to be relatively weak and/or disorganized. The eroded power base of labor common at this stage of the cycle is a carryover from the previous long-wave cycle low, during which labor suffered unbearable pain and setbacks. This is a prime time, therefore, for business to take advantage of low labor costs and of the relatively disorganized state of labor unions. During the next long-wave cycle, organized labor will likely regain its strength at a more rapid pace than it has in previous cycles, benefiting from what has been learned during this current experience.

6. Growth in real estate tends to begin in earnest. It is during this stage that real estate and land prices tend to begin their upswing. The combination of low interest rates and low real estate prices is what makes investment in this area the single most promising action an investor can take for the long term.

7. Tariffs and government control are at a minimum. During the previous long wave, government controls were relaxed in order to effect the economic stimulation necessary to reincarnate a healthy uptrend. It takes time for controls to be reinstated. It takes legislation as well as public support. Since excessive government control is seen as something inhibitory to economic growth, there is an unwillingness to move toward overregulation. This adds to the

favorable business climate. Incentives to industry are numerous. Anti-trust and anti-monopoly legislation is minimal. It is wise, therefore, to take advantage of this situation by venturing into businesses that fare well in the absence of excessive government control. The combination of low labor costs, minimal government control, a relatively low tax base, and the low cost of raw goods is now at the best mix of the entire long-wave cycle.

8. Deficit spending stages a comeback. Just as it is profitable for individuals and businesses to assume debt, it is also profitable for the government to do so. In fact, it helps to stimulate the economy. Remember, however, that there is bound to be considerable caution and opposition to deficit spending since it will generally be felt that deficit spending was one of the culprits at the last economic peak. Given the record level of deficit spending in the 1980s, the next long-wave cycle is certain to see substantial resistance to deficit spending (provided the current debt is ever diminished). Government spending tends to stimulate the economy. There is a clear shift toward increased government spending as politicians become more liberal.

9. Leisure-time activities tend to increase during Stage #2. Therefore, investments in businesses that capitalize on this increase tend to do well. The greater the growth in disposable income, the greater the potential profit in businesses of this type.

10. Precious metals prices are still likely to be relatively low or declining; however, industrial applications tend to increase demand. It is not possible to make strong generalizations about precious metals based on previous long-wave experiences. For one thing, industrialization has become increasingly dependent upon the use of precious metals. Their role is no longer confined to that of a hedge against uncertainty. In other words, precious metals are also likely to be a good long-term investment in Stage #2 of the long-wave cycle. Figures 8.3 and 8.4 show the severe declines in platinum and silver prices during the last long-wave cycle. Because of the likely continuation of technological demand for precious metals, even during the next long-wave decline, we are not likely to see the same percentage decline in prices as has been true in the past. In fact, the price lows are apt to be considerably higher than the lows witnessed during the last long-wave bottom.

Figure 8-3. *Platinum prices during the last long-wave decline.*

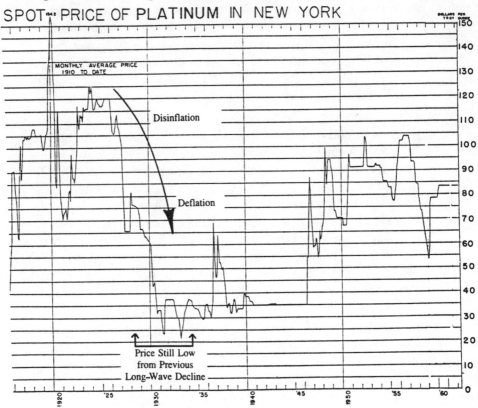

Source: Chart courtesy of Commodity Research Bureau.

Copper prices, which suffered severe declines during the last long-wave decline, are also likely to bottom considerably higher than their previous lows because of the continued demand necessary to maintain even the most rudimentary level of industrial output in our considerably larger world economy. My point is simply that precious metals investments for the long term are likely to be advisable earlier in the coming long wave than they were in previous long waves.

The so-called "strategic" metals, given their scarcity, as well as the continued march of technology (even at a slower pace), are also likely to increase in price and may, therefore, be good areas of investment in Stage #2 of the coming long-wave cycle.

The role of copper prices previous to Stage #2 and subsequent

Figure 8-4. *Silver prices during the last long-wave decline.*

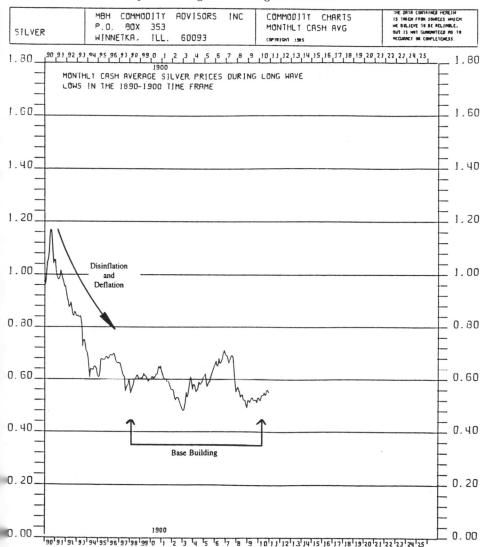

to Stage #2 for the last several long-wave cycles is shown in Figures 8.5 through 8.7. You can see that long-term investments in copper during Stage #2 are certainly a worthwhile consideration.

Clearly, Stage #2 is a prime time for long-term investments. The general rules for Stage #2 bear repetition. Remember that not all

Figure 8-5. Copper prices during the last two long-wave declines.

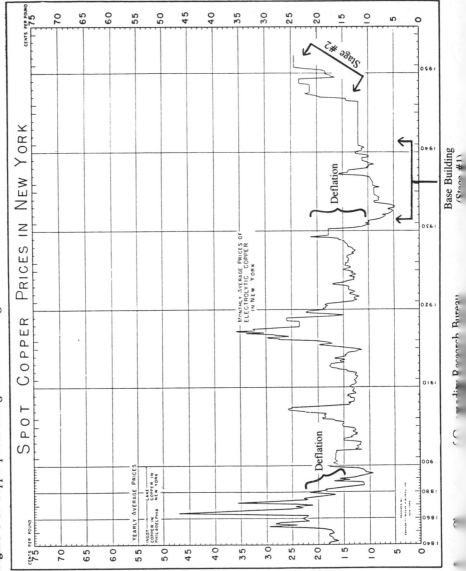

Figure 8–6. *Copper prices during Stage #2 in the 1830–1845 time frame.*

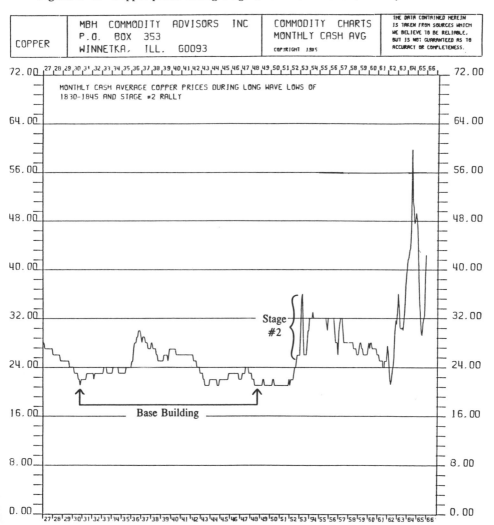

long-term cycles or stages are the same length and that not all Stage #2 fundamentals are similar. Here are the guidelines for Stage #2:

1. *Borrow heavily* and *for the longest period of time possible.*
2. *Borrow short-term money early in the decade* because of the historical patterns in short-term interest rates. Avoid borrowing for the short term late in the decade.

Figure 8–7. *Copper prices during the long-wave decline and Stage #2 of the long-wave lows of 1890–1900.*

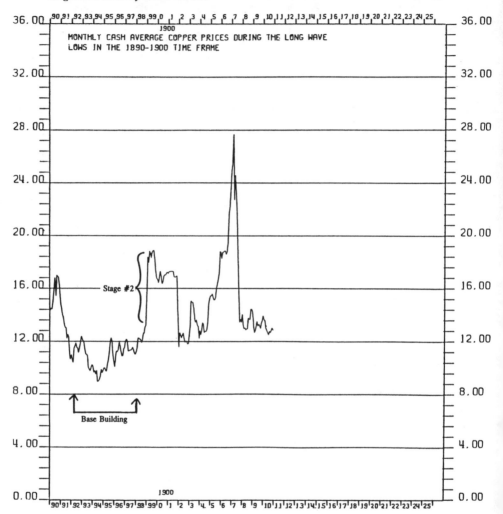

3. *Borrow for the long term near the mid-decade point,* given the pattern in long-term interest rates.

4. *Invest in land, real estate, rental properties, single- and multiple-family dwellings, and farm land.* All of these are likely to be at very low levels compared with their previous long-term cycle peaks.

5. *Invest in businesses subject to the lowest degree of government control.* These businesses are likely to thrive for many years.

6. *Take advantage of relatively low labor costs and the decreased level of labor union power.* This does not mean that one must take ruthless advantage of labor, rather that fair wages and low costs will yield high profits.

7. *Consider investments in precious metals and strategic metals* in expectation that technology will grow at a rapid pace.

8. *Invest in areas of new technology.* If the long-wave theories of innovation clustering are correct, then the plethora of new technological processes and products developed during the end of the current long-wave cycle will be among the fastest-growing industries in the next long-wave cycle. Stage #2 is a good time in the long-wave cycle to take advantage of such opportunities. In reality, the very best time will likely be during the declining phase of the long wave itself; however, it may take quite a few years before these investments can bear fruit.

STAGE #3: RAPID ACCELERATION AND INFLATIONARY INCREASE

While it is, indeed, true that transition from one stage to the next may be imperceptible, it is possible to determine the approximate timing of each stage by an examination of extant conditions and events. The present must be evaluated in terms of the past. Yet we must be careful not to become so entrenched in historical precedent that we fail to deal with current events. In spite of the fact that cycles and history set the tone of the future, they do not determine the precise events of the future. Figure 8.8 lists some general guidelines for Stage #3. Again, I caution you that these items are not written in stone. Some may be more important than others, and some may not occur at all. All of the items listed have a direct bearing on investors, business, and the economy. Here are some points to consider in connection with each of the items listed in Figure 8.8.

1. The rising trend in interest rates is clearly an indication that inflation has taken a strong hold, that it is not going to come to an abrupt end, and that the end of the long-wave cycle is inevitable. Speculators can profit from this trend by placing funds in areas that will take advantage of increasing interest rates. In spite of the fact that the cost of money is rising, there is likely to be a continued and

Figure 8-8. *Aspects of inflationary phase: Stage #3.*

1. Rising trend in interest rates
2. Rising trend in Consumer Price Index
3. Increase in liberal movements
4. Increase in civil rights movements
5. Growing federal aid programs
6. Growth in foreign trade and exports
7. Reduction in protectionism and tariffs
8. Rising land and housing costs
9. Rapid growth in price of prime farm land
10. Influx of foreign workers and refugees
11. Accelerating price of commodities
12. Steady increase in speculation across all sectors
13. Rising precious metals prices
14. Rising cost of collectibles
15. Exponential acceleration of growth toward end of inflation period
16. Gradual decline in purchasing power of the dollar
17. Steady rise in energy needs
18. Increased military spending
19. All culminating in "peak war" that is unpopular

persistent demand for land, real estate, single-family dwellings, and farm land. There are numerous relatively short-term opportunities (*e.g.*, of two to five years' duration) that can be attractive to those interested in taking more risk.

Leverage can be used profitably by those willing and able to take risk. Futures trading, which offers maximum leverage, can yield tremendous profits as interest rate futures drop precipitously on rising interest rates. Yet, there is also the risk of loss. During the long-term interest rate peak of the 1980s, a short position in interest rate futures (which moved down as interest rates moved up) would have produced tremendous profits, but not without considerable risk of loss. Figures 8.9 and 8.10 show how Treasury bond and Treasury bill futures behaved during this period. The more conservative investor or businessperson can hedge against the rising cost of money by using these markets wisely and effectively as a direct offset against rising costs. Note also that the spectacular increase in interest rates during long-wave cycles previous to the 1980 peak would have provided excellent profit opportunities to those who knew how to take advantage of the rising rates. Figure 8.11 shows how short-term interest rates acted during the 1929 peak and the subsequent economic deflation.

As the yield on long-term bonds increases to record levels, investors can lock in high yields by buying government bonds. The eventual and substantial decline in interest rates over the coming years will make this long-term investment a most secure and productive one.

2. The rising trend of consumer prices as evidenced by the CPI (Consumer Price Index) is, of course, further evidence of inflation. By comparing the rate of CPI increase with historical rates of CPI increase, it would be possible to determine just how near we are to the long-wave cycle peak. The investor should use the CPI as a measure of when to exit from investments. When acceleration of the CPI and WPI (Wholesale Price Index) reaches record levels, or near record levels, it is best to begin your exit from most businesses, to increase holdings of precious metals, and to avoid long-term commitments of any kind, other than those that tend to capitalize on disinflation. This does not necessarily mean that holdings of stock market investments should be sold. The stock market must be treated as a separate entity. Remember that stocks have been prone to peak a number of years after commodity prices. In fact, stocks could very well keep moving higher as the last wave of speculation takes hold.

3. Liberal movements tend to increase, and with them social behaviors tend to become more liberal. This tends to increase profits from such things as liquor-related businesses, travel and leisure businesses, legalized gambling, stock and commodity brokerage (because of increased speculation), and other concerns that cater

Figure 8-9. *Treasury bond futures during the long-term interest rate peak of the 1980s.*

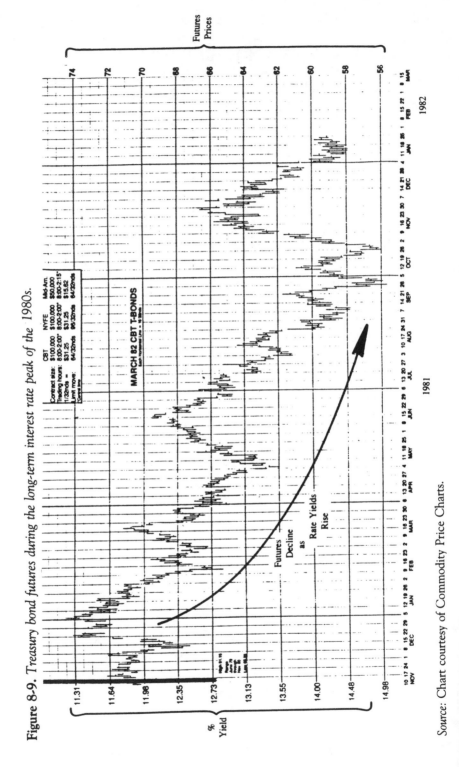

Source: Chart courtesy of Commodity Price Charts.

Figure 8-10. *Treasury bill futures during the long-wave peak of the 1980s.*

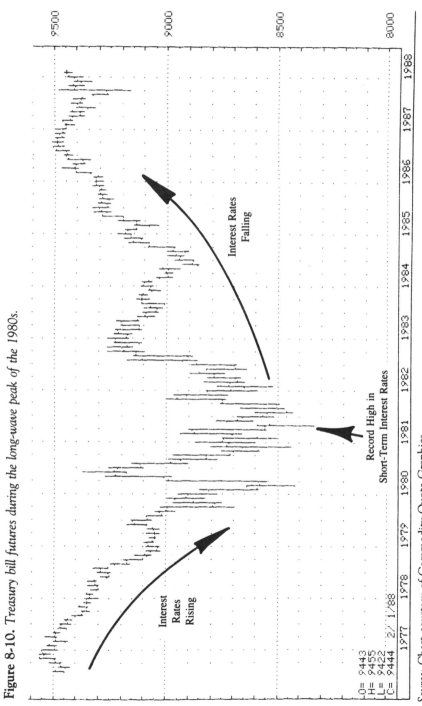

Source: Chart courtesy of Commodity Quote Graphics.

Figure 8-11. *Short-term interest rate peak and decline during long-wave cycle top in the 1920s.*

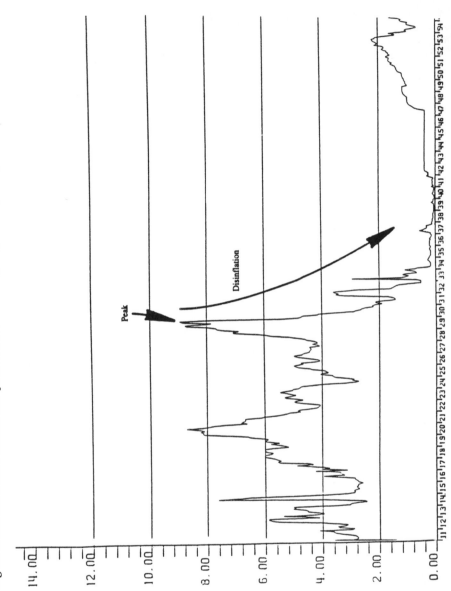

184

to more liberal attitudes. In the current cycle, for example, women's magazines and products directed at a more sexually liberal public have performed well.

4. Civil rights movements increase. This is essentially the same as #3 above. The investor should be alert to changes in social and political attitudes. They will help pinpoint timing of the long-wave cyclic peak.

5. Growing federal aid programs are not a direct concern of the investor; however, some industries may benefit as a consequence of these programs—in particular, the medical-care industry and its suppliers. The prospect of profits from this business as well as the possibility of profits from the purchase of stock in such concerns should also be considered.

6. There is growth in foreign trade and exports. This opens the door to a thriving export business. It also increases the potential of profitable import/export business opportunities. Foreign producers could profit from increased exports. As a consequence, the investor should consider the purchase of stock in foreign manufacturing concerns.

7. There is a reduction in protectionism and tariffs. Whereas government attitudes are prone to be liberal well into the final phases of Stage #3, they tend to change markedly once the top has been reached. The relative lack of controls, particularly on foreign competition, tends to make investments in foreign corporations profitable during this stage, particularly if their economic cycle is in a different stage. Their ability to manufacture and market more cheaply should be considered a prime indication that overseas investments are likely to be profitable.

8. Rising land and housing costs are typical in Stage #3. In fact, it is during Stage #3 that costs begin to accelerate very rapidly. For the short-term real estate speculator, the opportunities can be numerous and particularly promising as the rush into real estate continues, seemingly without regard for price or the cost of money. This is generally a good time to take short-term positions in land and real estate. It is also a good time to begin looking for buyers who will relieve you of the land and real estate you purchased in Stages #1 and #2.

9. Prime farm land prices tend to peak, falling sharply thereafter. It is unfortunate that many farmers are prone to buy land at this time. Many have increased their "on paper" wealth considerably during the inflationary times of Stages #1–#3. When the incentive is greatest to buy more, the proper action should be to sell all. Figures 8.12 and 8.13 will give you an idea of how farm land and real estate prices fared in previous long-wave cyclic upturns and downturns.

10. There will be an influx of foreign workers and refugees. This has also been typical during Stage #3. Because of increasing demand from industry for cheap labor, laws are relaxed and an influx of foreign workers fills the void. Government is not opposed, but organized labor is vehemently against the infusion of cheap labor. This causes increased tension not only between blue-collar workers and foreign laborers but also between labor and industry. The influx of cheaper labor is generally an indication that business is beginning to feel the pinch of increased costs. The businessperson should take this as further evidence that the long-wave cycle is coming to a peak.

11. Accelerating price of commodities is a clear and unmistakable sign that all is not well. The investor should take this as another

Figure 8-12. *Farm land and farm product prices during the long wave.*

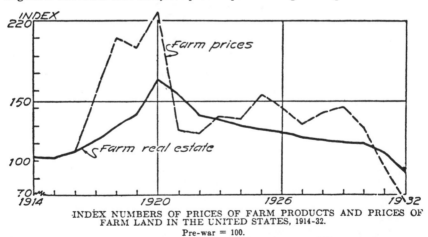

INDEX NUMBERS OF PRICES OF FARM PRODUCTS AND PRICES OF FARM LAND IN THE UNITED STATES, 1914-32.
Pre-war = 100.
With rising commodity prices, land values rose. Conversely, with falling prices they fell. Land values move more slowly than farm prices, and do not fully reflect changes in profits.

Source: Warren, G. F. and Pearson, F. A., "The Price Series" in *Prices*, Book 1, John Wiley & Sons, Inc., 1933, p. 258.

Figure 8-13. *Construction trends during the long wave.*

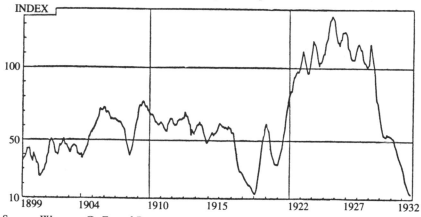

Source: Warren, G. F. and Pearson, F.A., "The Price Series" in *Prices*, Book 1, John Wiley & Sons, Inc., 1933, p. 268.

indication of the inevitable long-wave peak. The 1970–75 time frame witnessed a rapid rise in commodity prices similar to commodity price behavior during previous long-wave cycle peaks. Figures 8.14 through 8.17 show peaks in a number of commodity and commodity price indices for the last few long-wave cycles. The "blowoff" type behavior typical during this period often precedes the economic downturn by a number of years. It is, therefore, a sign of things to come. Those speculating in futures should be prepared to switch from the long side to the short side. Those involved in agriculture should take the "blowoff" behavior as a sign that their markets have likely peaked. The behavior of inflation-sensitive commodity prices should be given particular attention. Nonessential items such as sugar and cocoa tend to make exaggerated peaks, only to fall precipitously during the declining phase of the long wave. See Figure 8.18 for a look at cocoa price "boom and bust" history in relation to the last few long-wave peaks and troughs.

12. Speculation tends to increase across a broad front. No market is immune from the spreading frenzy of rampant speculation. Whether stocks, futures, land, tulips, or petroleum, speculation runs rampant. And this should sound a clear warning to all investors and businesspersons. The type of speculation varies from one cycle to another. Whereas some of the Stage #3 long waves witnessed land and railroad speculation, the 1920s era was one of

Figure 8-14. The "blowoff" in sugar prices during long-wave tops of 1800s and 1900s.

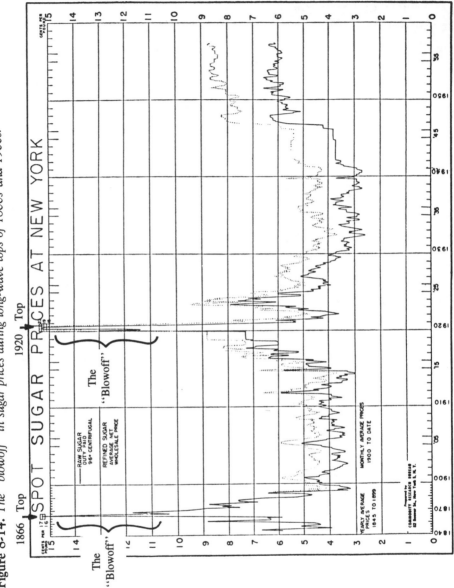

Figure 8-15. *The "blowoff" in wheat prices during long-wave tops of 1866 and 1919.*

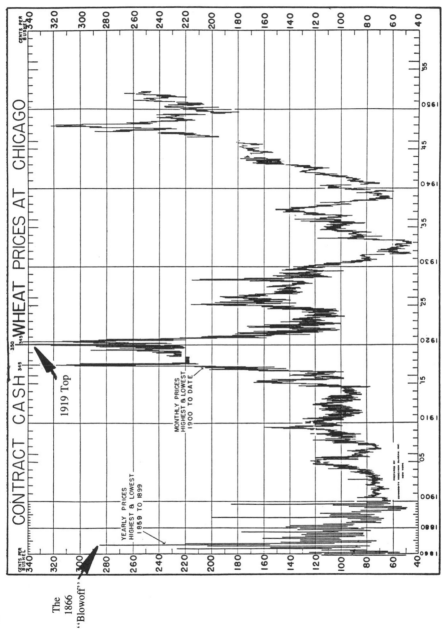

Figure 8-16. *The Wholesale Price Index during long-wave tops of 1814, 1864, and 1920.*

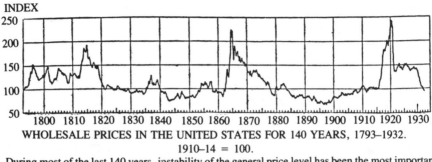

WHOLESALE PRICES IN THE UNITED STATES FOR 140 YEARS, 1793–1932.
1910–14 = 100.

During most of the last 140 years, instability of the general price level has been the most important problem of agriculture and industry. The periods of rising prices have been periods of prosperity, and periods of falling prices have been periods of distress.

Source: Warren, G. F. and Pearson, F.A., "The Price Series" in *Prices*, Book 1, John Wiley & Sons, Inc., 1933, p. 10.

rampant stock market speculation. In 1970, a wave of speculation hit the commodity futures markets, and in 1986–87, speculation in stocks, options, and stock index futures reached record proportions as reason and sound thought were left behind. The conservative investor must view these developments as clear and unequivocal indications of a major economic peak in the offing. Although speculation does not cause the coming economic decline, it is a sign of things to come.

13. Precious metals prices tend to rise. In fact, the price of virtually all metals tends to increase dramatically as fear of inflation grips investors the world over. The precious metals, copper, and, in fact, virtually all commodity prices reach record high levels, or levels that have not been seen in years. Furthermore, inflation-sensitive investments such as coins, *objets d'art*, antiques, diamonds, collectibles, and the like all reach record levels as investors flock into anything that holds the promise of increasing its value during the inflationary trend. Later, I will discuss the role of precious metals in an ideal or hypothetical portfolio. Although some holdings of gold should be carried through the disinflationary period, the odds favor a top in precious metals toward the end of Stage #3 or in Stage #4. Investors should, therefore, begin to liquidate holdings on a scale up, making certain to hold a small percentage (about 10 to 15 percent).

14. The rising cost of all collectibles is another mark of inflationary times. Items that were near-worthless twenty years earlier are suddenly sought after by collectors. Absurdly high prices are paid for all manner and sort of collectible items by inflation-worried investors.

15. There is clear evidence that growth has reached unreasonable proportions. In fact, it is clear to the experienced eye that the situation will soon be out of control and that a turn in the opposite direction is likely. Again, the astute investor should be prepared to lighten holdings of inflation-responsive items, while reducing debt and preparing to lock in high interest rates for long-term yields in U.S. government bonds.

16. Slowly, but surely, currency begins to lose its purchasing power. The decline in purchasing power is a trend that, though clearly evident during the rising portion of Stages #1, #2, and #3, becomes even more obvious and exaggerated in Stage #3 and into Stage #4. This should serve as another warning sign to the investor and businessperson. Certainly, government will ignore the warnings until it is too late.

17. Energy needs and energy prices have likely been on a sustained increase as industry has placed severe demands on available supplies in order to fuel its growth. The rising cost of energy prompts increased exploration for fuel and alternative energy sources that eventually meet the demand. When demand begins to decline steadily as Stage #4 takes hold, energy prices begin to tumble. This is another certain indication that the top is near. Those who have taken investment positions in energy-related stocks or businesses during Stages #1, #2, and early in Stage #3 should begin to liquidate their holdings while prices are rising. Once the top is in place, prices could fall so rapidly that liquidation of holdings might bring considerably lower prices than expected. Figure 8.19 shows the behavior of fuel oil prices during the current long wave.

18. Increased military spending is a trend that is undeniable and predictable. Although a cause-and-effect relationship may not be discernible, such increases have accompanied previous long-wave tops. They have culminated in . . .

Figure 8-17. *The behavior of sugar prices during long-wave peaks and declines.*

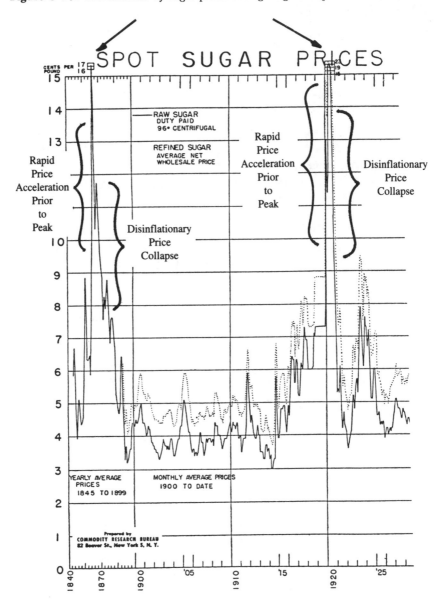

Figure 8-17. (cont.)

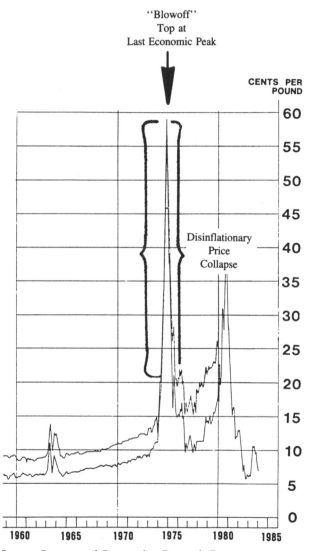

"Blowoff"
Top at
Last Economic Peak

CENTS PER
POUND

Disinflationary
Price
Collapse

Source: Courtesy of Commodity Research Bureau.

Figure 8-18. *Cocoa price peaks during long-wave economic tops.*

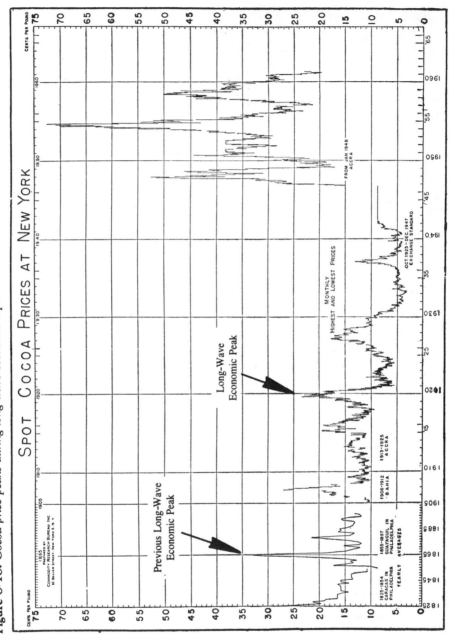

Source: Reprinted with permission from Commodity Research Bureau.

19. The top war. The various top wars associated with each of the long-wave cycles have already been discussed in this book. Implications for the investor are clear. During Stage #3, investments in military-related stocks are likely to do well. Yet as the conflict begins to prompt public protest, it is best to liquidate such holdings.

What has been presented in the preceding pages is, by no means, a complete chronology of major events during Stage #3 of the long-wave cycle. Nor is it intended to serve as an investment guide through all of the long-wave cycles to come. For the investor who is willing to study previous long-wave cycles and trends, putting events into their proper perspective, the potential rewards are immense. Not only will this investor be prepared for virtually any economic eventualities, but he or she will also have reaped handsome profits during the long-wave cycle by following the very simple and obvious rules of previous cycles. Assumptions that every stage of every long-wave cycle will be similar will surely lead the investor astray. Furthermore, each individual has different investment needs and abilities that are the result of current socioeconomic level, salary, savings, age, and personal preference. This is why no single strategic investment program can be recommended as a panacea. However, this should not be used as an excuse for complacency. In the short run and in the long run, those who are not prepared will suffer under the weight of disinflation and economic chaos.

STAGE #4: THE "BLOWOFF" TOP

In terms of time, Stage #4, the "blowoff" top, tends to be rather short-lived. By virtue of the extreme emotionalism and speculation that accompany this stage, it is more violent than it is long-lasting. It is during this stage that the investment world is in a state of great turmoil, turmoil that sets the trend for a number of years to come. The economy and the markets behave like an adult past middle age who cannot accept the fact that physical health is beginning to decline, that hair is turning gray, that the prime of life has passed. Denial and cosmetics are invoked as quick-fix solutions. Just as the balding forty-five-year-old man may buy a hairpiece or suffer the pain of hair transplants, the economy is patched up and painted to look healthy. Yet this is not because there are

Figure 8-19. *Fuel oil prices at most recent Stage #4 top.*

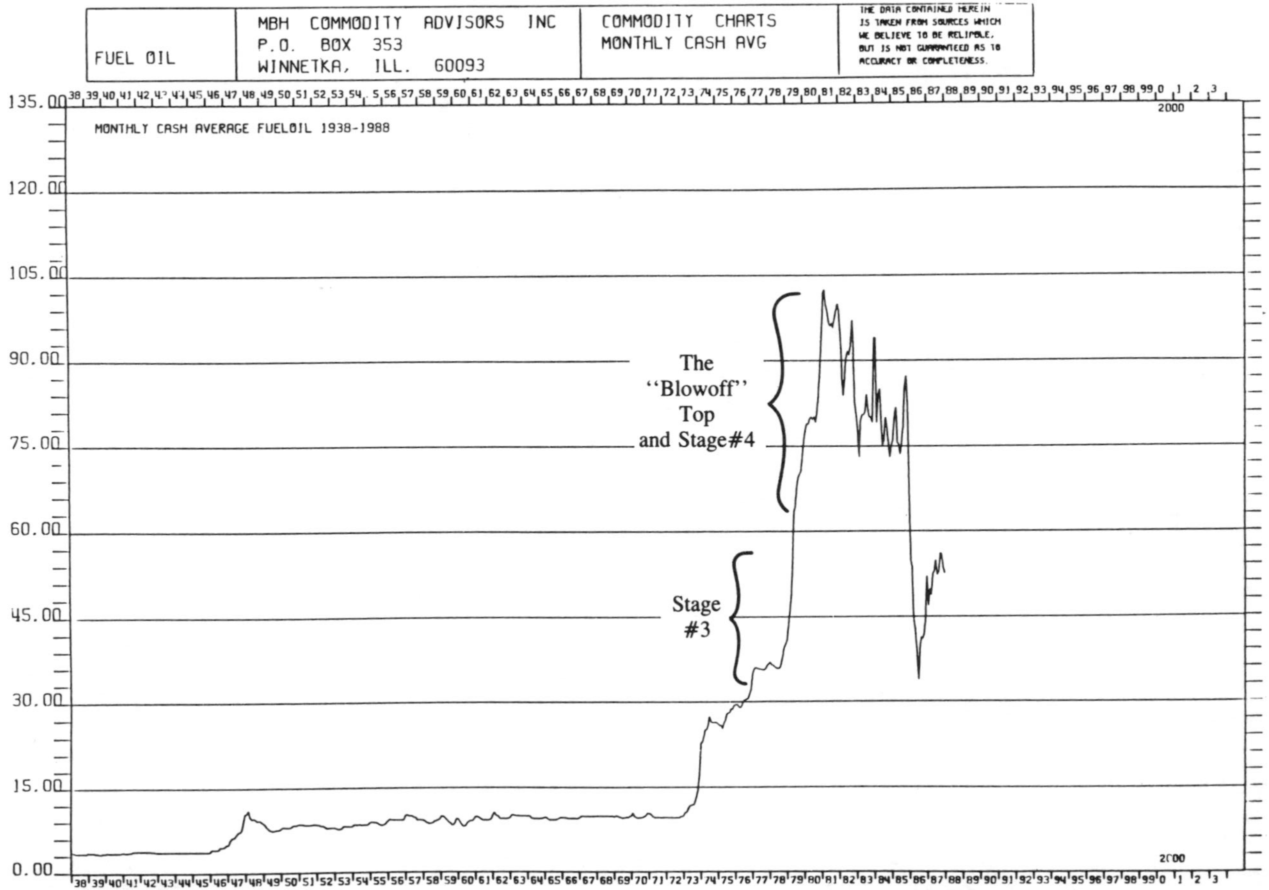
FUEL OIL
MBH COMMODITY ADVISORS INC
P.O. BOX 353
WINNETKA, ILL. 60093
COMMODITY CHARTS
MONTHLY CASH AVG
THE DATA CONTAINED HEREIN
IS TAKEN FROM SOURCES WHICH
WE BELIEVE TO BE RELIABLE,
BUT IS NOT GUARANTEED AS TO
ACCURACY OR COMPLETENESS.
MONTHLY CASH AVERAGE FUELOIL 1938-1988
135.00
120.00
105.00
90.00
75.00
60.00
45.00
30.00
15.00
0.00
The
"Blowoff"
Top
and Stage#4
Stage
#3
2000

no solutions. Rather, it is because the solutions are not easily implemented. Nor are the solutions popular with the public.

Good health is not recaptured without pain. Physical aging in adults can frequently be retarded by the application of simple, well-known, and sensible techniques. Diet, exercise, rest, a slower pace of living, vitamins, reduction of stress, and so forth are obvious solutions. But their benefits are not realized without effort, time, and a gradual but total change in lifestyle.

Economies age as well. Stage #4 marks the top of the growth phase and the beginning of the declining phase. The diet of the growth phase, its pace of life, and its excesses have all come home to roost. The problems *can* be solved, yet years of political expediency and inaction cannot be overcome with one stroke of the presidential pen or with one act of Congress. It takes austerity, rational economics, a slow but steady return to budget balance, slow but relentless economic contraction, a reasonable tax structure, and sufficient incentives to business to cure the problems. A sound monetary policy is also of primary importance. The years of deficit spending and/or fiat money will eventually bring chronic disease, the cure for which is to reverse the process. Yet, this is not popular with the public, politically expedient, or attainable without concerted and careful action. It is far easier to patch up leaks in the dike than it is to tackle the entire problem in one fell swoop. Efforts at cosmetics can work to hide the problems for many years. They can make a sick economy look healthy, just as makeup can make an old actor look young again. But cosmetics will only work for so long and the dike will eventually collapse under the force of discontented waves and a tidal wave of illness. The structure will be demolished. At first, only bits and pieces will collapse. Water will rush in, destroying large segments of the structure. Investors and businesses caught in the avalanche will either be destroyed or, if they are fast enough, will move out of the way. But the chain reaction will eventually take its toll as wave after wave of seething waters rush in to threaten the stability of an already unsound structure.

With each wave, more and more businesses will fail. All social classes will suffer. Unemployment will increase, and, eventually, what started as a trickle will end as a flood. The old will be buried, save for a few pillars of the past that will remain sufficiently stable to support a new foundation and a new structure. Stage #4 marks the start of deterioration. It is during this stage that investors, businesspeople, and governments can take definitive actions that will save them, yet they rarely do so, perhaps more out of fear and ignorance than out of stupidity.

Historical precedent suggests that the general list of symptoms and events shown in Figure 8.20 tends to characterize Stage #4. These are reviewed individually with suggestions as to what the investor and/or businessperson might do to avoid their negative consequences and, perhaps, even to profit.

1. Interest rates have reached record or near-record levels. This has been a result of record demand for money by government, business, and the public. The investor should take advantage of this opportunity to lock in a high rate of return on funds. The purchase of government bonds or other relatively "safe" vehicles is recommended. There is also bound to be some question about the safety of banks during this crisis period. It would be advisable to review the financial stability of any banking institution in which you have placed funds.

2. The various measures of inflation are all at or near record levels. This is a key indication to the businessperson and investor that all is not well, that there are serious problems, and that the time has come for many inflation-related investments to be liquidated. This includes such things as precious metals, rare coins, *objets d'art*, most real estate, and the like. It is at this point in the long-wave cycle that a transition from intangible assets to tangible assets should take place. Yet the primary tangible asset should be cash, as opposed to most other things (*e.g.*, metals, coins, etc.).

3. Most commodity markets peak in a dramatic fashion during this stage. The history of commodity price peaks is clearly shown by Figure 8.21, which depicts the Commodity Research Bureau Futures Price Index previous to, during, and subsequent to the current long-wave cyclic peak. Although some markets will make another peak over a period of several years after the Stage #4 top, most markets will decline precipitously. This does not necessarily include the stock market. Stock prices tend to peak well after commodity prices. Regardless of which markets peak first, the fact remains that this time frame is one during which tops are made in a great majority of the markets. It is vital for the investor and businessperson to be cognizant to the trend change and, above all, to take action promptly and assertively.

Figure 8-20. *Characteristics of Stage #4.*

---

1. Interest rates tend to reach record levels with violent swings and immense volatility.
2. The rate of inflation, the Wholesale Price Index, and the Consumer Price Index all tend to reach record levels.
3. Most commodity markets peak in a dramatic fashion.
4. Demand for loans is at record levels.
5. There is growing concern for the stability and safety of banks.
6. Credit is hard to come by, and businesses begin to fail.
7. There is consumer resistance to excessively high prices.
8. There is rampant speculation in virtually all markets and investments.
9. Domestic productivity is low while wages are high.
10. There are numerous stock and bond offerings.
11. Government begins to recognize that there may be a problem and begins to tighten spending.
12. Tighter government controls put further strain on an already taxed business sector.
13. To meet its own debt obligations, government seeks to raise taxes.
14. Economic slowdown begins to take hold toward the end of Stage #4.
15. The top war ends.
16. An initial disinflationary or recessionary decline develops.

---

4. Demand for money and loans is usually at record levels. This is also a very clear sign that the long-wave peak has arrived. Not only does government demand for money add to the problem, but the government makes it harder to get money by keeping interest rates high. The very high level of loan demand clearly indicates that all is not well. It suggests that business is suffering and that a credit crisis is in the making. Few signals or indicators of an economic peak are as reliable or telltale as this one. Do not ignore it!

Figure 8-21. *Commodity Research Bureau Futures Price Index prior to and subsequent to the 1980 long-wave economic peak.*

Source: Reprinted with permission from Commodity Research Bureau.

5. There is growing concern for the stability of banks, and rightfully so. Typically, banks are loaned to their maximum, and there is concern about the ability of many lenders to repay loans. During the current long-wave cycle, foreign governments have been the largest lenders unable to repay loans. In addition, farm loan payments have been in jeopardy, thereby placing considerable strain on the stability of rural banks. The credit situation tends to deteriorate even more after Stage #4 is over. Bank failures increase. The 1983–87 time period witnessed record bank failures.

6. Credit may be difficult to obtain as banks tighten their requirements and reach their lending limits. The demand for credit is so high that banks are loath to take additional credit risks. Their requirements are more stringent, and their willingness to take on unnecessary risk is diminished because of concern about the ability of many borrowers to repay loans. There are clear indications that a banking crisis is developing. The investor should be aware of the developing crisis and must act accordingly.

7. There is consumer resistance to excessively high prices. It is precisely this resistance that eventually stimulates the decline and causes the initial selling wave.

8. There is rampant speculation in virtually all markets and investments. The most recent economic peak was marked by wild speculation in futures, land, precious metals, strategic metals, and by stocks prior to the 1987 crash. As a point of information the stock market peak of 1987 was preceded by a peak of commodity prices a number of years earlier, repeating the scenario of the previous (1920s) economic peak.

9. Domestic productivity is low while wages are high. This situation continues to plague businesses in the United States even in 1988, while foreign productivity remains high with wages relatively low.

10. Previous to the 1987 Stock Market Crash, stock and bond offerings were plentiful. The scenario mimics similar situations during previous long-wave peaks.

11. Government begins to recognize that there may be a problem and begins to tighten spending, although deficit spending is clearly recognized as a problem, the alternative, which is a balanced budget, is unpalatable but necessary.

12. Tighter government controls put further strain on an already taxed business sector. Bureaucracy continues to plague business, further increasing its inefficiency. The net result is a further strain on the productivity and profitability of U.S. business.

13. To meet its own debt obligations, government seeks to raise taxes. This, of course, comes as no surprise to any student of economic history. It is not until the destructive effect of excessively high taxes are recognized that changes are made.

14. Economic slowdown begins to take hold toward the end of Stage

#4. Figure 8.21 illustrates what tends to occur toward the end of Stage #4.

15. The top war comes to an end, initially bringing optimism but thereafter signaling the start of an important disinflationary trend.

16. An initial disinflationary or recessionary decline develops. This is plainly visible upon examination of Figure 8.21. (See also item #14 above.)

STAGE #5: THE INITIAL DECLINE

Following Stage #4, a period of initial decline tends to occur. The decline can be quite severe, which was witnessed after the 1980 peak; however, it is usually seen as a welcome relief to inflation. Stage #5 should be seen as a warning sign that all is not well and that the long-wave decline probably has started. At this point, the reduction of debt is perhaps the single most important thing that the average individual can do.

STAGE #6: THE RECOVERY PERIOD

Usually after several years of the initial decline, disinflation tends to abate and the recovery period begins. Rather than respond to the discovery by breathing a sigh of relief and claiming that the worst is over, the intelligent investor should consider the recovery period as an opportunity to further reduce debt, while moving into disinflation-type investments.

STAGES #7 TO #9

The precise time span for Stages #7 to #9 is difficult to predict since government action, or lack thereof, can significantly impact their time span. Typically, however, these are the worst years of the long wave: years during which substantial economic contraction, panics, and repudiation of debt are not uncommon. Low debt, a high cash position, and disinflation-type investments are favored during this period.

Chapter 9

Long-Term Cycles:
An Overview

The student of periodic rhythms in human affairs has a tool which the law of averages itself puts into his hands. If trends have continued for decades, or if the oscillations of cycles around the trend have repeated themselves so many times and so regularly that the rhythm cannot reasonably be the result of chance, it is unwise to ignore the probability that these behaviors will continue.

—*Dewey and Dakin, 1954*[1]

Timing is the crucial issue no matter what the investment and no matter who the investor. While there are some who act on impulse or emotion, those who take the time to study the history of price cycles will find that their timing will improve markedly as a result of their efforts. Entering an investment too early ties up capital and increases exposure to losses. Entering an investment too late often requires that one pay a higher price and, as a consequence, that one take more risk. Accurate timing is essential to the long-range success of any investment program. Timing is not as serious an issue in some markets as it is in others, yet its importance cannot be overestimated. In the area of real estate, for example, triming can be off by as much as a year without a significant impact on the final result. In precious metals futures, however, where margin requirements are 3 percent or less, and leverage is high, timing cannot be off by more than a day or two at the most.

[1]Dewey, Edward R. and Dakin, Edwin F., *Cycles: The Science of Prediction*, Foundation for the Study of Cycles, 124 South Highland Avenue, Pittsburgh, PA 15206.

There are many ways in which timing may be improved. Most methods for improving timing require study, concentration, consistency, discipline, and follow-through. Today's availability of home computer software and hardware can help ease the workload. Many excellent programs provide technical timing signals for short-term entry and exit in stock and futures trading. However, no programs I know of will provide the long-term investor with most of the answers he or she needs. The fact is that few investors or traders are interested in the ultra long term. Their concerns are in the here and now; their thinking extends as far as next week or next year. Mention the ten-year outlook or the long-wave cycles and their eyes glaze over. There are few sources of reliable long-term advice or information. We're on our own. We must forge ahead without much help from economists, government, bankers, advisors, and/or friends. In so doing we must be guided by the following three rules:

1. *Observe* the historical trend and behavior of markets and prices.
2. *Evaluate* and *analyze* price trends in order to isolate repetitive patterns and behaviors that may improve timing.
3. *Project* future trends and patterns using relationships that you have found reliable over the course of your study.

CYCLES AND PATTERNS

Virtually every market or data series has its own patterns and/or cycles. In some cases the patterns are readily discernible, whereas in others they are occult or otherwise not obvious. Although it is true that some patterns and relationships can be found only through the application of complex statistical and mathematical formulae, I've found that a good majority of relationships are visible with nothing more than the naked eye guided by motivation and persistence. Let's take a look at a few of the patterns to which I have just referred.

Cycles are the most common of patterns. Whereas it would be convenient to think of cycles as relatively perfect and highly predictable, the fact is that this is not true for most economic data. Chronobiology, the study of cyclic behavior in biological organisms, has uncovered literally hundreds, if not thousands, of highly regular biological cycles, but economists and investors are not fortunate enough to have had the same experience. Economic cycles, market cycles, and the cyclic behavior of prices are irregular at best but predictable within a reasonable margin of error. The ability to forecast prices and/or price trends to within 10 to 15 percent accuracy is a valuable asset. What cycles lack in precision can be compensated for by improving timing techniques.

Cyclic analysis and forecasting is still not considered an orthodox technique among economists and businesspersons. In spite of the accurate and at times astounding work of such cyclic investigators as Ned Dewey and Gertrude Shirk of the Foundation for the Study of Cycles, this approach to market analysis is largely ignored or grossly misunderstood by the vast majority of businesspersons, traders, investors, economists, and bureaucrats. Their ire is aggravated by the erroneous belief that cyclic analysis and forecasting are highly deterministic, that cycles are rigid, and that they do not consider changes in fundamental events and underlying conditions.

My Work with Economic Cycles

In 1981 I wrote *The Handbook of Commodity Cycles: A Window on Time* (John Wiley & Sons, Inc.). This book was designed to increase investor and trader awareness about the role of cycles in the futures markets and to provide those so inclined with timing methods for using cycles in their trading and/or investing programs. At that time I made the following observations about the importance of cycles:

> We live in uncertain times. Hardly a day passes without leaving its mark on the pages of history. The pace of life appears to be on a never-ending upward spiral that goes hand-in-hand with technology. And yet, at the base of all sophistication lies simplicity. Cyclic analysis offers the opportunity to return to basics. It is my firm belief that repetition is the key to analysis in virtually all areas of science, philosophy and art. Were we to know all of the cyclic variables in a given area we would predict with near 100 percent accuracy. But the state of knowledge is itself governed by complex cycles and alternates from low to high and back to low again, hence making our task even more difficult. The history of humanity is the history of cycles. We have moved from humble one-celled beginnings to complex mega-celled human machines only to now sit on the verge of possible self-destruction

and a return to the one-celled form. Technology itself tends to undo progress just as complexity eventually self-destructs leaving only gears, springs, wires, nuts, and bolts. . . .

There are no guaranteed answers, assured profits, totally safe methods, or ultimate systems in this or any other speculative or invest-ment area. We are all subject to emotion, confidence, self-doubt, conceit, and overconfidence. In the proper measure these traits can be valuable, but in extremes they can undo even the most promising method of market analysis. Cyclic analysis and the methods I discuss in this book have definite limitations. There will be times when they are more effective than usual, and there will be times when their results are less than desired. But these results can be significantly altered for better or for worse by the human factor. And the human psyche itself is subject to cyclic variation. The world of cycles is at one and the same time complex and simple. [Bernstein, 1981]

Today, more than seven years later, the role of cycles is even more important than it was then. Why? Because there is increasing evidence that virtually every market, economy, economic indicator, natural event, and/or sociopolitical event exhibits cyclic tendencies. My knowledge of and experience with cycles, which began in the early 1970s, prompted me to publish, in 1978, a relatively brief but timely forecast entitled *Commodites—Now Through 1984*. The study was directed at futures traders who were interested in and concerned with the direction of long-term price cycles for the period through 1984. Here is a summary of my comments from the 1978 study:

It is interesting to note that many markets will be reaching their ideal cyclic peaks at or about the same time. This time frame is late 1980 to late 1981. There is often considerable economic, political and mili-tary turmoil at such peaks. And this one should be no different. I am making the assumption that many markets have not as yet seen their cyclic highs. If they have, then these highs will be tested. Interest rates, for example, have most likely peaked, but a second top is a historically reasonable expectation. It is not possible to use cycles of such lengthy duration for precise timing. Only a good trading and timing system can help in this respect. We should be more concerned about riding the major trends after first identifying them without too much concern about how high or low prices are going. I have at least five general expecta-tions. They are as follows:

1. Continued economic turmoil and inflation through mid-1980;

2. The start of a major bear market well before late 1980 in most of the agricultural and metal markets;

3. The start of a Kondratieff Wave down cycle which could have serious long-term deflationary consequences;

4. Continued strength in metals most likely until late 1980; and

5. A second attempt at the highs in interest rates and secondary rise in inflation rates. It is too early to tell whether these peaks will surpass highs already seen. [Bernstein, 1978]

Today we can see that the forecasts given in 1978 were, without question, accurate. In fact, their accuracy has given me much food for thought. But the importance of the 1978 forecasts is not in their accuracy but rather in the techniques used to generate them. The principles of cyclic analyses that were applied to the economy, interest rates, and the commodity markets were validated and verified by actual market behavior.

In August 1986, the forecasts were updated and new long-range forecasts, based on cycles, were given through the year 2001. *Futures— Now Through 2001*, of which only 450 copies were printed, underscored my commitment to cyclic analysis as an analytical tool, one that, if properly used, could markedly improve the lot of traders, investors, and economies the world over. Here are my comments as stated in *Futures— Now Through 2001*:

We live in a world of uncertainties; a world which grows unstable with each passing moment. Rarely a day passes without news of violence, civil unrest, or other destabilizing events. Virtually every aspect of human life has in the last 25 years come under pressure either from vocal proponents of change or from militant forces intent upon massive and disruptive political reformation. Whether these forces will ultimately bring about positive or negative change is a major issue, yet, there are more immediate and pressing needs which affect civilization. I might add that I use the term "civilization" merely in an obligatory fashion since the question could appropriately be raised as to whether humankind is indeed acting in a civilized fashion.

The world today is one of sharp contrasts. While grain warehouses in the United States bulge with supply and the prospect of unharvested grain due to lack of storage space looms as a persistent reality in 1986, thousands die a degrading and merciless death from starvation in Africa. While some nations thrive others can barely survive. While efforts to ensure freedom are carried to excess in some nations, others perpetuate a tightening police state. The contrasts become more exaggerated daily and there are fewer and fewer neutral spots to be found.

On an economic level most so-called "free world" nations are in a state of disinflation following an inflationary bubble which besieged most economies in the 1970s. Many commodity markets have been at low levels for a number of years. Though this situation was unexpected by many analysts, the cyclic forecasts I offered in my 1978 study *Commodities—Now Through 1984* clearly indicated the expectations. Now that 1984 has come and gone, it's time to look ahead to the end of this millennium in order to determine the status of my long-term cycle studies.

I hasten to add that what I am offering herein is not based upon an occult or arcane methodology, but rather upon a cyclical and technical analysis which, at best, is only quasi scientific but certainly not subjective. I understand that my forecasts will change over time. Knowing this I have attempted to provide you with some alternate scenarios, again, based on technical price and indicator studies.

The use of price cycles for the purpose of forecasting is not nearly as scientific as we would like it to be. Yet, in spite of its limitations, it has its assets as well and should not be discarded. As computer technology grows, and as our ability to understand cycles improves, it will be possible to make more precise and accurate forecasts. But at this time we must do the best with what we have. [Bernstein, 1986]

Several years after the publication of *Futures—Now Through 2001*, many of the forecasts have been verified. Yet the methodology I employed is not mystical, magical, complex, or particularly difficult. It is a methodology that any interested and motivated investor can apply to any market indicator, statistic, or data series. The only things required are a sufficiently long data history (which can be difficult to obtain), the willingness to study these data, and the discipline to apply the results to our individual investments and needs.

One result of my literally thousands of hours of work and analyses with historical data has led me to the conclusion that the single most important aspect of any market or economic indicator is its price cycle. In fact, my studies and analyses have yielded the following conclusions:

1. There are cycles and cyclic tendencies in every market indicator, economic statistic, and/or data series.

2. There are repetitive patterns and relationships in every market, economic statistic, and/or data series.

3. The cycles and patterns can be determined by observation and/or by application of various statistical methods.

4. Once found, the cycles and patterns can be observed and statistically validated.

5. Investors and speculators can use these patterns to their advantage.

More Preliminaries

Chapter One has already presented the aforementioned list as it applies to the study, analysis, and application of cyclic phenomena to economic cycles. This chapter will give you an overview of the important long-term cycles in a variety of markets. Whereas the balance of this book has been dedicated to an examination of economic cycles, this chapter will pinpoint the most important and reliable long-term cycles in markets that are likely to be affected by economic trends in the years ahead. I suggest that you study the cycles and patterns, evaluating them with specific reference to your individual situation. If you are a businessperson, for example, then you will be most concerned with the interest rate cycles and projections, and with the cyclic analyses and forecasts that pertain specifically to your type of business. If you are involved in agribusiness, then you will want to pay particular attention to several of the agricultural market forecasts inasmuch as they are likely to affect your business. If you're primarily interested in the precious metals, then pay particular attention to the cycles and forecasts specifically provided for these markets. In studying the analyses and forecasts that follow, please note that:

1. *Forecasts are not 100 percent accurate.* We would be fools if we believed, even for a fleeting moment, that any forecast represents reality. Forecasts are expectations based on what we assume to be logical deduction and inference, based on quasi-scientific methodologies. Forecasts will change, events will affect forecasts, and new data will make forecasts obsolete. Our goal is to be correct within a reasonable margin of error (*i.e.*, 10 to 15 percent). But we must also remember that publishing a forecast is like buying a new automobile. Once the auto has left the dealership, it has lost a percentage of its value. It is not as valuable. It must be maintained and kept in

running condition. If the car was well built, then only minimal maintenance will be necessary. It will run well for many miles and years, performing to expectations. If, however, the proverbial "lemon" has been purchased, then major surgery may be necessary to make it function to specifications and expectations.

2. *Forecasts will change* over the course of time. By the time you read these forecasts, they will be somewhat out of date. One hopes that they will be reasonably correct; however, *you must keep them current, or you must find an individual or service that will keep them up to date for you.* You are best off doing the work on your own.

3. *Markets interact with one another.* Therefore, what's happening in one market will have an impact on other markets. No forecast should be taken in total isolation. Attempt to achieve an overview of "the big picture."

4. *Cycle lengths change.* The fact that a cycle has been accurate for an extended period of time does not necessarily indicate that it will continue to be accurate in the future. It is likely *but not certain* that the cyclic lengths will remain relatively constant.

5. *Cycles interact.* There are numerous cycles in each market. They interact with and affect one another. This forecast shows only one or several of the important cycles. Remember that the influence of one cycle on another may result in tops or bottoms earlier or later than expected.

6. *Cycles forecast time and not price.* In other words, timing is considered more important than price. If we know when to do something, then the price at which to do it must necessarily be right. Cycles are about time. I will not sink too deeply into the quagmire of forecasting prices, as this is really unnecessary. Because this is a most important issue, consider the following comments given in *Cyclic Analysis in Futures Trading*[2]:

Are Price Targets Necessary?

We all know that in the markets, "timing is everything." If the time for taking a particular action is right, then the price must necessarily also be right. Therefore, it makes little difference to those

[2]Bernstein, J., *Cyclic Analysis in Futures Trading—Contemporary Methods & Procedures*, John Wiley & Sons, Inc., New York, 1988.

trading with cycles how high or low prices may be. If the time has come to take action, action must be taken without regard for price. In fact, if one allows price to affect judgment, the resulting decision can be inconsistent with one's original intentions. Assume, for example, the case of an individual who purchased gold at $300/oz. with a price target of $379/oz. Although the market may have risen to within $10 of the objective with the cycle peaking, the original price target has now become a benchmark. It prompts the investor to hold the position, awaiting the price target, even though market cycles may be saying that the trend has most likely turned lower. I conclude that projecting price targets is not necessarily a practice that fosters sound investing or successful speculation. Price targets have a way of fostering dependency. The more you establish a specific price target for your trading or investing, the less attention you are prone to pay to the important aspects of timing. [Bernstein, 1988]

7. *Fine tune the cycles.* As the ideal time frame of an anticipated cyclic turn approaches, attempt to fine tune your expectations with other methods, technical and/or fundamental. To cover this topic adequately would require several additional books; however, you can consult any number of excellent texts to learn more about market timing.

8. *Don't be swayed by the news.* The news will almost always be contrary to what the cycles are saying. Cycles will be topping when the news is most positive, and cycles will be bottoming when the news is most negative. Reading the newspapers or listening to the ramblings of bureaucrats can help you considerably. Simply evaluate the majority opinion, determine how strong these opinions are, and look at the projected cycle. Odds are that majority opinion will be opposite from the anticipated cyclic turn. There is great value in determining what the majority is doing or expecting, and then doing the opposite, particularly if the cyclic expectations call for price movement opposite from that expected by the crowd.

9. *Remember to maintain a balanced portfolio.* Don't become too heavily concentrated in one area or group of investments. Attempt to isolate time frames during which many cycles in different markets converge to an expected low or high point at about the same period of time.

Cycles in Gold

The cycles in gold are not as readily determined as they are in other markets, because the data history of gold prices is not as continuous or complete as we would like. This is due to the volatile history of gold prices and the fact that prices were fixed by government decree in the United States for a number of years. An excellent overview of the historical behavior of gold prices was provided by David Williams in *Cycles* (September/October 1981). Williams notes the existence of an approximate 22.83-year cycle in gold prices as measured from peak to peak. Figure 9.1, reprinted from Williams's article, shows the approximate cycle tops for this pattern, as determined by Williams. In 1981 Williams projected the next theoretical top in gold prices as due in approximately 1983.21. Figure 9.2 shows the actual behavior of gold prices. A slightly different analysis of Williams's results yields the following longer-term cycles:

Figure 9-1. *Average between peaks: 22.83 years. The next theoretical peak might come around 1983.21.*

The 22.83-Year Cycle of Tops in U.S. Gold Prices

Date	Price	Years Between Tops	Notes
5-31-1781	Astronomical		$400-1000 in notes for $1 of Hard
		34	Currency (Revolutionary War)
1815	$23.07		War of 1812
		22	
JUN 1837	22.70		Panic of 1837
		20	
SEP 1857	Premium		Panic of 1857
		16	
SEP 1873	23.30		Panic of 1873
		20	
OCT 1893	20.67		Panic of 1893. Discount Rate up
		24	36%. U.S. gold stocks increased.
SEP 1917	20.67		World War I. Free export of gold
		17	barred. U.S. gold stocks increased.
1-31-1934	35.00		U.S. off the gold standard. Price
		26	fixed at $35 for next 37 years.
OCT 1960	40.00		

Source: Reprinted from *Cycles*, The Foundation for the Study of Cycles, 3333 Michelson Drive #210, Irvine, CA 92715.

1. 1781–1837 = 56 years, top to top
2. 1837–1893 = 56 years, top to top
3. 1893–1934 = 41 years, top to top
4. 1934–1980 = 46 years, top to top

Although there is still only limited evidence in support of an approximate 46- to 54-year cycle, there is a hint that such a cycle may be present in the gold data. A more useful analysis can be gleaned from the approximate 6.6-year cycle in gold prices.

The question on the minds of virtually all investors throughout the world is "Where will prices go, and when will they get there?" Unfortunately, I do not have the answer any more than anyone else does. Certainly, one could adopt the "buy on a scale down and hold indefinitely" attitude, which will eventually be right. As absurd as this sounds, some well-known analysts have done just that. All the way up they touted the virtues of gold, projecting $1,000/oz. or more. All the way down they urged their followers to buy more. This type of financial behavior is more cultist than it is investment or trader oriented. Gold is not a religion. It's just another market. Figure 9.3 shows futures monthly, and Figure 9.4 shows a combination of gold shares index 1941–74 and monthly cash average gold 1974–88.

1. *The approximate 6.62-year cycle:* There has been much discussion and controversy regarding the gold cycles. It appears that each faction sees a gold cycle consistent with its vested interest. My work shows a rather unreliable cycle of 6.62 years, low to low. A major peak is expected in the 1991 to 1992 time frame, followed by what could be record highs in the 1997–98 time frame. The 1997–98 highs could be the result of serious banking problems or from the expected "bottom war."

2. *Projections:* I suspect that it will take considerable time to overcome the record peak in gold prices. Such a move is not likely until the next cycle approximate high period in the 1991 to 1992 time period or perhaps as late as the cycle top thereafter in the 1997–98 time frame. A projection of $980–$990 is likely for the next top, and a projection of $1,590–$1,605 as the top thereafter, yet these projections depend either upon a new wave of intense inflation and/or major disruption of world gold supplies. The $260 level is important as long-term support.

Figure 9-2. *Gold prices in England, 1343–1980.*

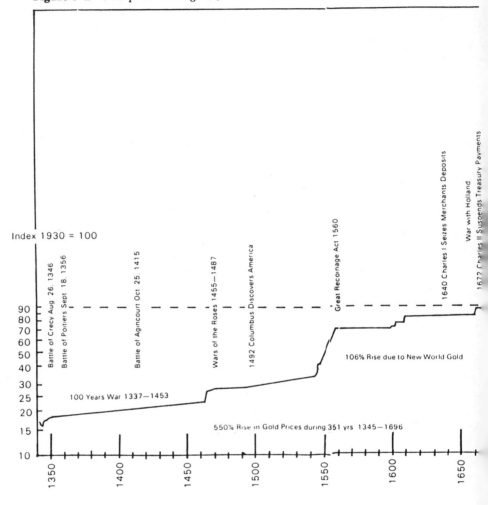

My comments are not designed to underplay the role of gold as an investment. Nor are they intended to reduce the significance of gold as a hedge against uncertainty. They are, however, directed at bringing gold more closely into the realm of all markets. Certainly the percentage size of up and down moves in other markets has been just as significant as that in gold.

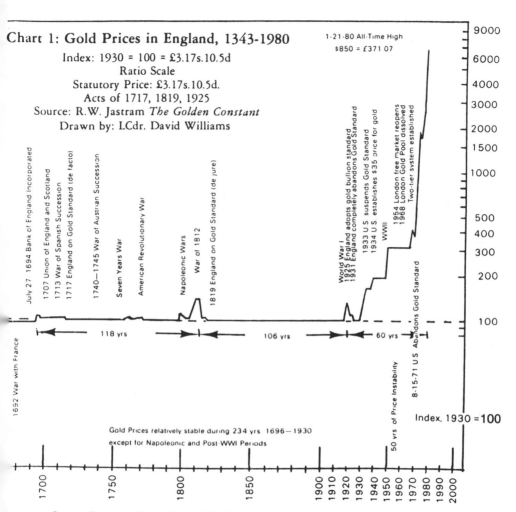

Chart 1: Gold Prices in England, 1343-1980

Index: 1930 = 100 = £3.17s.10.5d
Ratio Scale
Statutory Price: £3.17s.10.5d.
Acts of 1717, 1819, 1925
Source: R.W. Jastram *The Golden Constant*
Drawn by: LCdr. David Williams

1-21-80 All-Time High
$850 = £371 07

Index, 1930 = **100**

Source: Reprinted from *Cycles,* The Foundation for the Study of Cycles, 3333 Michelson Drive #210, Irvine, CA 92715.

Cycles in Silver

The history of silver prices is more readily studied than is the history of gold. Silver prices have been free to fluctuate for many years. The January/February 1981 issue of *Cycles* featured a most thorough analysis of silver price history by David Williams, who presented evi-

Figure 9-3. *A closer look at the gold cycle—futures prices (monthly),* 1976–86.

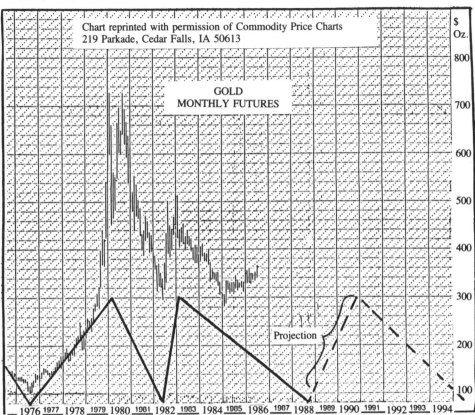

dence of 31-, 15.36-, 9.26-, and 5.58-year cycles. My work has confirmed the existence of these cycles. Note the following commentary on the silver cycles by Williams.

> It will also be noted . . . that all four cycles, i.e., 31, 15.36, 9.26 and 5.58 years, peaked in 1919. In addition, the 31- and 15.36-year cycles peaked in 1859, 1890 and 1951, while the 9.26- and 5.58-year cycles peaked together in 1912, 1935, 1946 and 1974. The 1951 peak of the 5.58-year cycle also coincided with the peaks of the 31- and 15.36-year cycles in that year. These cycles are believed to be real because: (a) There have been 3 repetitions of the 31-year cycle and 7 repetitions of the 15.36-year cycle since 1850; (b) there have been 8

Figure 9.4. *Monthly gold index/gold prices 1941–88 and cycles.*

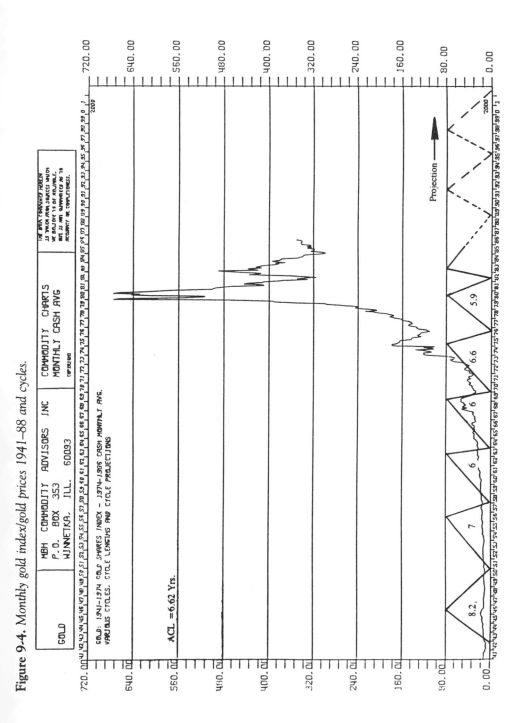

repetitions of the 9.26-year cycle and 12 repetitions of the 5.58-year cycle since 1900. Shirk estimates the next ideal peaks to occur: 31-year cycle in 1980.5, 15.36-year cycle in 1981.58, 9.26-year cycle in 1983.5, and 5.58-year cycle in 1985.62. By a slightly different method, the author's forecast is: 1981.7, 1983.7, 1983.09 and 1985.66 for the respective cycles. The ideal low of the 5.88-year cycle is due at 1982.8 according to Shirk. [1981, p. 8]

My analysis of the silver cycles suggests the following:

1. *Approximate 10-year cycle:* Because of the nature of these charts (Figures 9.5 and 9.6), the cycle lows of the approximate 10-year cycle are shown by numbers 1 through 7. Note that these lows typically have come early in the start of each decade. Based on this pattern I expect the next major silver low to occur during 1991. This is, of course, the ideal time frame for the low. From this low the approximate 10-year cycle should peak in the mid-1990s and move to another low in the 2001 time frame.

2. *Approximate 5.58-year cycle:* This cycle has been somewhat variable, at times running well in excess of 5 years, at times less than 5 years. The lows of this cycle are indicated by 1–7 and A–G. As you can see from Figure 9.5, the 1987–88 time frame marked an ideal low in the approximate 5.58-year cycle. This should be followed by a top in the late-1989 to early-1990 time frame and, from there, a low with the approximate 10-year cycle as shown.

   In analyzing all of the cycles in silver you would do well to remember that silver is first and foremost an industrial metal. Hence, its price will be more closely related to economic trends than to international political instability and like factors. The precious metals, however, are sensitive to both aspects, economic and political.

3. *Projections:* Based on the cycles above and upon my understanding of the long-wave economic cycles, I have the following price projections for silver. Low 7 marked the last approximate 5-year low, top H was the top of the 5-year cycle, and low G is forming now. It is likely to be followed by projected top I. The top of this cycle should not exceed top H because we are in a disinflationary long-wave cycle. An optimistic projection would be about $11. On the downside, there is considerable long-term support between 4.85 and 3.50. For

Figure 9-5. *Long-term silver cycles (monthly futures).*

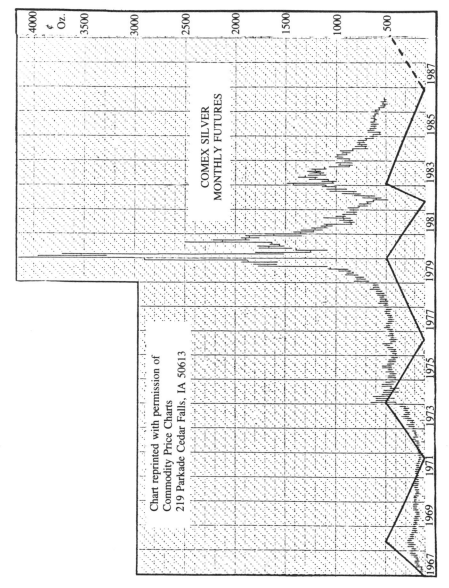

COMEX SILVER
MONTHLY FUTURES

Chart reprinted with permission of
Commodity Price Charts
219 Parkade Cedar Falls, IA 50613

219

Figure 9-6. *Long-term silver cycles—monthly cash average.*

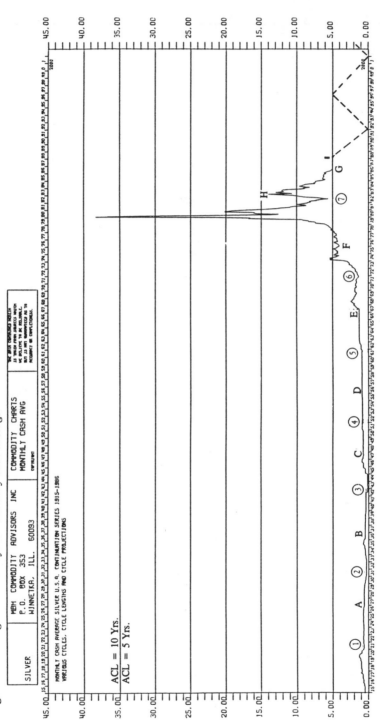

220

those buying and accumulating long-term positions in silver this is a moot point, because historically prices are very cheap.

Based on the approximate 10-year cycle, more optimistic projections are possible on the upside, with the downside support area still as stated above. I suspect that a serious challenge to the all-time highs can occur in the 1994–96 time frame. A monthly cash average price above $19 could easily trigger such a challenge, but it would take a major bull market in other metals to trigger such a move. This could be stimulated by a banking crisis in the early 1990s during the declining phase of the long-wave cycle.

Cycles in Copper

Copper has had a long history of reliable cycles. The Foundation for the Study of Cycles and others have performed literally hundreds of studies on copper prices. There is a fairly continuous data history available. My conclusions and projections are as follows (see Figures 9.7 and 9.8):

1. *Approximate 12.8-year cycle* lows and highs are shown. This cycle has been somewhat variable at times, but it is fairly reliable overall. It suggests that a low was made in 1984. A top is due in the early 1990s.
2. *Early-decade-low pattern.* Copper has shown a tendency to make lows early in each decade, most often in the years numbered 2 or 3. Though the subsequent upmove may at times be small, it does, nevertheless, appear to be consistent (lows marked 1–7).
3. *Approximate 4.5- to 6-year cycle* lows and highs are also shown. This cycle bottomed in 1987. A top is due in 1989.
4. *Projections:* Copper prices are very low on a relative historical basis. This clearly reflects the disinflationary economic trend in recent years. In fact, copper has retraced more than 50 percent of its move from the 1932–33 lows to the 1979–80 highs. In the event of a declared war, prices could easily test the record highs.

Note that I have not provided any analysis of the cycles in platinum or palladium. There is an insufficient or noncontinuous data history for both of these markets.

Figure 9-7. *Long-term cycles in copper.*

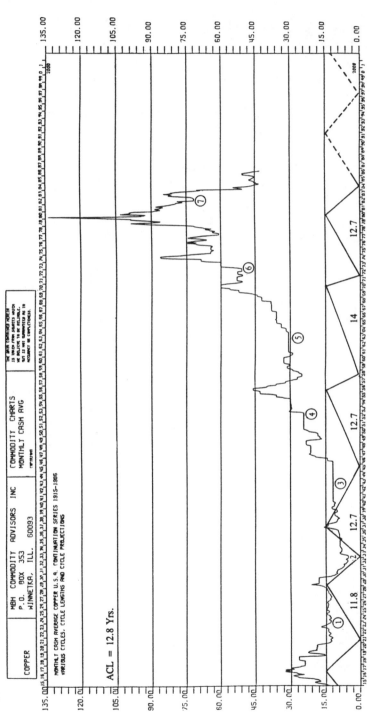

222

Figure 9-8. *The 5–6-year cycles in copper.*

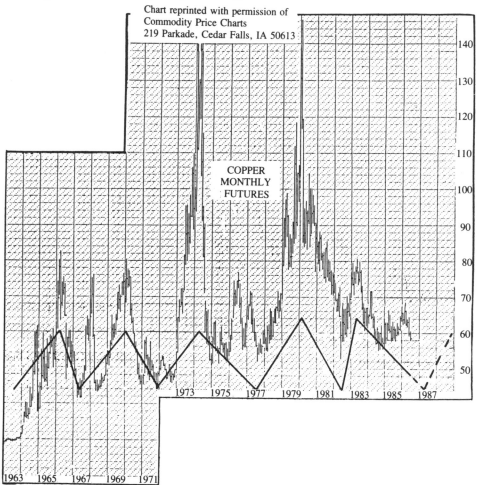

Chart reprinted with permission of
Commodity Price Charts
219 Parkade, Cedar Falls, IA 50613

COPPER
MONTHLY
FUTURES

Stock Prices

A major area of concern to investors is the stock market. Of all the markets, stocks have received the most attention. There are literally hundreds of studies on cycles in stocks. Cyclic lengths range from as long as forty-two to fifty-four years to as short as three to four days. Many of the cycles in stocks are highly reliable. Perhaps those having the greatest importance to investors are the approximate nine- and four-year cycles. Clear statistical evidence of both the nine- and four-year cycles has been presented by many analysts. Although the cycles have changed somewhat over the years, they are still reliable. Note the following analyses and projections. See Figures 9.9 and 9.10. (Figure 9.10 shows an approximate 19-week cycle.)

1. *Approximate 8.52-year cycle* lows and highs are shown. Low and high projections are shown by the dashed line.
2. *Approximate 4-year cycle* lows and highs are numbered 1 through 15. The last low at 15 formed the bottom of a very short cycle. Both the approximate 4-year and 8.52-year cycles are likely to top and bottom as projected.
3. *Projections:* Cycles in stock prices are not only among the most well researched, but they are also among the most reliable and repetitive. Based on these cycles an important top is due in late 1988 or by mid-1989.

Did the "Crash of '87" signal a top in the 8.52-year cycle? Perhaps it did. Yet, a test or possible penetration of the 1987 top could still come.

Cycles in the Canadian Dollar

Here is an analysis that may surprise many readers: Few investors pay attention to the Canadian dollar, yet if the cycles are correct, then the Canadian dollar could well become one of the strongest currencies in the world.

Figure 9.11 shows Canadian dollar monthly cash price, 1915–86. Figure 9.12 shows monthly Canadian dollar futures. I expect a significant appreciation in the Canadian dollar based both on the cycles and on my understanding of the long-wave world economic situation. Essentially these translate into the expectation that Canada and its currency will, at some point in the future, become dominant in world economics. The charts and expectations are based on the following factors:

1. *Approximate 22.23-year cycle:* Though there have only been 3 repetitions of this cycle since 1915, I suspect that the cycle will prove to be a valid one. Based on this cycle we are now at what should be the

Figure 9-9. *Long-term cycles in stock index.*

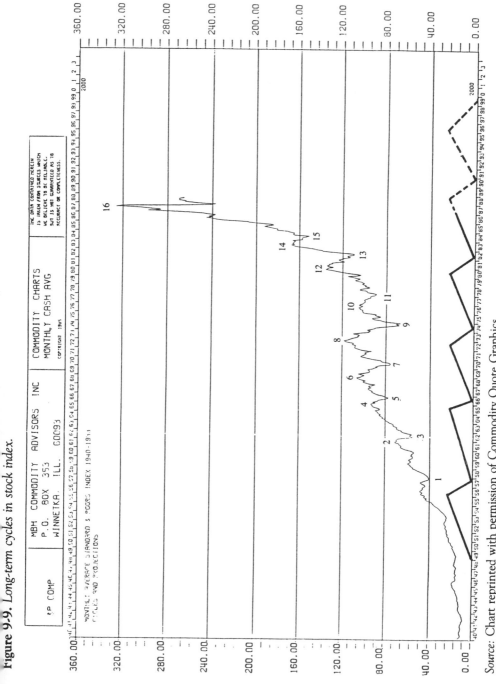

Source: Chart reprinted with permission of Commodity Quote Graphics.

225

Figure 9-10. *Long-term cycle in stock index.*

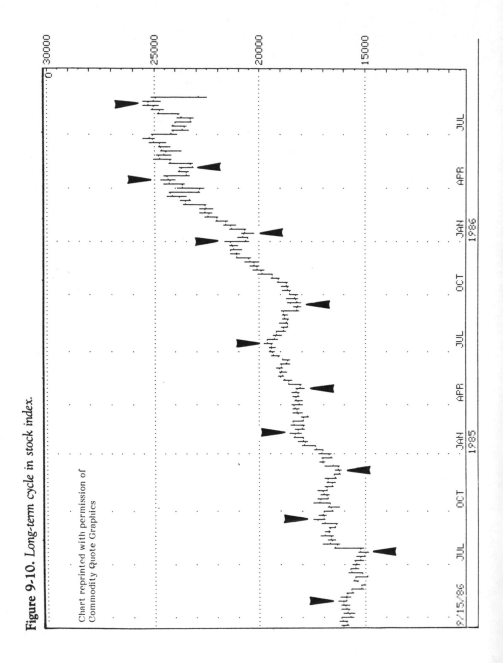

Chart reprinted with permission of
Commodity Quote Graphics

Figure 9-11. *Long-term cycles in the Canadian dollar, 1915–86.*

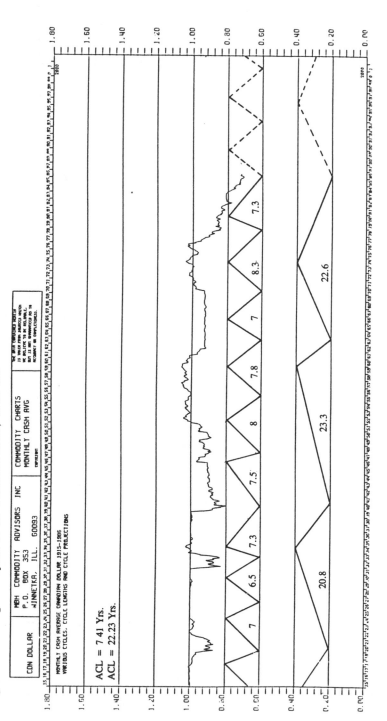

227

start of a major bull market in the Canadian dollar that is likely to take the market to new all-time highs and a peak in the mid-1990s.

2. *Approximate 7.41-year cycle:* This cycle is part of the approximate 22.23-year cycle. It is shown as likely to bottom now as well with a projected top in 1989–90. Additional cycles are shown and projected accordingly. Penetration of point "A" (Figure 9.12) was important as an indicator that the 7.41-year's low had been made.

3. *Projections:* I expect the Canadian dollar to become one of the strongest currencies in the world, if not, in fact, the strongest. I say this for several reasons. First, the cycles are lining up for important lows as stated above. Second, Canada is a country with immense natural resources and production capabilities. Not only does the country have massive agricultural capability, but it also has petroleum, minerals, and vast undeveloped areas of land. These important resources are the building blocks of economic growth that will mark the next period of expansion once the current long-wave cycle has bottomed. In terms of upside projections, I can see the possibility of $1.20 to $1.40 as a minimum projection.

Cycles in the Swiss Franc

My data history on the Swiss franc is extensive and readily amenable to long-term cyclic study. This is not the case with some of the other currencies, where various historical factors stand in the way of a complete and lengthy data file. Given this continuous data string, a thorough analysis and projection of the Swiss franc can be made on the basis of several cycles. The analyses and projections are as follows. See Figures 9.13 and 9.14.

1. *Approximate 12.9-year cycle:* This cycle has not shown much variability, though the assignment of lows and highs during the period of stability from about 1939 through 1970 is somewhat arbitrary. Yet, given these limitations, the cycle appears to have made its last low in late 1984 to early 1985. As you can see, we have started a longer-term bull move that has carried the Swiss franc to new highs against the U.S. dollar.

Figure 9-12. *The long-term cycles in the Canadian dollar as seen on monthly futures chart, 1972–86.*

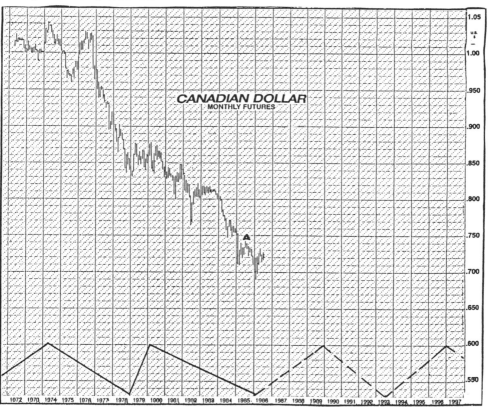

Source: Chart reprinted with permission of Commodity Price Charts, 219 Parkade, Cedar Falls, IA 50613.

2. *Projections:* In 1986 I projected a new all-time high in the Swiss franc vs. the U.S. dollar. Remember that the fate of the currencies relative to the U.S. dollar is closely related to the long-wave economic cycle. Should disinflation become a serious factor (which the odds still appear to favor), then prices could readily set back to secular support in the 24–28 area. (See Figure 9.14.)

Do not discount an early top for the 12.9-year cycle.

Figure 9-13. *Long-term cycles in the Swiss franc, 1915–86.*

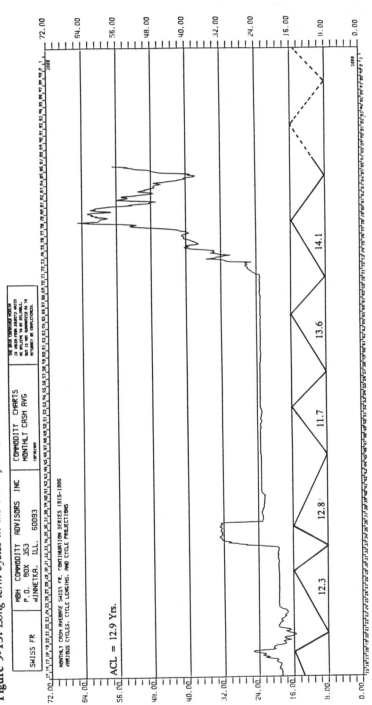

Figure 9-14. *Monthly Swiss franc futures and cycles, 1915–86.*

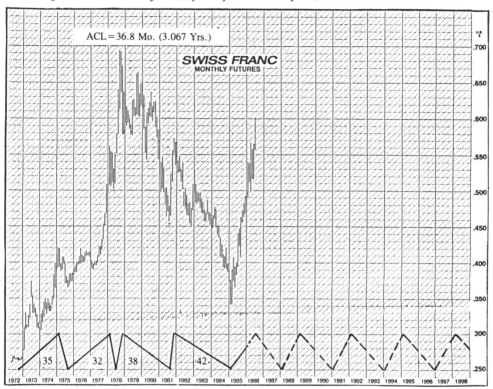

Source: Chart reprinted with permission of Commodity Price Charts, 219 Parkade, Cedar Falls, IA 50613.

Cycles in the British Pound

As in the case of some of the markets covered in this report, there is a lack of useful continuous data on the British pound. Yet it appears that there is a relatively reliable approximate 8.65-year cycle, low to low. The last cycle low was made in early 1985. See Figure 9.15. The monthly futures chart, Figure 9.16, shows the same cycle and projection through 1991.

Projections: The British pound has been in a major downtrend since the mid-1960s. It is well overdue for a substantial correction to the upside. The record lows made at the last cycle bottom should hold; however, if they do not do so on a monthly cash average basis, then the 1.00 level will likely be the next target.

Figure 9-15. *Long-term cycle in British pound as seen on monthly cash chart, 1951–86.*

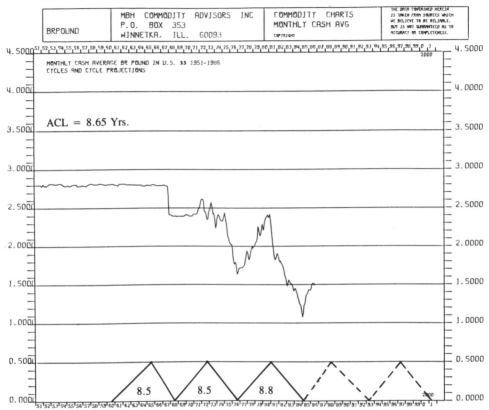

Cycles in Corn Prices

For many years, corn has been one of the most reliable cyclical markets. The major cycles and projections are reviewed here. See Figure 9.17.

1. *Approximate 27-year cycle* lows and highs are shown by the letters A through E. The next top for this cycle is projected at high G past the year 2000. In spite of the length of this cycle it has been very reliable.

2. *Approximate 5.65-year cycle* lows and highs are shown in Figure 9.17. This cycle has also been reliable. It projected a major low (F) of the

Figure 9-16. *Monthly British pound futures and cycles.*

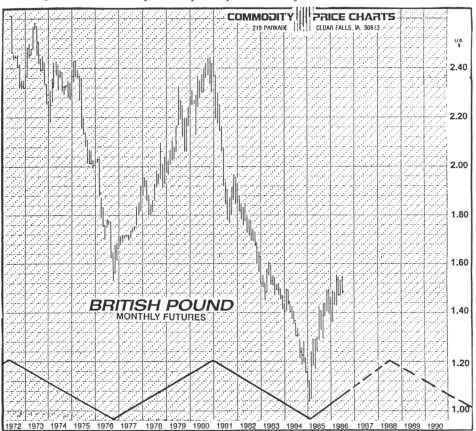

Source: Chart reprinted with permission of Commodity Price Charts.

approximate 27-year cycle. The 5.65-year cycle lows and highs are shown and projected on the monthly futures price chart as well. It is possible that a low was made in 1987.

3. *Projections:* A major cyclic low on two cycles is due in 1988. This low may have come early. From this low I expect prices to recover to as high as $2.20 and then $3.30 by the time the 1990–91 top is in place. The 1995–96 top should see a new all-time high (although it could come earlier, depending on weather cycles). Ideally projected 27-year top G should see prices at the end of an explosive upmove not dissimilar from the surge that came prior to tops A, C, and E.

Figure 9-17. *Long-term cycles in corn, 1915–86.*

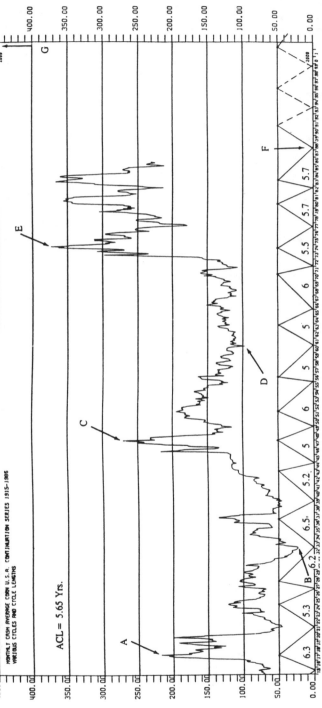

In closing, it should be remembered that corn prices are closely related to the overall trends of the long-wave fifty-four-year economic cycle (as are virtually all markets). The timing and projections given above will, therefore, be a function of the lows and highs of the long-wave economic cycles. Note also that most commodity markets made their fifty-four-year cyclic lows in 1932–34, about eight years before the economic lows were in place.

Cycles in Lumber Prices

There is much to say about lumber price cycles. In addition to the fact that this is a very reliable market from a cyclical standpoint, it is also a market which is directly related to inflation and deflation. The inflationary economic peak was marked by top #9 in lumber and the recent economic low, though likely not a major one came at about the time of low #5. But this barely scratches the surface. The following cycles and patterns are relevant in lumber.

1. *Approximate 8.37-year cycle:* This pattern has now shown much deviation from its average length during the data history. The next low is due in 1990, with the current cycle due to peak by mid-1988. Thereafter a major top is due in the late 1990s—one that should be well in excess of the record high at top #9 (Figure 9.18).

2. *Approximate early-decade lows:* There has also been a tendency for lows to be made early in each decade. See as examples lows market 1 through 5. Low 5 was a bit late. Most of the important lows have been made in the first or second year of the decade (Figure 9.18).

3. *Approximate late-decade highs:* There has been a tendency for tops to occur during the eighth through last year of the decade. These highs are marked 6 through 9 (Figure 9.18).

4. *Projections:* The current 8.37-year average cycle should peak in the next year or two in the technical resistance area of about $220–$240. The next cycle low, due approximately in 1990, should be a major low, perhaps as low as the $80 area in conjunction with anticipated economic lows. From these lows new all-time highs should be made well in excess of top #9, possibly as high as the $420–$480 area (Figure 9.18).(See also Figure 9.19.)

Figure 9-18. *Long-term cycles in lumber, 1938–86.*

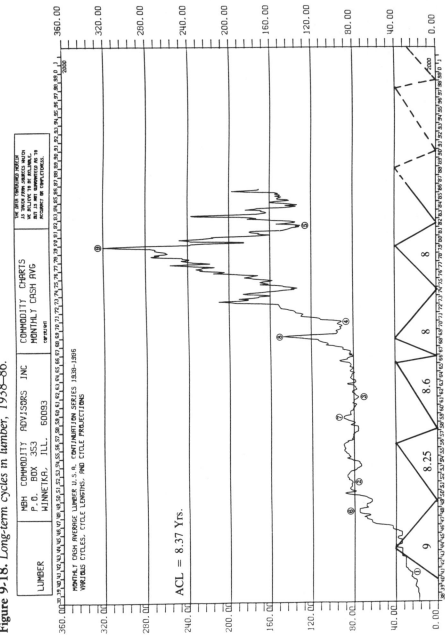

Figure 9-19. *Long-term cycles in lumber shown on monthly futures chart.*

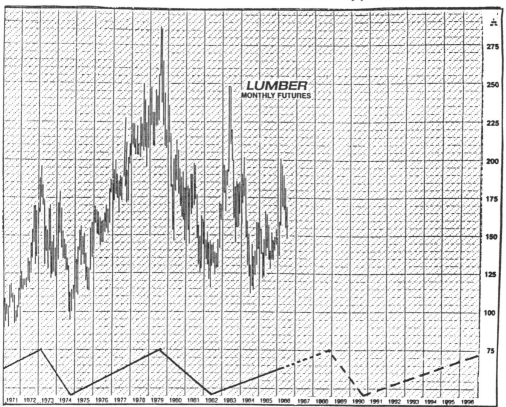

Source: Chart courtesy of Commodity Price Charts.

Cycles in Long-Term Interest Rates

Interest rates have several reliable cyclical patterns.

1. *Approximate 10-year cycle* lows and highs are shown and projected in Figures 9.20 and 9.21. Note that an alternate count for the current cycle is possible, projecting a low in early 1987 as opposed to a low in 1985 (see B, C). Low A was the bottom of a shorter-term cycle. It is likely that the 10-year cycle has bottomed.

2. *Projections:* A low should be in process at this time. This should be followed by top in the early 1990 time frame and a low about

Figure 9-20. *Long-term cycles in bond yields, 1915–86.*

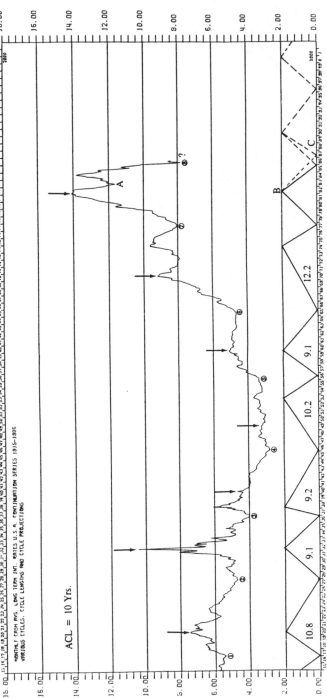

Figure 9-21. *Long-term cycle in T bond futures, 1978–86.*

mid-decade per the mid-decade-low pattern. There should be good long-term support in the 6 percent area, then in the 5 percent area. A long-term cycle low should be made in line with the economic lows in the areas mentioned. Expect long-term resistance in the 11 percent area. Look for record highs in the 1999–2000 time frame. Further updates will be necessary depending upon the inflationary trend and developments with the long-wave economic cycle.

Cycles in Short-Term Interest Rates

There are several important patterns and cycles in short-term interest rates. These are as follows. See Figure 9.22.

1. *Approximate 10-year cycle:* The continuation of an approximate 10-year cycle is shown by the dashed line. This cycle suggests that a low is in process to be followed by a top in the 1989 time frame and another low in the 1996–97 time frame.

Figure 9-22. *Long-term cycles in T bills, 1915–86.*

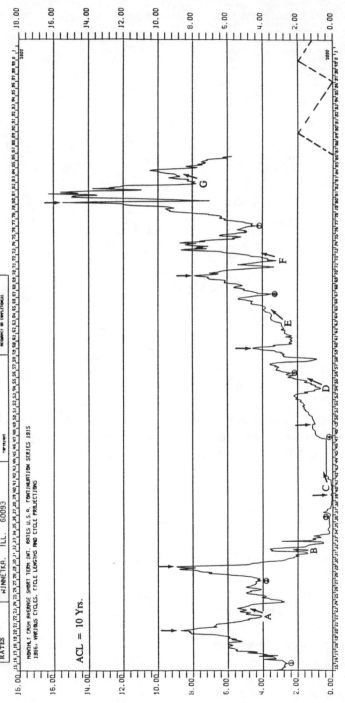

240

Figure 9-23. *Long-term cycle in T bill futures, 1976–86.*

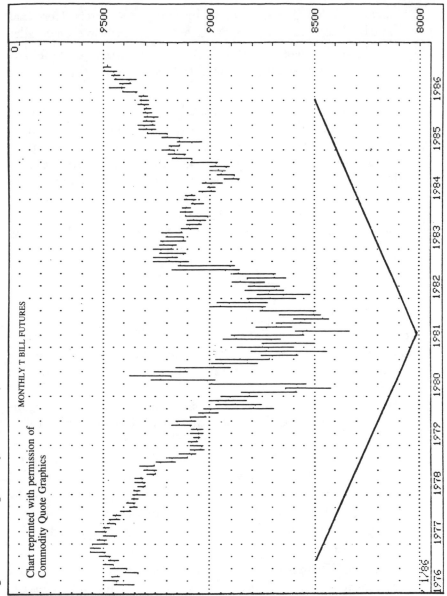

Chart reprinted with permission of
Commodity Quote Graphics

MONTHLY T BILL FUTURES

2. *Early-decade-high pattern* is shown by arrows and letters. Note that there has been a tendency for prices to bottom early in each decade.

3. *Late-decade-high pattern* is shown by arrows at the tops. Note that there has been a tendency for highs to be seen toward the latter part of each decade.

4. *Projections:* The cycles are projected to bottom the current time frame, topping in around 1990. This should be followed by a decline into the 1996–98 time frame. *It is possible that a low will be seen early in the 1990's* in line with the pattern described in #2 above. I expect that by the time this low is reached, short-term rates will have tested the 4 percent level. On the top side there is likely to be resistance in the 8 percent area, then in the 11 percent area. Record highs should ideally not be surpassed until after the 1997 time frame or later *unless* a hyperinflationary scenario develops. (See also Figure 9.23.)

Cycles in Petroleum Prices

Though the price of petroleum was stable for many years, making cyclic analysis somewhat difficult. Since the 1950s, however, petroleum prices have become more volatile and there are now a number of important and fairly regular patterns in prices. See Figure 9.24.

1. *Approximate 11.45-year cycle* lows and highs are shown in Figure 9.24. As you can see, the next low is likely to occur in 1993, followed by an approximate 1997 top. Remember that this cycle has shown only 4 repetitions since 1938 and should be regarded with a considerable degree of skepticism.

2. *Approximate 11.45-year cycle, alternate count:* The long-term cycle in fuel oil could be counted in a different fashion from the indicated zigzag. Lows numbered 1 through 5, top 7, and projected low 6 indicate the alternate count.

3. *Projections:* There is also an approximate 4-year cycle and an important 13-month cycle in petroleum prices. The alternate long-term cycle count projected a low around 1986–87, followed by a significant rally into the early 1990s, perhaps to as high as the $.72 area. After projected low 6, the market should be poised for a move to record highs, well in excess of $1.05.

Figure 9-24. *Long-term cycles in fuel oil, 1938–86.*

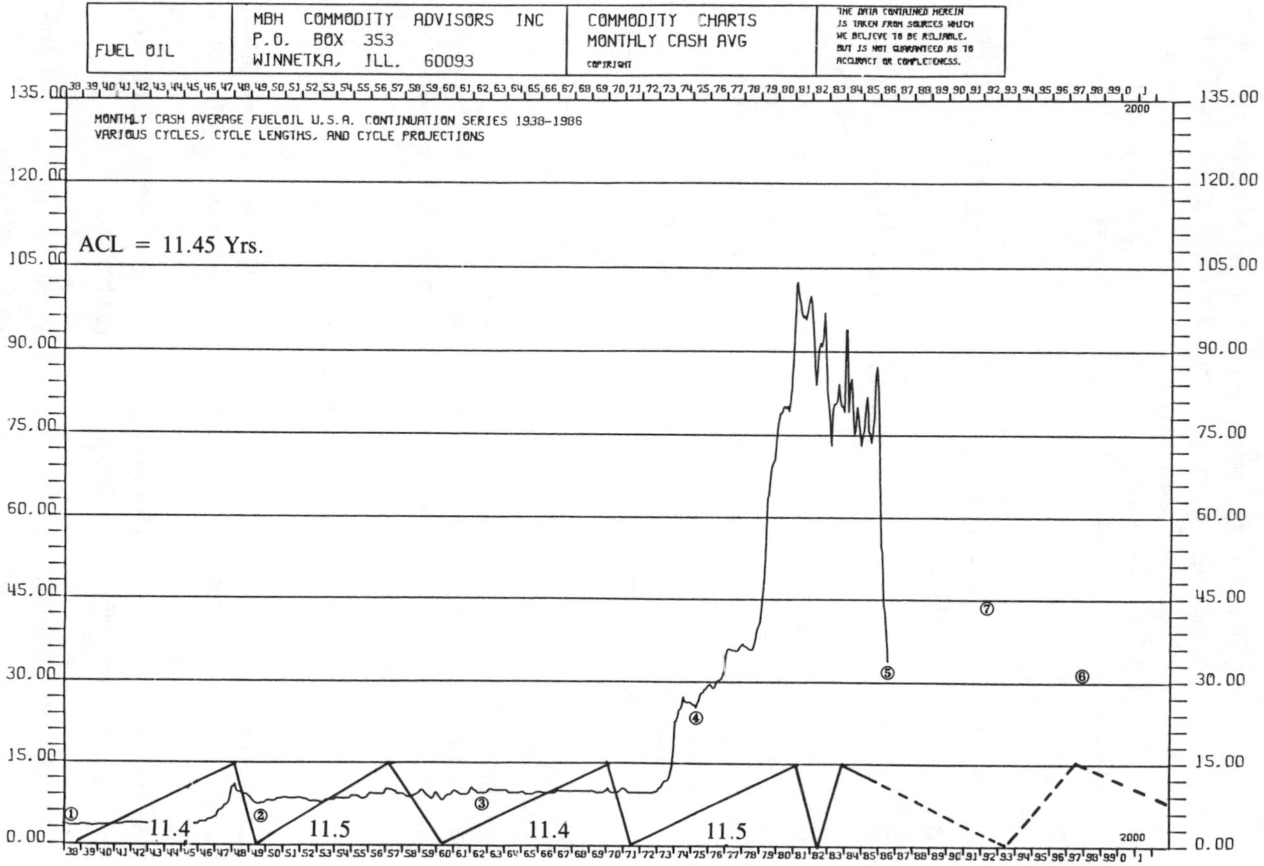
FUEL OIL
MBH COMMODITY ADVISORS INC
P.O. BOX 353
WINNETKA, ILL. 60093
COMMODITY CHARTS
MONTHLY CASH AVG
COPYRIGHT
THE DATA CONTAINED HEREIN IS TAKEN FROM SOURCES WHICH WE BELIEVE TO BE RELIABLE, BUT IS NOT GUARANTEED AS TO ACCURACY OR COMPLETENESS.
MONTHLY CASH AVERAGE FUELOIL U.S.A. CONTINUATION SERIES 1938–1986
VARIOUS CYCLES, CYCLE LENGTHS, AND CYCLE PROJECTIONS
ACL = 11.45 Yrs.
11.4
11.5
11.4
11.5
135.00
120.00
105.00
90.00
75.00
60.00
45.00
30.00
15.00
0.00
2000

In closing, it should be remembered that the Mideast will continue to see destabilizing pressures and military confrontations. These factors could easily distort the cycles or could very well confirm low 5 as the bottom of the long-term cycle. The most important consideration in petroleum is that not only could the price cycles be affected but the price magnitude could be affected as well by military action.

CONCLUSIONS ABOUT THE INDIVIDUAL MARKETS AND THE LONG WAVE

The long-wave cycles are a reflection of many different economic trends and indicators. No single market or indicator best tracks the economic trend. Interest rates and stock prices, however, tend to be two of the most closely correlated indicators. The long wave is more of an idea than anything else. There is no one sector of the economy to which we can point and say, "This is the long wave." The long wave will always be determined by how individual markets and economic indicators behave within their own cyclic patterns. Most markets should move in the direction of the long-wave cycles, but there will be exceptions. It is for this reason that I recommended a balanced portfolio consisting of various investment vehicles and various types of cash market instruments. The purpose of this chapter, which was to provide you with an overview of the long-term cycles of less than fifty to sixty years' duration in various markets, has been achieved. In examining the cycles, you will note the following:

1. Most agricultural commodity markets most likely bottomed in the late 1980s.
2. Interest rates are still likely to go lower over the long term, following a relatively brief return to higher levels. This suggests a continued disinflationary trend.
3. Petroleum prices, which also reflect economic growth, could decline persistently, suggesting a declining economic trend.

All of the above can be significantly affected by national and international developments. However, the cycles appear to be on course with long-wave lows due in the mid-1990s. This forecast will, of course, be subject to adjustment in the years ahead.

Chapter 10

Psychology of the Long Wave

All fruitful ideas have been conceived in the minds of nonconformists. . . . The truth of today was the heresy of yesterday. . . .

—*Immanuel Velikovsky*

Few economists willingly acknowledge the fact that human psychology has played an important role in the history of economic trends. While it may very well be true that human emotion has not been the single most important factor underlying economic trend changes, it is indeed true that some significant historical events relating to economics, finance, stock prices, and monetary relationships have been, in part, prompted by mass human psychology. While one might correctly argue, for example, that the "Crash of '29" or the "Crash of '87" were not caused by human emotion, there is no doubt whatsoever that they were exacerbated by the panics that came on the heels of the initial declines.

When Charles MacKay wrote his now-classic *Extraordinary Popular Delusions and the Madness of Crowds,* in 1889, he chronicled several of the most glaring instances of mass human economic folly. Those who have not read this most important historical record should, by all means, make it part of their education. The examples cited by MacKay represent only a minor sampling of the countless incidents that have characterized human economic folly and mass psychology during times of prosperity and poverty alike.

Why study human psychology in relation to economics? To what end can such studies lead? How can we learn from the past in order to make the future less of an obstacle course? Perhaps this chapter will answer some of these questions. I suspect, however, that it may very well raise more questions than it resolves. Learning without concomitant stimulation of curiosity is not complete learning. The questions I may leave unanswered are those that I cannot answer or that have not crossed my mind. As I have stated repeatedly throughout the course of this book, I do not have all of the answers. My work is somewhat theoretical and speculative, though based on a firm footing. I am unable to ask all of the pertinent questions because, most likely, of my own relative ignorance. But armed with an extensive background in human psychology, personality testing, and clinical application, I can bring to light numerous important issues that have either surfaced as a result of my economic research or that are still *sub rosa* but begging to be brought to light.

A PERSPECTIVE ON INVESTOR PSYCHOLOGY

This is not the first book about long-wave economic cycles, nor will it be the last. Virtually every economist, investment advisor, or politician nowadays has his or her thoughts and opinions about what is and what's to become. As conditions become more volatile, and as reactions within the economic underpinnings become more pronounced, opinions and attitudes become more polarized. While some experts would have you believe that the long-wave cycles have their origin in the teachings and theories of various economists or philosophers, others claim that economic trends are random, unpredictable, and, therefore, incapable of being effectively analyzed. Still others would have you believe that economic salvation is embodied in the virtues of the gold standard, or in the rational policies of a balanced budget. While books, theories, opinions, and advice on this especially relevant subject are plentiful, little concrete information deals with the emotional aspects of investor behavior. Nor is there a confluence of opinion regarding the optimum methodology by which an investor or businessperson may implement specific investment strategies without the potentially destructive consequences of emotion, lack of discipline, fear, or greed.

Advisors and economists have, for many years, assumed that investors are reasonable, relatively normal, well-adjusted, non-neurotic, and self-disciplined individuals. Could it be that the opposite is true? Could so many investors and speculators be losers because they lack the necessary emotional prerequisites to investment success? Certainly the experience of futures traders provides us with strong evidence that 80 to 90 percent of speculators in these markets tend to lose their starting capital. Could it be that the rate of losers is just as high in the stock market? Perhaps not. Perhaps only 50 percent of stock investors are net losers. Certainly, the percentage of losers is a direct function of the types of investments that are selected. It appears to me that several variables may either exacerbate losses or facilitate profits. They are as follows:

1. The nonprofessional investor is likely to fare well in longer-term investments as opposed to shorter-term speculation.

2. The investor who maintains a balanced portfolio is likely to fare better than the investor who puts all of his or her eggs "in one basket." Diversification spreads risk and makes profitable results more likely.

3. Mutual fund investments appear to be the ideal area for a majority of investors inasmuch as they spread risk, diversify, and practice the discipline necessary for successful investing.

4. Investors with larger starting capital tend to do better in the long run inasmuch as they can diversify their holdings more quickly than can the individual beginning with limited capital.

5. The investor who is aware of his or her personal limitations, assets, and liabilities tends to fare better than the investor who plunges headlong into the markets without regard for the potential emotional consequences of his or her behavior.

6. Investors who follow a given plan or strategy tend to be successful more frequently than do those who place their money haphazardly or without regard to a given plan, system, or strategy.

7. Those who are capable of selling or selling short as well as buying tend to fare better than those who can trade only from the long side or those who are always bullish.

The fact that there are still losers in the stock and futures markets tends to belittle the value of our purportedly great strides in business science and investment analysis. Computer technology, modern economic theory (whatever that is), and a veritable watershed of investment messiahs have not been able to make winners out of all of us. When I stop to consider the events that are foreshadowed by what transpired during the late 1970s and what has transpired during the early 1980s, I shudder to think of the consequences that are apt to become stark realities in the months and years ahead. Yet I know from personal experience that strategy, theory, advice, analysis, trading systems, and investment schemes are only minor aspects of the success equation (although many would disagree with me).

J. Peter Steidlmayer, whose success in futures trading is known to few outside the field, has noted repeatedly that the formula for market profits is dependent upon the discipline and emotional maturity of the trader. Although Steidlmayer was not the first to assert the importance of human emotion in the achievement of success, he did so in a concise and easily expressed fashion when he noted the following:

> Some broad observations of the characteristics of the human race at this point in our evolution include:
>
> Man's powers of observations are no longer crucial to his survival and thus have declined through underuse.
>
> Man's ability to think for himself analytically has also declined through lack of use. The structure of civilized society combined with technology's impact on humankind's environment does not encourage either observation or independent thinking.
>
> Man as a class would prefer to be led and told what to do rather than think for himself. The success of modern advertising attests to this.
>
> Man as a class is inconsistent in his behavior: he will respond differently to the same situation and set of data depending on mood, stimuli, etc. Furthermore, his capacity and perceptions will change throughout different stages in his life.
>
> Man as a class does not enjoy the feeling of being either physically or ideologically alone, especially in stressful conditions.
>
> Man as a class does not want to be left out or left behind.
>
> Man as a whole tends not to have an accurate sense of his own self-worth. He tends to overinflate or underinflate his self-worth, thus impacting his perceptions of reality.
>
> Man as a class has a natural tendency towards lack of self-confidence.
>
> Man as a class is jealous of those who have more than he.
>
> Man as a class often thinks he is improving when he is not.
> [Steidlmayer and Koy, *Markets and Market Logic*, Porcupine Press, Chicago, IL, 1984, p. 139]

Avoiding Emotional Decisions

It is important to remember that in all areas of practical life, reason and logic are regularly overwhelmed by the natural tendencies of hesitation, euphoric overconfidence, anxiety, ambition, prejudice, melancholy, laziness, jealousy, egotism, and the need for self-gratification. These tendencies occur in individuals involved in the marketplace as they do elsewhere. Indeed, they may be compounded in the futures markets and the investment field in general, since when the individual uses leverage, success can spell quick wealth while failure can mean correspondingly quick financial ruin.

The Trader's Biggest Problem

Conventional wisdom emphasizes that the emotions of fear and greed motivate every market and that these two emotions are the trader's greatest enemy. These statements do not display a deep understanding of human psychology. The key emotional factor in market behavior is also the biggest roadblock to effective decision making. It is the hardest emotion for every trader to control: the propensity toward hesitation, toward being late. [Steidlmayer and Koy, *Markets and Market Logic*, Porcupine Press, Chicago, IL, 1984, pp. 141–142]

While you may learn more about virtually all fields of investing from the many books you can obtain on this subject, you will find a painfully obvious void in the area of investment psychology, particularly as it relates to the long-wave economic cycles. Although one chapter in my book cannot erase the misconception that better investment methods will automatically lead to success, I think that my analyses of human psychology and the long wave can provide valuable assistance to those who accept the notion that success does not immediately follow market understanding unless it is accompanied by self-understanding and discipline.

A QUESTION OF ORIGIN

While there are those who contend that human behavior does not determine economic trends, there are also those who argue in favor of economic determinism. Determinists claim that economic conditions result in stresses and strains that have a marked effect on human behavior and emotion. Poverty, for example, may breed frustration and aggression. Wealth may breed complacency and the need for more stimulation; this may, in turn, promote alcoholism and/or drug dependency as well as anxiety and psychophysiological responses such as ulcers and migraines. On the other hand, psychologists may argue that emotion influences economic behavior. Their line of reasoning might be stated as follows: "Human needs such as anxiety and stress produce the need for such things as liquor consumption, movie watching, and overindulgence in food. Such activities are compensatory or defensive mechanisms that are inspired by psychological needs. Insecurity, for example, may stimulate certain types of economic behavior such as the accumulation of material possessions as a form of compensation. Irrational fear may cause investors to liquidate stocks, futures contracts, real estate, collectibles, and the like, thereby causing market crashes. Insatiable greed may stimulate excessive buying of stocks and other investments regardless of price and regardless of potential return."

Each of these positions, however, is deterministic. They are unacceptable lines of reasoning inasmuch as they take an extremely narrow view of humankind. They fail to consider the fact that human behavior is composed of inputs from all of the senses and from virtually every aspect of the environment. Just as emotion and psychology alone cannot be seen as the stimulus of economic activity, we cannot view economic activity as the sole cause of human behavior and emotion.

Some theorists have claimed that the fundamental basis of long-wave economic activity is war. Their works have been cited earlier. Yet such a narrow interpretation is also faulty. Life, economics, history, and systems are neither simple nor readily relegated to constant causes. Whereas one long-wave cycle may have been precipitated by a given event or events of specific origin, another long-wave cycle may have been precipitated by entirely different causes.

Some theorists have claimed that the origin of long-wave cycles rests in technological breakthroughs. Some of these works have also been cited. I find these assertions equally fallacious. In reality, long-wave economic behavior arises from a multiplicity of inputs—some psychological, some economic, some technological, some sociological, some religious, and so forth.

In spite of the clear fact that long-wave economic cycles are the result of multiple inputs and causative forces, the fact remains that some of these inputs are more important than others, that some aspects are more readily visible than others, and that some incidents are more timely than others. Hence, the question regarding long-wave cycle origins is an academic one, one that may in the long run and in the short run generate more heat than light. Human psychology, emotion, and behavior patterns are both a partial cause of and a partial effect of economic trends. Psychology and emotion are important factors of the long wave that have received little if any attention from previous studies, regardless of what I consider to be their immense value.

A FEW THINGS TO CONSIDER

In evaluating long-wave cycles and the psychological factors that are at one and the same time inputs and outputs of long-wave structure, I have reached the following very general conclusions:

1. Long-wave economic cycles exert a variety of stresses and strains on human behavior and emotion.
2. The specific nature of these emotional and psychological reactions is a function of the long-wave cyclic phase or stage. Each stage appears to have its specific influences on human behavior.
3. In addition to economic cycles influencing human behavior, human behavior in turn influences economic trends to a certain extent, resulting in a "backlash" effect.
4. Mass psychology in the form of panic is not uncommon during the declining phases of the long wave.
5. Fear, greed, hoarding, and other human responses are not uncommon during the various phases of the long wave.

In addition to the above, there are various socio-psychological interactions and counterreactions to economic conditions, some of which tend to appear with fairly predictable regularity during the long waves and others that have been unique. The discussion that follows will highlight some of the above-mentioned psychological phenomena with an emphasis upon how the knowledge of human psychology in relation to economic trends may be beneficial in your long-range investment strategy, regardless of which phase of the long wave is currently in process.

The Role of Fear

Although you may feel that you know everything you need to know about fear, there are things that you may, perhaps, have over-looked unless you have training in the field of psychology. When we think of fear, we rarely attach it to such things as bankruptcy, losing money, financial consequence, or a "run" on the banks. Fear is com-monly a reaction reserved for more tangible or direct threats, such as the threat of crime, impending failure, or perhaps an auto or airplane accident. But fear of the unknown is more pervasive than any of us would care to admit. When we logically examine our fears, we find that only a few of them are based on realistic interpretations of reality. Fear of flying, for example, is not logical, given crash statistics. Fear of failure is learned in response to the fashion in which failure has been approached during childhood and adolescent days. Fear of a given situation, such as combat, is shaped by either a true-life event or the imagination of dire consequences. Regardless of the type of fear an individual is experiencing, some form of treatment can lessen its impact on behavior. It is important to realize that fear, for the most part, is a result of ignorance. Ignorance allows the imagination to magnify and distort expectations.

It is frequently the anticipation of negative consequence that leads to fear. Fear results in behaviors that may not necessarily be appropriate to the given situation. In other words, there are rational fears and irrational fears. The soldier in the battlefield, for example, may flee or fight in response to fear. In such a case, fear and its resultant mobilization of the defensive processes may lead to beneficial, life-saving results. However, less obvious situations, wherein the threat is not clear and, therefore, subject to distortion, the resulting defensive behavior may not be appropriate to the situation inasmuch as the "enemy" or threat is not realistically or clearly visible.

As an example, consider the plight of the investor who responds to the fear of financial loss. Assume that an investment in a given stock has been made. Assume also that shortly thereafter, stock prices begin to decline on a broad front. The investor just happens to hear, either from his or her broker or from another source, that stocks are declining sharply. In fact, the news is very negative indeed. The decline now taking place is one of the worst on record. What to do? Clearly, there are several possible courses of action. The logical response to this perceived threat would be to do nothing. Why? Because logic would have previously dictated the type of action that would have anticipated such an event and that would have prompted the investor to liquidate stock investments well in advance of the market decline, to have substantially lightened up his or her holdings, or to have placed protective stop loss orders with a broker. Regardless of what action may have been taken in advance of the market decline, the fact is that preparatory action, anticipation of such events, and planning are logical ways of avoiding potentially irrational behavior(s) that may be the result of fear.

The illogical response to the hypothetical situation I've presented would be panic liquidation. When panic grips many investors at the same time, market behavior is exaggerated and magnified many times over. The consequence is a decline much worse than might have been the case had reasonable preparation and planning been done in anticipation of a possible severe market decline. "But how is it possible to plan for such an event?" you may ask. Here are some things to consider:

1. Major stock market declines have, for the most part, taken place during the declining phase of either the approximate nine-year or four-year cycles.

2. Stock market "crashes" have most often occurred during or in close contiguity to long-wave economic cycle peaks.

3. Most stock market crashes and severe declines have been the result of overspeculation and blatant investor disregard for negative economic and fundamental considerations.

4. Stock investments should constitute only a specific percentage of your assets. Even if you are more heavily invested in stocks than in other areas, you will know when to lighten your portfolio if you heed the clear warnings of rampant speculation, stock market cycles, and economic cycles.

5. Most, perhaps all, severe market declines have given warnings for a considerable period of time prior to their occurrence.

6. Few markets decline severely without a respite or upside correction. Therefore, liquidation of stocks in response to fear is likely to be an incorrect response inasmuch as fear will likely not set in at its greatest level until the worst is about over.

I am certain that you can imagine many other situations in which fear may lead to illogical behavior. Yet, the lessons to be learned are as follows:

1. Fear is an emotional response to either real or imagined threats. If fear is the motivating factor in response to an imagined situation or to imagined consequences of a situation, then the resultant behavior will, a great majority of the time, be inappropriate, leading to undesirable results.

2. Preparation, planning, logical anticipation, and discipline are actions and behaviors that will limit or entirely eliminate the illogical responses that tend to characterize the fear response.

3. The lessons of economic history, though by no means totally perfect or 100 percent applicable to every future situation, are important guidelines to future behavior and planning. The lessons to which I refer must be learned. In order to learn them, each individual who is intent upon planning ahead must study economic history, cycles, and market history.

4. Economic cycles and market patterns are fairly obvious to students of market behavior. Although they are neither perfect nor 100 percent reliable, they are sufficiently predictable to permit planning and development of a general investment "road map" or timetable.

Clearly, then, the way to avoid the potentially destructive consequences of fear is to be prepared, to combat fear with logic, and to replace emotional response with intelligent and well-planned programs.

Panic

Panic is a form of fear. Economic panics and panics in response to perceived economic threats are no less destructive than are panics in response to other potential or actual threats. When someone yells "Fire" in a crowded theater and virtually all of the terrorized patrons rush to the same exit, the result will most certainly be death and destruction. Economic panics are no different. There have been literally hundreds of panics in the history of world economics. Without too much thought we can remember such panics as the 1929 and 1987 stock market crashes, as well as the banking panics during the 1930s' economic decline. History has clearly shown that panics are the worst form of fear. Although varying levels of fear may be experienced at any one time, only the most intense and pervasive fear leads to panic. History also teaches that panics have more often than not been witnessed during the declining phases of long-wave economic cycles and during the declining portion of shorter market cycles. The most ideal or logical way to cope with panic is to act in a fashion that will either minimize its impact on your finances or that will entirely avoid its negative consequences. The best way to do this is to apply the same rules as I've stated previously for anticipating and minimizing the effects of fear on your finances.

Remember also that financial panics (whether real or in response to perceived threats) are not necessarily related only to bear markets or to the declining phase of long-term cycles. Although clearly less obvious, buying panics can also develop during the rising portion of economic cycles and trends. The fear that a given investment, buying opportunity, home, stock, or food will be in short supply can drive prices to dizzying heights. Buying panics are no strangers to economic history. Whether they take the form of such events as the Tulip Mania, the South Sea Bubble, Sutter's Folly, or the rampant speculation that has accompanied most stock market peaks, buying panics develop more slowly and are more obvious to the informed investor earlier in their inception than are selling panics. Regardless of whether panics are subtle, obvious, inspired by news, or inspired by rumor, their negative consequences are, for the most part, avoidable by logic, planning, and preparation.

The Role of Denial

Psychiatry and psychology have long known the role of defense mechanisms in human behavior. When the impact or perceived impact of given events or experiences is too difficult to cope with, the mind may opt to deny or minimize the reality. An investor may place funds with a money manager who fails to perform well. Perhaps 20 percent of the initial equity may be lost, yet the investor ignores the poor performance, fails to analyze the losses, and continues to believe that success will come. In spite of continued losses, in spite of obviously poor judgment on the part of his or her money manager, the investor continues to believe that success is imminent. After several years of losses, the investor clings to visions of success, denying the reality of the situation. Why has reality been denied? What has caused the investor to ignore the obvious?

Consider the following situation: You read a book or an article on gold-mining stocks that prompts you to buy shares in a mining concern. Your investment begins to deteriorate. It appears that the company whose shares you have decided to buy is losing money because of a weak cash market for gold. Your technical indicators have turned bearish. Your investment has reached the point at which you decide in advance to liquidate and take your loss. Yet you fail to follow through. You sway from your plan. You deny the reality of the situation, deciding instead to "give it one more day." "One day" becomes several weeks. You are still holding your "investment." Once again you have altered your plan, lost your discipline, denied the reality of your situation. Why?

Denial is perhaps the single most pervasive factor in the investment world. Almost every one of us has, at one time or another, fallen victim to denial in speculation and/or investing. What are the mechanisms and motivations that govern the use of this defense mechanism? Here are some ideas for you to consider:

1. Unwillingness to accept a loss causes us to deny the existence or importance of that loss. Denying the loss or its importance, we open the door to further losses and additional breaches of discipline.

2. Accepting a loss is ego deflating. By denying the importance of a loss or by negating its existence, we "save" our ego from having to face the reality of the situation. We feel, unconsciously, that everything is well when, in fact, our rational mind knows that all is *not* well.

3. By denying a situation indefinitely, we need not deal with it. This is an approach used all too often in everyday life. Procrastination is a way of denying the importance of events and required actions.

4. Denial is not reality based. It is a manifestation of the childhood mind. In other words, denial constitutes a regression to techniques we may have used when we were very young. The fact that denial may have worked for us in our childhood makes us believe—mistakenly—that it will work for us as adults. But this is not, as you know, a realistic approach to life.

5. Denial leads to more denial, and more denial leads to more mistakes. Denial can only, therefore, lead us to losses or to inappropriate decisions as far as investments are concerned.

6. Denial has no place in the investor's repertoire. While denial can be valuable in day-to-day emotional life, for limited periods of time or for brief periods during extreme crisis, it is counterproductive when used in place of decisive action.

If and when the economic events I am expecting come to pass, investors, politicians, and economists will all be especially inclined to employ denial as a method of dealing with the painful realities. When stock prices crash again, investors will watch the growing cataclysm, frozen with inaction by denial. They will tell themselves that the worst is almost over. They will still own stocks by virtue of their many weeks of denial prior to the next crash. By denying the warnings, *which will be clear and unmistakable prior to the next stock market crash*, investors will find themselves in a worse situation than if they had accepted the reality when it was there for the seeing. But denial will be rampant in virtually every sector of the economy, whether in the banking industry, in the business world, or in monetary policy. In order to avoid the serious consequences of denial, I suggest the following:

1. *Come to terms with your own psychology.* Think about times in your life, past and present, in which you have used denial as a defense. Has it served you well? Did denying reality make things better for you, or did it make things worse?

2. *Are you a procrastinator?* Procrastination is a form of denial. Do you let your investments take care of themselves? Do you procrastinate in spite of knowledge that suggests specific action? If so, analyze your behavior and take steps to eliminate this aspect.

3. *Denial can be avoided by planning and organization.* Although there is no guarantee that organization, direction, planning, and systematic preparation will lead to avoidance of denial, they will facilitate action, minimizing the possibility that denial may interfere with your behavior.

4. *Get a partner.* Two heads may be better than one when it comes to denial. A partner may help you admit to things that you won't want

to see. Your partner may prove a strict taskmaster, and this may be what's required when the going gets tough.

5. *Plan well ahead of time* in order to reduce the possibility of denial. If you act before pain has set in, then you will avoid the need to employ denial as a mechanism of coping with the pain of loss or with the ego-deflating consequences of being incorrect about the markets.

6. *Work long and hard on accepting the reality of your financial situation.* Avoid delusions, fantasies, and/or unrealistic expectations. Know where you stand and evaluate your situation regularly. In so doing you will limit the possibility of denial creeping into your behavior, subtle and unnoticed at first, if you are unaware of or unwilling to accept the limits of your financial conditions.

In short, logic, preparation, acceptance of reality, realistic expectations about the future, and the avoidance of unrealistic expectations will help you deter the potentially serious consequences of denial. In the dark days ahead, those who continue to deny the seriousness of reality will be those who are first felled by its arrows. Denial has been the *modus operandi* of governments throughout the world for many years. Regardless of ideology—communist, socialist, or capitalist—governments throughout the world have denied the existence of basic economic principles, long-wave economic cycles, the needs of their people, and the importance of sane economic policies. The bitter fruits of their denial are only now beginning to appear. The terrible harvest is soon upon us. Denial of its ultimate reality can serve only to make the ultimate situation worse than it might have been if dealt with appropriately and within a reasonable amount of time.

Intellectualization

A more subtle form of defensive behavior on the part of the investor is "intellectualization." By using what is believed to be logic, reason, and rational evidence, the investor attempts to justify a given situation intellectually. Although the logic may be correct, and although theoretically a given position should lead to given conditions, reality may not coincide with theory. The individual or individuals who practice this form of defensive behavior are avoiding reality by taking refuge in what should be, not in what is. There is no doubt that markets are frequently predictable and logical; however, anyone who has had even the slightest exposure to the markets knows that there are times when logic and intellectual considerations do not play an important role. When panic, greed, and emotion dominate a market, the logic of earnings, price/earnings (PE) ratios, fundamentals, and chart patterns go out the window. Replaced by fear, poor judgment, and irrational behavior, intellectual considerations have little effect. Yet, there are those who sit and watch the reality of the marketplace, taking solace in the intellectual facts and figures. Their thoughts might be as follows: "The charts and statistics indicate that this price decline was not supposed to happen. I'll just hold on until things go the way they should." This line of reasoning might be acceptable from a scientific point of view, but the fact is that the economy, the markets, and price trends are not totally scientific. Although in the long run the laws of supply and demand may reign supreme, prices may deviate from the ideal for extended periods of time. To cling tenaciously to ideal expectations, to explain away reality by invoking intellectual excuses, is just another form of denying what is real.

Scientific reasoning, logic, and "intelligent" behavior are held in high esteem by many people. Although these qualities may serve us well in the business world, they may actually prove counterproductive when quick response and quick decision making are required. The clear-thinking, logical business-school graduate may find his or her logic useless during panics. In fact, to take intellectual refuge in "what should be" may result in financial ruin. Although it is correct to practice emotional control and self-discipline, it can be financially disastrous to use intellectual arguments to support an obviously incorrect and illogical position in one's investments.

PSYCHOLOGICAL PREPARATION

Each individual has different needs, wants, and emotional makeup. We understand, interpret, and respond to similar situations in different ways. Inasmuch as we have distinctly different response and coping styles, no single solution or set of rules will be sufficient in preparing all of us emotionally for the economic crises I've described in this book. There are, however, a number of general considerations and guidelines that can help point you in the right direction. Here, for your analysis and consideration, are a number of suggestions derived from my understandings of both human psychology and long-wave cycle history.

1. *Be prepared well ahead of time* if you want to avoid the errors that tend to occur when you respond with emotion. If you accept my conclusion that the "Crash of '87" was merely the harbinger of a more severe and extended crash that is yet to come, then you must own as little stock as possible when the decline begins again. In order to do this you will need to be deliberate about what stocks you own, how long you own them, how and when you liquidate, and if and when you want to be on the short side of stocks. You may be better off being a bit too early than a bit too late.

2. *Keep in close touch with your financial situation.* Know where you stand financially. If you know your situation, you'll avoid acting without knowledge. When emotion and panic grip the financial markets you'll be less likely to respond emotionally if you know your financial condition.

3. *Set your goals and objectives.* You won't need a precise road map, but it will be a very good idea to have your goals clearly in mind. Naturally these goals will differ based upon a multiplicity of variables, such as your age, profession, tax bracket, and so on.

4. *Avoid being influenced by those who offer simplistic solutions.* Every major turn in market events will usher in a cadre of financial "prophets" who claim to have the ultimate answer to the problems confronting the economy. Some may offer valid recommendations and alternatives, but it is more likely that their solutions will not be effective. They may suggest, for example, that placing all of your funds in gold bullion will protect you from falling victim to economic collapse. Some economic "messiahs" may advise putting your money into gold-backed bonds, or in Treasury bills, or in rare coins. In all probability, putting all or most of your assets into one investment will not serve you well. There is no ultimate answer to the problem of protecting your assets. Although they will be attractive and logical, simple solutions are not likely to work.

5. *Believe in yourself!* When others claim to know what's right for you, don't follow their lead until you've had an opportunity to fully evaluate their claims, analyses, and forecasts. Develop your own

specific strategies and act on the basis of your own observations. Trust in your opinions, but don't trust blindly. If you take the time to learn about the history of the long-wave cycles, your own work will serve you best. Keep an open mind, evaluate all reasonable inputs, and then make up your own mind.

Chapter 11

An Investment Strategy for the Long Wave

There are only two kinds of freedom in the world: the freedom of the rich and powerful, and the freedom of the artist and the monk who renounces possessions.

—Anaïs Nin
The Diaries of Anaïs Nin, Vol. IV

Given the complexity of the long wave, its numerous stages, imprecise timing, and the frequent criticisms that have been leveled against its essential concepts, you can understand why the "experts" disagree about which investment vehicles and/or strategies will best protect you during the coming hard times. Although some advisors and financial planners would have you believe that all will turn out for the best no matter what happens, this is simply a dream. Still other well-intentioned professionals strongly contend that our government will protect and shield us from the tumultuous times that await us in the not-too-distant future. I would ask of these individuals, "What have governments done to protect their people from the violent economic up and down swings of the last fifteen years?" Perhaps governments would protect us if they could. Perhaps governments would enact legislation designed to help smooth the economic rough spots if they had such powers. But the plain truth is that governments do *not* have sufficient ability to always take the appropriate actions at the right time, or in the right amount, to make the bad times less difficult and the good times less extreme. Although the ideas of Keynesian economics are attractive (perhaps Utopian), they have not helped curb the destructive effects of extreme economic excesses.

Governments throughout the world, in so-called "free-world" nations and in communist nations as well, are large and lumbering bureaucracies. Their machinery moves slowly and with great effort. The legislative process takes many months. By the time responsive action has been taken to cope with a given economic crisis, the crisis has often resolved itself, and the action is too late. Governments don't anticipate, they respond. Because the time lag between economic stimulus and government response is so long, actions taken to resolve a crisis tend to foster a new crisis. It is as if governments are taking aim at targets that are no longer in their original positions by the time the gun is fired.

Furthermore, governments the world over are motivated by dogma, the tunnel vision of self-interest, corruption, and political favoritism. There is a general absence of economic direction and policy. Goals are loosely stated, and even when they are stated in specifics, they are rarely met.

International conflict further hampers government ability to act effectively to avoid or otherwise deal with economic crises. Combined with the natural cycle of industrial plant growth and decay, as proposed by Jay W. Forrester, economic conditions in the 1980s have reached emergency proportions. Consider the following list of economic concerns that confront the United States and most free-world nations in the late 1980s:

1. The U.S. dollar is at or near record lows. This situation puts considerable pressure on foreign economies because it makes U.S. goods more competitive. Competition in turn accelerates foreign inflation as well as labor–industry discord.

2. U.S. firms are more vulnerable to takeovers by foreign firms that can get more for less. A wave of foreign buyouts has swept through the United States. This has prompted an increase of foreign influence in U.S. economic affairs.

3. Foreign confidence in the United States decreases, making us more vulnerable to military and terrorist aggression. This, in turn, places more strain on the U.S. economy as government acts to increase military spending in response to perceived and/or real threats.

4. Petroleum shipping during the 1980s has been disrupted almost daily by major military confrontations in the Persian Gulf. This places more stress and strain on nations that are oil dependent (*e.g.*, Japan) while it continues to erode the international political situation.

5. Government corruption at the highest levels continues in many "free" nations of the world, but particularly in the Americas. This undermines the confidence of other nations and the citizenry. It also opens the door for disruptive military actions, confrontations, revolutions, coups, and potentially serious economic embargoes (*e.g.*, Nicaragua and other Latin American nations).

6. The U.S. banking system is in serious trouble. Not only are many banks loaned to the hilt, but there are far too many foreign loans that will never be repaid. This reduces confidence in banks, which is already at a relatively low level. Low trust and low confidence are conditions that foster a possible "run" on the banks.

7. Foreign competition from the Far East continues to strain the U.S. economy. Although there is nothing intrinsically wrong with foreign competition, it creates both visible and invisible barriers. This increases the likelihood of political and possibly military conflict in the future. It also stimulates "trade wars" and political sanctions.

8. Trade protectionism is on the increase both in the United States and abroad. Protectionism is a historically predictable response to increased foreign competition. Retaliation by economic sanction is the typical reaction of nations that are targeted by protectionist legislation. In the long run a "trade war of attrition" is likely to develop. Trade wars yield no victors; rather, they injure all participants.

9. Many state, local, and federal governments are grossly inefficient, lugubrious anachronisms riddled with corruption, graft, and nepotism. Although the systems still operate, they are wasteful and overstaffed. When the coming disinflation grips nations that have not rectified this situation, many employees and bureaucrats will be forced out of office regardless of political ideology or affiliation. This will add to economic stress and strain in the short run; however, it will be beneficial in the long run.

10. Although many commodity and raw-goods prices have declined since the late 1970s, these price reductions have not been passed on to the consumer. Rather, the notorious "middleman" has continued to mark prices up, placing continued imbalance in the economic system. Ultimately this situation may correct itself in one fell swoop as demand virtually disappears and retailers are forced to mark prices down well below cost in order to move merchandise. Although this has not happened as yet during the present long-wave decline, historical precedent suggests that the "day of reckoning" is coming.

11. Instability in world financial and stock markets has become commonplace with exceptionally large day-to-day volatility. Instability is a symptom of underlying economic disease. Many analysts view the extreme fluctuations as a cause rather than as an effect. They are wrong. Volatility and instability reflect underlying and chronic economic disease.

12. Political instability is the rule rather than the exception throughout the world. In fact, only a few nations' governments are sufficiently stable to run day-to-day operations with reasonable efficiency and success. Normal and efficient economic interactions, both domestically and internationally, are therefore hampered.

13. Social instability is also becoming more evident as labor–management conflict tends to become more frequent and more lengthy. This is typical during long-wave declining phases. The worst is yet to come as labor and management are destined to compete for ever-shrinking profits.

14. The threat of war, whether by design or accident, increases every day. Hence, government policies are frequently directed at military strategies rather than at domestic issues.

   In addition to the items just outlined, numerous financial and economic concerns, as well as those more national and international in scope, confront state and local governments. The individual investor or businessperson must make plans that will minimize the impact of these potentially severe economic reactions. Provided such strategic plans are developed and deployed, it will be possible to both survive and profit during the highly unstable economic times that are likely to afflict all world economies in the months and years ahead.

Rhetoric and theory are not answers to the problems I have cited. Action, planning, and preparation are the only effective weapons in our arsenal. I am going to present a list of general suggestions you may wish to consider in developing your personal financial strategy. However, before we deal with specifics, the following prerequisites and caveats should be considered:

1. *No one answer or solution will be ideal for all investors or businesses.* Inasmuch as we all have different levels of assets and liabilities, both financial and personal, there cannot be a single best strategy or solution that will best serve us all during economic crises.

2. *It is up to each individual to perform a thorough and honest assessment* of his or her financial situation. Development of an effective strategy cannot be achieved in the absence of such an appraisal.

3. *Remember that your plan must consider personal resources and ability,* as well as financial factors. What may be a potentially effective strategy for a thirty-year-old father of two may be totally inappropriate for a fifty-five-year-old divorcée.

4. *Risk must be minimized.* Your plan must be a conservative one designed to minimize risk and maximize the safety of assets.

5. *Work, study, pain, and persistence* are the personal contributions that will be required. Without them your plan cannot be put into motion.

6. *Fear of the future* is something you will need to fight virtually every day. As conditions become worse, or panic grips the markets, you will be tested repeatedly. But you must not capitulate.

7. *There will be many temptations* to sway you from your course. You will be lured by the promise of vast short-term profits, and you will be tempted by the expectation that the worst is soon to end. You may even be influenced by the politically motivated rhetoric of self-interest groups and bureaucrats. But you must not be diverted from a conservative, realistic, and diversified program unless you can see clear and unmistakable evidence that change for the better is taking place.

8. *You may need to take some losses* in order to put your plan into action. Many of us have made investments that are either unprofitable or that result in negative cash flow. These may need to be disposed of at

a loss in order to prevent a continued financial drain as well as a larger possible loss in the future.

9. *Prepare to be scorned and ridiculed* for your opinions, views, actions, and expectations, particularly if they run contrary to current short-term trends. It is normal for others to lash out at those whose ideas threaten the stability of their own ignorant bliss.

THE PLAN

With these caveats in mind, let's examine some general guidelines that should be followed in your development of a strategic financial plan. As you read my suggestions, remember that they are:

1. Based on economic history and precedent.
2. Presented with the expectations that long-wave history will repeat or is repeating itself.
3. Not guaranteed to be complete or 100 percent effective, because no strategy can make such a claim or offer ultimate success.
4. Dependent to a great degree upon your abilities, discipline, skill, organization, finances, and patience. Many a good plan has been ruined by improper erratic and/or undisciplined implementation.
5. And that you alone must take the necessary actions once you understand, accept, and visualize the long-wave past, present, and future. You must not take action until you are convinced that my theories and expectations are likely to be proved true.

I suggest that you study and evaluate each and every one of the following suggestions in relation to your specific situation:

1. Diversify your assets into a variety of areas. To have a majority of your funds in one or two investments is dangerous and senseless. Be especially cautious of claims by various advisors or programs which promise that "total" safety and high return can be achieved by putting most of your cash into their program. It is unlikely that any single area or investment will perform well during each stage of the long wave.

2. Seek safety, not yield. When making investments, consider safety of funds as your primary goal. Yield and return must come second. Whereas the goal during inflationary times is yield as opposed to safety of funds, the objective during times of disinflationary or deflationary crisis is safety of funds. This means that you will need to be highly selective in your choices. Specifics are provided below.

3. Avoid banks or other financial institutions whose financial stability is in any way questionable. You can obtain the financial statement of any bank or financial institution with which you plan on doing business. Take the time to read the statement and avoid any institutions with large unsecured loans to domestic and/or foreign entities. Take particular care in your dealings with savings and loan banks. If you plan to place funds with a brokerage firm, then do your homework in determining its stability. I do not recommend keeping funds with any brokerage firm other than in the amount immediately necessary for your trading and/or investing.

4. Precious metals are likely to offer safety and yield at the right time. However, it may be difficult to determine precisely what the "right" time may be. Certainly during a period of inflation, precious metals are apt to rise; however, during a declining economic trend, precious metals are also likely to decline. If, on the other hand, a serious threat to bank stability once again develops, then precious metals may be a good refuge for some of your funds. Therefore, I recommend that a percentage of your assets be placed in the premier precious metals, such as platinum and gold.

5. Make certain that your investments are liquid. Liquidity allows buyers and sellers to enter and exit markets with ease and relative speed. Illiquid markets, on the other hand, are difficult to enter and/or exit quickly and at or near your desired price. Remember to limit investments to liquid vehicles only. You'll want ease of buying and selling when the time to act is right. Although some investments may appear more attractive than others in terms of yield, price, or potential, lack of liquidity may destroy their advantage. So place your funds only in areas that are likely to remain relatively liquid in the years ahead. Do you remember the "strategic metals" craze of the late 1970s and early 1980s? Here is

an example of how liquidity or lack of it can work against you. Although the potential of exceptionally high yield was a positive feature, the poor liquidity, lack of a central marketplace, and absence of active trading in many of the strategic metals were obvious drawbacks to investments in these promising but illiquid vehicles. On the other hand, markets such as most listed stocks, futures, many stock and futures options, and bonds offer high liquidity and relative ease of entry and exit. If and when the occasion requires you to switch funds from one area to another, and if the exchange must be a quick one, then high liquidity will be your ally.

6. Be prepared for panics well ahead of time. I have already indicated that panic declines and sharp bear market rallies are characteristic of long-wave declining phases. My work and studies suggest that some significant panics could be seen through the mid-1990s, particularly in stocks, futures, options, the banking system, and real estate. The stock market crash of 1987 could very well be repeated on an even larger scale. Be prepared by heeding some of the suggestions I've given you throughout this book.

7. Organization, structure, and planning will help you avoid emotional response to panics, both on the upside and on the downside. The structure you have established for your assets will help keep you on track in spite of the fact that many of your peers may be acting strictly out of fear, not from a base of good sense or intellectual reasoning.

8. Expect a "crash" in real estate prices if and when a severe economic contraction takes hold. Whereas some areas of the United States have already experienced a "crash" of sorts (*e.g.*, Texas and Oklahoma) in real estate values, other areas of the country are still in the midst of a price surge and, therefore, are vulnerable to a substantial decline. Furthermore, real estate prices in Japan, Hong Kong, and other countries have risen to absurdly high and unwarranted levels because of inflation in those countries. I expect a record-breaking real estate "crash" in these countries if and when disinflation spreads into their economies.

9. Overseas investments may not be favored, particularly in the Far East, because of their rapidly overheating economies. When consumer and industrial demands in the United States and Europe "dry

up," Japan, Taiwan, Hong Kong, and even China will feel the impact in a big way. I do not, therefore, favor foreign investments other than, perhaps, in Canada.

10. Reduce your long-term debt in order to increase your financial liquidity and cash flow. The best time to do so is when brief inflationary rallies bring prices higher, allowing you to exit burdensome investments quickly and at a favorable price. If history is any guide to the future, then high debt will differentiate those who survive and prosper from those who fail and/or falter.

11. Cash will, most likely, be "king." Another aspect of the long-wave declining phase will be the relative scarcity of cash in spite of deflating prices. At first the need for cash will be reflected in higher interest rates; however, as the economy contracts, cash will still be needed to meet high debt in spite of falling interest rates. In other words, there will be less demand for money because of decreased business expansion, home financing, and consumer spending, but these will be the result of high unemployment, contracting business, and price deflation. Money will, therefore, be more difficult to acquire and more difficult to save. There will be less borrower demand because of deflating business conditions. Those who have saved their cash will be in the advantageous position of being able to accumulate all types of investments at "bargain" prices *at the right time*. Those who have little or no debt will have the confidence to borrow at low rates in order to take advantage of these "bargain" prices, but again, *at the right time*. Having cash and/or the ability to acquire it will differentiate the winners from the losers.

12. Evaluate your current sources of income in order to determine their stability in the years ahead. Are you employed by or do you own a business that is dependent upon inflation for its survival? If so, it may be time for a change.

Now that you have had a chance to review and study my suggestions, take the time to evaluate them as they apply to your own situation. Formulate a specific plan and then, most important of all, put it into action.

Chapter *12*

Some Straight Talk
About the Long Wave

Why cannot all men develop and become different beings?
*   The answer is very simple.* Because they do not want it. *Because they do not know about it and will not understand without a long preparation what it means, even if they are told.*

—P. D. Ouspensky

What I've presented in this book has, for the most part, been based on theory, fact, or on a combination of the two. While theory and fact are helpful, they are often too general to permit specific application to individual situations by those who are either new to the topic or limited in their actual experience. In order to help translate theory and fact into pragmatics, I will address my attention to various relevant questions; questions that may or may not now be on your mind. The questions I'll present are either my own or those I've been asked repeatedly through the years. In addition, I will provide some of my random thoughts about the future based upon various aspects of individual market cycles and the long-wave economic cycle.

WHY IS THERE A LONG WAVE?

Those who are dedicated students of investing need not know the answer to this question, yet there are many who are still intrigued by the question "Why?" The need to know "why" things are is a normal need of the inquisitive human mind. It is, to a great extent, typical of Western thinking.

From the days of our earliest childhood experiences we ask "Why?" Once we have matured, once our attitudes have been shaped by the educational system, we travel the road of life's experiences by the maps that have been engrained on our minds by parents and the educational system. The Western system of education is more concerned with the "why" of things than with the "because" of things. Rather than how to observe nature and discern its patterns and rhythms, we are taught to dissect and understand the "cause and effect" of systems. We want to know what makes a car work, how chemical reactions produce their results, and why biological systems function as they do. This miscroscopic or analytical view of the world within and without obscures our ability to understand the world as a system, viewing it on a microscopic level instead. It is only through a macroscopic or global view that we can see how systems function and integrate to form the whole.

Perhaps the most accurate answer to the question "Why is there a long wave?" is: "Because there is a long wave." This answer would not, of course, satisfy the inquisitive Western mind. Some academicians will object, saying that we have not statistically demonstrated the existence of the long wave and that the answer is, therefore, meaningless. Others would object by saying that we are avoiding an answer to the question. Though my feeling is that the question requires no more of an answer than "Because," let me advance some explanations for those who feel that they need them.

Standard explanations for the existence of the long-wave economic cycles relate to the life span of what Forrester has termed "the capital goods sector." Such things as machinery, equipment, manufacturing facilities, and so forth are ingredients of the capital goods sector. It takes approximately thirty years for the capital goods sector to become worn out, or to live out its useful life. Thereafter, the capital goods are written off the record books, discarded, or otherwise eliminated from the production equation. The result is a period of declining productivity and consumption as business becomes inefficient and production unprofitable. In the words of Forrester:

> Literature on the Kondratieff cycle is filled with debate and conflicting assertions. Economic evidence has been interpreted differently

by different observers. There has been no cohesive theory to explain how an economic pattern spanning a half century could be systematically and internally generated. Because no theory of the long wave existed to show how the many aspects of reality could fit into a unified pattern, controversy was unavoidable.

We believe the National Model now provides a theory of how the economic long wave is generated. The process involves an overbuilding of the capital sectors in which they grow beyond the capital output rate needed for long-term equilibrium. In the process, capital plant throughout the economy is overbuilt beyond the level justified by the marginal productivity of capital. Finally, the overexpansion is ended by the hiatus of a great depression during which excess capital plant is physically worn out and financially depreciated on the account books until the stage has been cleared for a new era of rebuilding. [Forrester, in *Design, Innovation, and Long Cycles in Economic Development* by Freeman, 1986, p. 129]

and

Under economic stresses that reach a climax in the 1920's, previous trends faltered and reversed in the 1930's. The earlier pace of capital investment slowed. Overcapacity appeared in many sectors of the economy. Prices fell under the pressure of oversupply. Wages were driven down by falling profits and high unemployment. Defaults and bankruptcies cleared out the excess debt load. Expansion ceased because agriculture and consumer sectors had excess capacity. . . . Labor was drawn from consumer sectors into capital sectors, thereby producing a tight labor supply and still more incentive for consumer sectors to become more capital-intensive. Demand for capital was self-reinforcing: in order to expand, capital sectors themselves required new capital plant, thus creating further demand on capital sectors. A long, powerful regenerative process drove expansion of the capital sectors. [Forrester, in *The Futurist*, December 1978, p. 382]

While this explanation seems logical, I find it somewhat insufficient. I suspect that various other forces interact to produce long waves. Among these I include human psychology, population trends and cycles, weather patterns as influenced by sunspot cycles, and cycles in innovation. Because of the differential influences on each element at different times, their total impact on the long-wave cycles varies. This is most likely what makes each long-wave cycle slightly different from the last while each cycle still retains most basic elements of the long wave.

Consider the important influence of human behavior as a major element of the cycle. As society becomes more affluent, trends in consumption increase, and family size tends to decrease. The result of steady demand is overproduction. As population trends decline with production still on the upswing, prices begin to decline. In the interim, expansion in capital facilities has reached a high level, one from which a retreat is not easily made. Now, with massive capital facilities in place, demand begins to decrease. While demand decreases, supplies are still high. Prices begin to react downward. Business profits decline, and unemployment increases. As unemployment increases, there is less disposable income, and consumer demand declines further. This places an added burden on business as more employees are laid off. The downward spiral continues and eventually becomes accelerated. The decline continues until prices become sufficiently attractive to stimulate new consumer interest. Slowly attitudes begin to improve, and demand increases. The cycle begins anew.

Why is there a long wave? There is a long wave because there are people. People drive the long wave. As Don Hoppe notes:

> Modern economic theories (Keynesianism, monetarism, supply-side) all fail, or make things worse, because they attempt to deal with an economy objectively, as a "thing" composed of taxes, interest rates, money, exports, imports, rules, regulations, etc., when it is actually a *phenomenon* of human behavior. (That is why psychological approaches, such as contrary opinion, tend to work better than objective market analyses based on statistics.) At least if there was some understanding of the long wave we would not make the mistake of deliberately stimulating more capital investment when overbuilding of the capital sectors is already becoming a problem. But I really don't expect such understanding to become widespread for many more decades, if ever. [February 1988, p. 19]

CAN WE ALTER THE COURSE OF THE LONG WAVE BY MANIPULATING GOVERNMENT POLICIES?

Keynesian economic theory asserts that excessive periods of expansion and contraction could be avoided by government manipulation of economic policies. By simply expanding and contracting the money supply, federal spending programs, banking regulations, aid to farmers, and tax regulations, the government can, indeed, affect the course of economic trends and cycles. However, as time and experience have shown, there are both advantages and disadvantages to this approach. On the one hand, government intervention and manipulation can act to forestall a situation; however, there is clear evidence that it cannot delay indefinitely certain economic consequences. For example, government can increase the money supply to stimulate the economy, but such stimulation is artificial—it creates nothing and eventually forces an overextension in the opposite direction.

In many respects, economies follow the laws of physics and chemistry. Every action has an equal and opposite reaction. By making changes in one sector of the economy, government is likely to affect another sector in the opposite way. Historical examples supporting this claim are numerous. In 1985 the U.S. Department of Agriculture undertook the task of raising milk prices in order to assist dairy farmers who claimed that their profits were insufficient. In order to raise milk prices the USDA instituted a dairy cow liquidation program, culling the dairy herd. The result was an oversupply of beef that severely pressured the beef cattle industry, bringing beef prices to their lowest levels in a decade. This, of course, resulting in the bankruptcy of many beef producers. In turn, beef producers decreased their production. Then, from 1985 through 1988 beef prices moved steadily upward as supplies of beef decreased with moderately rising demand (see Figure 12.1). In the end, consumers and livestock producers paid dearly for the dairy price support program. However, when cycles are allowed to run their natural course with a minimum of intervention, they eventually run their course without artificially prompted push/pull and its concomitant volatility.

The 1960–88 time frame was marked by persistent government intervention that fostered a sharp increase in economic volatility. All sectors of the U.S. and world economies have been affected by the long reach of government manipulation. While I do not advocate a totally *laissez-faire* or libertarian approach, I do feel that government regulation is not only excessive but also out of control, damaging, and counterproductive.

Some areas should be regulated by government policy, but a vast majority of the regulatory programs should be scrapped. Wage and price controls should never be necessary other than, perhaps, during times of declared war. Such things as child labor laws, certain anti-trust legislation, fair housing and employment laws, anti-discrimination laws, and

Figure 12-1. *The fall in feeder-line cattle prices (futures) resulting from the USDA dairy liquidation program and the subsequent "explosion" in prices due to decreased cattle production.*

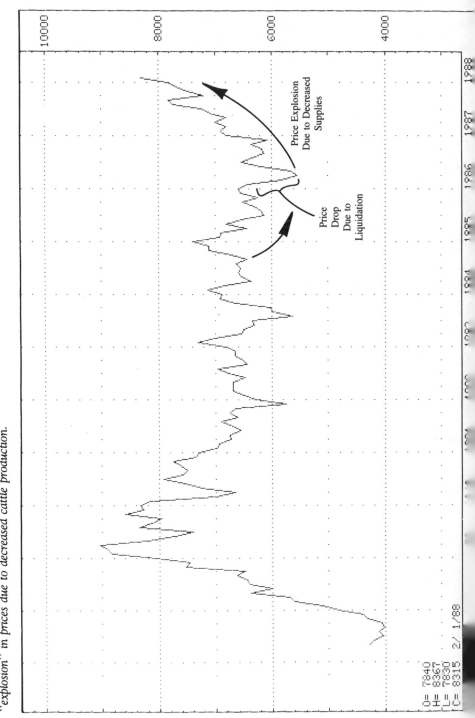

so forth should not be eliminated. I suspect that with the passage of time this will become abundantly clear once again. As economies grow, government regulation increases to the point of overcontrol and gross inefficiency. Then, after the economic peak, regulation begins to diminish, the evils of intervention are recognized as counterproductive, and there is a relaxation of inhibitory legislation toward the bottoming phase of the long-wave cycle.

I am a strong advocate of the motto "That government is best which governs least." This assertion is not based on alignment with any political faction or party. I am apolitical. My conclusions are based on the study of economic history and the long wave. R. Batra in his *Great Depression of 1990* concluded that the one way to avoid the coming economic depression is to tax away "excess" wealth in order to compensate for an "unprecedented concentration of wealth." It is difficult to believe that in this day and age of knowledge about the evils of overtaxation any thinking individual could propose such a preposterous and totally unworkable "solution." Why give the government more money to squander and misappropriate?

WHY DO GOVERNMENT EFFORTS AT ECONOMIC REGULATION USUALLY FAIL?

There are numerous reasons for the demonstrated ineptitude of government in controlling the economy. Among the more obvious reasons are:

1. Government tends to react to situations rather than to plan ahead. As inflation becomes rampant, it waits and watches the situation. Once the situation becomes severe, then government acts. *Rather than anticipating situations, government reacts to situations.* Preparation and preventive action are much more effective than reaction.

2. Government usually responds to statistics and indicators, which are necessarily delayed. The process of gathering, collating, and analyzing statistics takes time. By the time statistics reflect a change in underlying fundamentals, the situation is most likely to be changing of its own accord; it is about ready to take an opposite turn. This is when government steps in to take action. One such scenario is

taking place as I sit and write the final words of this book in early 1988. Many economists are concerned that the U.S. economy is entering a recessionary phase. Government statistics suggest a slow-down in an already volatile and declining economy. Interest rates are falling, reflecting decreased demand for money. Unemployment is on the upswing. This concerns the Reagan administration because of the impending elections. In the interim, however, many commodity prices have risen dramatically. Corn, soybean, soybean oil, wheat, oats, cattle, hog, lumber, copper, sugar, coffee, and feeder cattle prices have made significant price gains. Figures 12.2 through 12.5 show the price increases in some of these staples. Clearly these suggest that demand is up, which in turn indicates that the economy is about to turn higher of its own accord. The price of important commodities is rising. My work suggests that further increases are likely. This upswing will eventually be reflected in the government economic statistics. But government can't wait, particularly with presidential elections not far off. Therefore, the government is likely to take actions that will "stimulate" an already "stimulated" economy. The result will be overstimulation of an economy about to improve on its own.

3. Government policies are often implemented slowly. They take time. The effects of a new program might not be felt for several years. By then the situation that prompted the program will likely have been resolved through the natural course of economic events.

4. Government action is usually biased by special-interest groups, riders on legislation, graft, and corruption. These take their toll. Funds designed for one program are frequently misdirected to another program or into the pockets of special-interest groups and/or corrupt bureaucrats.

There are, perhaps, many other reasons behind the ineffective-ness of government regulation. I have made the assumption that most government officials are incompetent and that they do not know what actions to take given certain economic developments. This is, most likely, an exaggerated assumption. I am certain that some bureaucrats do know what they're doing, but a majority of them are incompetent.

Figure 12-2. *The increase in soybean oil futures prices from 1987 through early 1988.*

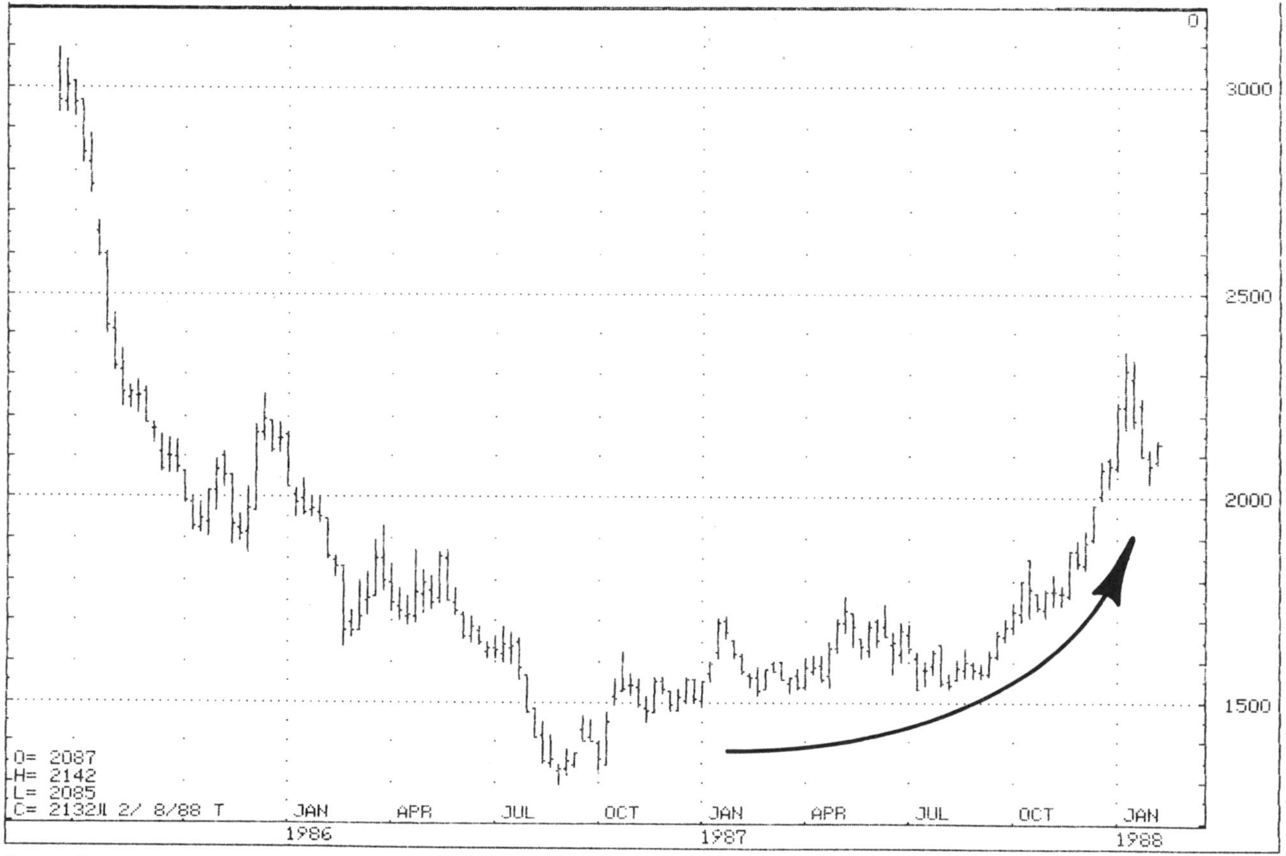

```
O= 2087
H= 2142
L= 2085
C= 2132( 2/ 8/88 T
```

Source: Reprinted with permission of Commodity Quote Graphics.

Figure 12-3. *The increase in corn prices, 1987–88.*

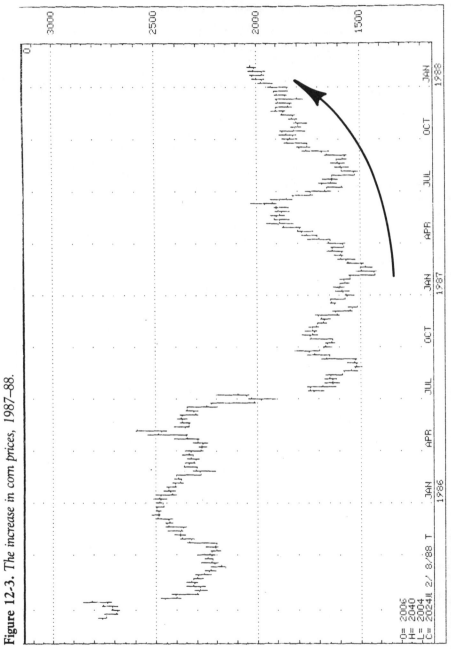

Source: Reprinted with permission of Commodity Quote Graphics.

Figure 12-4. *The increase in copper prices, 1986–87.*

O= 9450
H=10420
L= 8750
C=10285   2/ 1/88

Source: Reprinted with permission of Commodity Quote Graphics.

Figure 12-5. *The upswing in sugar prices from mid-1987 through early 1988.*

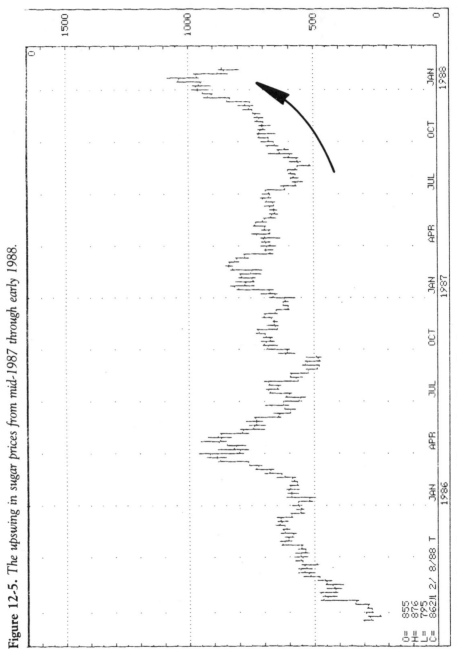

Source: Reprinted with permission of Commodity Quote Graphics.

IS THERE A SINGLE BEST WAY OF PROTECTING PERSONAL AND BUSINESS ASSETS DURING THE LONG WAVE?

No! This question is like asking if there is a sure-fire way of avoiding car accidents when you drive. You can take precautions, you can know the rules of the road, you can have experience with your vehicle, you can know how far to push your vehicle, you can know the roads you are traveling, but none of these guarantee accident-free driving. There's always "the other guy," the chance happening, the freak accident, and the fallibility of driver and machine. In the same way, there is no single best way to avoid economic or financial accidents. No one investment portfolio or investment will protect you against the happenstance of economic trends. However, by having a balanced and diversified investment portfolio, by knowing which investments tend to fare well in different economic climates, and by knowing in advance when economic trends are likely to change, you can adjust your portfolio accordingly. This will help you avoid an accident, but it will in no way guarantee accident-free investing.

ARE SOCIALIST AND COMMUNIST COUNTRIES LIKELY TO BE AFFECTED BY THE LONG WAVE?

Time has shown that the communist system does not foster sustained economic growth, incentives to labor, productivity, or independent technological progress. The Soviets have acquired much of their technology by stealing it or by buying it from the West or Far East. Their abysmal agricultural programs and pathetically anachronistic production methods do not make efficient use of either human or natural resources. Increasingly, socialist and communist countries have come to rely upon trade with the West, Far East, and Europe in order to fulfill their needs. Rather than uplift the condition of their peoples, they have created a restrictive, controlled, rigid, and totalitarian state. While their educational system is clearly far superior to anything offered in the West, they have been unable to efficiently implement their vast brainpower because of restrictive business and trade policies. As communist and socialist nations like the Soviet Union and others continue their dependence upon trade with capitalist countries, they are more likely to be affected by economic conditions in capitalistic countries as well. I suspect that any extended economic decline in capitalist nations will spread to the various communist and socialist nations throughout the world, affecting them in a similar fashion, but not necessarily to the same degree.

IF THE LONG WAVE IS SO IMPORTANT, WHY DO MOST RESPECTED ECONOMISTS AND GOVERNMENT POLICYMAKERS IGNORE ITS EXISTENCE?

First and foremost, there is a dearth of acceptable statistical evidence in support of the long wave. In spite of what I've presented in this book, the fact is that much more evidence is required by academia and government. Even then there will be disputes about which aspects of the long-wave cycles are important. There will be disagreement about how to avoid or solve these problems. The net result will likely be more heat than light, more confusion than solution, more haste and waste.

In addition, there is a general hesitation among economists and bureaucrats to accept any notion which so much as hints that they themselves may not be in total control of the situation. The long wave or, for that matter, any cycle suggests that there is a natural and perhaps unavoidable rhythm in economic movement. This is a difficult notion to accept. Politicians must campaign with slogans. They promise to "make things better," to support one special-interest group or another, to improve trade, to lower the budget deficit, and so forth. They make promises, and, in their own futile way, they attempt to fulfill their promises. But, alas, they cannot; the force cycle is too strong.

Economists must also justify their own existence as well. They must advise and formulate. They must solve problems. Eventually the problems will solve themselves by the simple process of economic equilibrium, by supply and demand acting in their normal way. But this is not good enough for those who must show their superiors or the public that they are "doing something" about the situation. Accepting the long wave, or any cycle, as a viable force seems, to these individuals, inconsistent with their needs and profession. But this perception is not true. There are so many cycles that have yet to be investigated and uncovered. There are numerous interactions of various cycles that are still to be studied and evaluated. There are many cyclic forecasting methods that must still be developed and there will, therefore, always be work for economists. But they do not see the light now, nor is it likely that they will. Human nature rarely changes. Economic philosophy is also unlikely to change. Unless it does, government, academia, or the general public will not accept long-wave theory. Refutation of cycles— long term, intermediate term, or short term—on the basis of statistical insufficiency is merely a convenient way of not having to deal with the obvious.

IS A SEVERE AND/OR EXTENDED ECONOMIC DEPRESSION A NECESSARY CORRELATE OF THE LONG WAVE?

No. I suspect that the severity of the declining phase is a function of several factors. They are:

1. the intensity of the upswing and the degree of inflation that accompanied it,
2. the degree of government control and regulation, and
3. the confluence of other cycles during the long-wave declining phase.

Let me explain. If the economic upswing is large (*i.e.*, with inflation running rampant), with economic indicators out of control, and exceptionally high price volatility, then it is likely that the downswing will act in an equal but opposite way. In other words, violent upswings beget violent downswings. This is frequently observed in individual markets, stocks, futures, real estate, collectibles, and so on. Figure 12.6 shows how the unprecedented upswing in silver prices during the 1970s was followed by an equally violent and extended downswing, a decline from which prices are still recovering. Figure 12.7 shows the violent upswing in sugar prices during the 1979–80 time frame and the equally volatile decline that followed it. Economies

Figure 12-6. Upswing in silver futures prices during the 1970s, and reaction to lower levels during the disinflation of the 1980s.

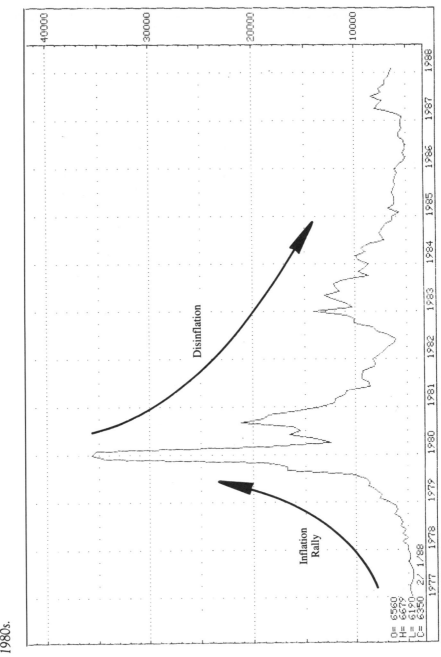

Source: Reprinted with permission of Commodity Quote Graphics.

Figure 12-7. *Severe decline in sugar prices following major price upswing.*

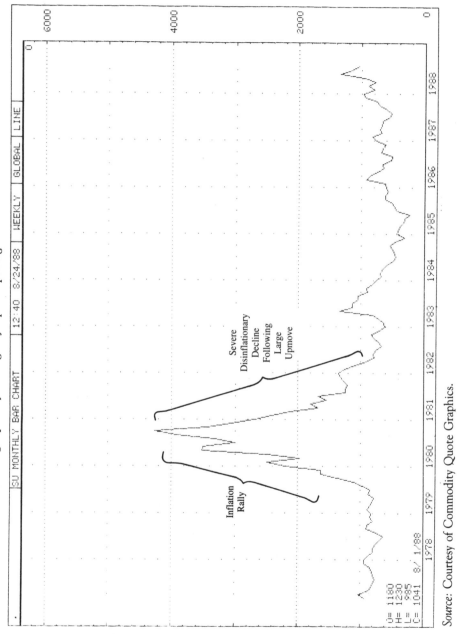

Source: Courtesy of Commodity Quote Graphics.

behave in a similar fashion. There are numerous examples of this in economic history. Figure 12.8 shows several periods of substantial price increases in copper followed by equally severe declines. Note that my copper examples are drawn not only from recent history, but from many years ago as well.

Figure 12-8. *Several violent up- and downswings in copper prices.*

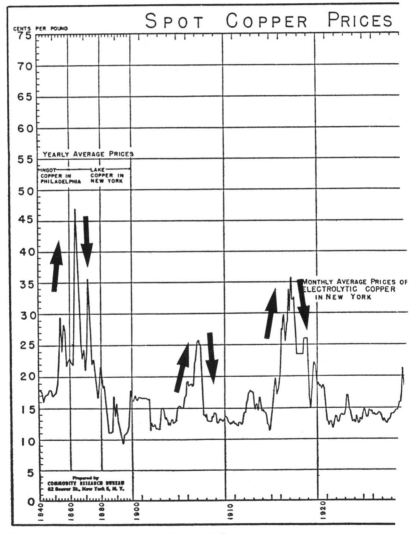

Source: Courtesy of Commodity Research Bureau.

Figure 12-8. (cont.)

Source: Courtesy of Commodity Quote Graphics.

291

I conclude from my study of cycles, prices, and economic history that the long-wave upswing must necessarily be followed by a long-wave downswing, but that the severity of the downswing need not be similar in each case. Typically, however, the larger the upswing, the larger the downswing.

DOES THE LONG-WAVE THEORY IMPLY ECONOMIC DETERMINISM?

I have touched on this issue previously. The fact that cycles exist and the fact that one accepts them as factual do not imply in any way that one has adopted a deterministic policy. Cycles are not the cause; rather, they are the symptom. Cycles don't cause events to occur; they are merely a reflection of what is happening. Just as fever is not the cause of an infection, cycles are not the cause of price movements or trends. Fever is measured in order to determine the underlying condition of a patient. There is a normal range of body temperature. If temperature remains within normal limits, the patient will be fine. If, however, temperature continues to rise, this is an indication that all is not well. If the rising trend continues, then greater concern about the patient's condition is justified. Once body temperature turns lower, symptoms begin to subside, the cycle ends, and the patient returns to baseline or normal health.

Cycles do not cause economic trends any more than temperature causes ill health. They are both reflections of underlying conditions, and, consequently, they cannot be deterministic. If, however, we use correlates of the long wave to determine social, political, religious, and economic policy in a rigid and pervasive sense, then we are guilty of determinism in its worst form. The long wave does not support a deterministic course of action based upon its findings. Rather, the long wave suggests that certain actions may be more effective at certain times than at others. It suggests that what is correct during one time frame is not necessarily correct during another. This is not deterministic; it is analytical, sensible, and rational.

IS THERE A "QUICK FIX" OR "SURE-FIRE CURE" FOR THE ECONOMIC AILMENTS OF THE 1980s AND THE COMING CRISES OF THE 1990s?

No. Just as there is no quick cure for cancer or AIDS, there is no quick cure for our current worldwide economic ailment. In fact, there may be no cure whatsoever. The strongest will survive, and the weakest will fall victim and die. Those who have not taken adequate precautions, made sufficient preparation, or avoided certain inappropriate actions will be those who suffer most. There is no quick cure or answer. This book has provided numerous corrective suggestions. Our best hope for tomorrow is to implement some of these solutions. As I have indicated, however, the application of these solutions is an individual matter, it is not something that government will do for us. It's everyone for him- or herself. In the words of Don Hoppe:

> Don't adopt the philosophy of "growth at any cost," because growth does have a price. If you try to grow too fast by resorting to borrowing massively from the future you create an unstable condition that leads ultimately to a panic collapse. If it wasn't for the final decade of euphoric speculation and overinvestment in capital goods on borrowed money, you could still have the long wave contraction, but it would be fairly mild, and at least would not begin with a panic financial collapse and severe business depression. *But having had the euphoria of the plateau decade there is no way to escape the consequences* [underlining added] . . . [February 1988, p. 19]

HOW DO SOCIAL ISSUES REFLECT THE LONG WAVE?

People change in response to their environment. Economic environment is just as real as is physical environment. In fact, physical environment can be affected by, and can, in turn, affect, environment. Social and psychological issues respond to and influence economic issues. Perceptions influence behavior and action. Hence, all aspects of human behavior are intertwined in a complex system of interaction.

I have previously stated that social behaviors and attitudes seem to reflect underlying economic conditions. The more I read of economic history, the more I find this to be true. Mind you, we are not necessarily talking about cause and effect. There may be a causal effect, but this is of no interest to me. I am concerned only with using social and economic correlates as a means of confirming or locating the approximate position of the long-wave cycle.

The trend in social behaviors, attitudes, mores, and customs tends to reflect the long-wave stage. During the early phases of the long wave, attitudes and behaviors are relatively conservative. As the wave continues and the economic growth accelerates, attitudes and behaviors become more liberal and permissive. There is a growing trend toward sexual freedom, increased freedom of expression, tolerance of conflicting or radical opinion, and a relaxation of business and trade legislation. As the long wave reaches its peak, so do liberal social attitudes and behaviors. When the downswing begins, so does a tightening of social attitudes, a decrease in liberalism, and declines in sexual freedom and freedom of expression. There is a return to isolationism, conservatism, and closed-mindedness. The "surprise" strength of religious conservative Pat Robertson in the 1988 Iowa caucuses was no surprise. It was to be expected, based on the fact that the long wave was in its declining phase at that point. If such a trend were to continue, then we would see all manner and sorts of social and political conservatism develop and increase through the mid-1990s. In spite of Robertson's short-lived popularity, it is likely that national sentiment has turned toward conservatism. Hence, we can expect the trend of U.S. and "free-world" leadership to become more conservative into the 1990s.

WHAT CAN WE LEARN FROM CONTRARY OPINION?

Market history is a reflection of human history. Human behavior, human attitudes, and human emotion are key elements at major turning points in economic, social, political, and speculative trends. When human sentiment is strongly aligned in one direction, there is a significant likelihood that the majority will be wrong. If you examine the role of sentiment during the Dutch Tulip Mania and during or previous to the crashes of 1929 and 1987, you will find that sentiment was strongly positive, that the public was clearly optimistic, bullish, positive, and euphoric about the future. If you examine public and professional sentiment at major economic lows and market bottoms, or near changes in downtrends, you will find a pervasive negativism, a plurality of bears, and a majority of sellers. This is common. This is how sentiment alerts astute traders and investors to changes in trends.

Students of the stock market have studied "odd lot" behavior for many years. When a majority of small nonprofessional speculators is most bearish and sells short, uneven lots (*i.e.*, under one hundred shares) of stock, there is reason to believe that stocks are bottoming. R. E. Hadady*developed what he called "The Bullish Consensus," a means of determining professional market consensus on the markets every week in order to determine the level of bullish or bearish sentiment. In his book *Contrary Opinion*, Hadady made the following assumptions about strong levels of consensus or agreement among the professional market watchers whose collective opinions he tracked weekly:

> Contrary Opinion, perhaps the most powerful of all tools for predicting the future course of events in business and economics, is more often than not misunderstood and incorrectly applied. Contrary Opinion is, in essence, an opinion that it is contrary to what almost all of the people believe the course of events will be. In a given market, if almost all of the people believe that the prices will rise, the contrarian will be expecting prices to go down . . . equally applicable in all areas of business and economics . . . when the consensus of speculators reaches one of the two extremes, i.e., when almost everyone is bullish (expects prices to rise) or bearish (expects prices to decline). It also, and perhaps even of more importance, deals with the situation between consensus extremes. Reiterating, Contrary Opinion is involved only when the Consensus nears an extreme. For those who are interested in the application of Contrary Opinion outside the commodity futures market, you are urged to read on anyway; the principles are the same for any sphere of activity. . . . [1983, p. 1]

Recently I have embarked on a program that monitors the daily market sentiment of individual futures traders rather than rely on the weekly assessment of newsletters and brokerage houses. With the assistance of M. Lively,[1] I have studied the daily opinions of futures market speculators, correlating the highs and lows in their collective sentiment with market turning points. Rather than assess the opinions of market professionals on a weekly basis as did Hadady, we weigh our daily survey to the public trader. We have found few instances of strong market sentiment, either bullish or bearish, that failed to correlate highly with a strong price movement in the opposite direction. Figures 12.9 and 12.10 are taken from Hadady's work, and Figures 12.11 and 12.12 are taken from my work with M. Lively on what we have termed the *Daily Sentiment Index*. Observe my comments on the charts.

[1]*Daily Sentiment Index*, P.O. Box 353, Winnetka, IL 60093.
*Hadady Corporation, "The Bullish Consensus," 1111 South Arroyo Parkway, Suite 410, Pasadena, CA 91105.

Figure 12-9. *The Bullish Consensus and sugar futures, 1981. Note how high Bullish Consensus came close to the top of this market (B) after first reading false (A).*

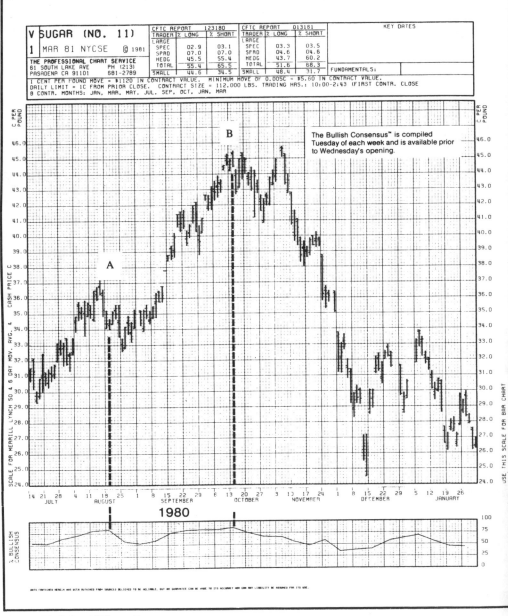

Source: Hadady, 1983, p. 7.

Figure 12-10. *A classic example of Bullish Consensus. Note that all three important tops developed on high Bullish Consensus readings (dashed lines).*

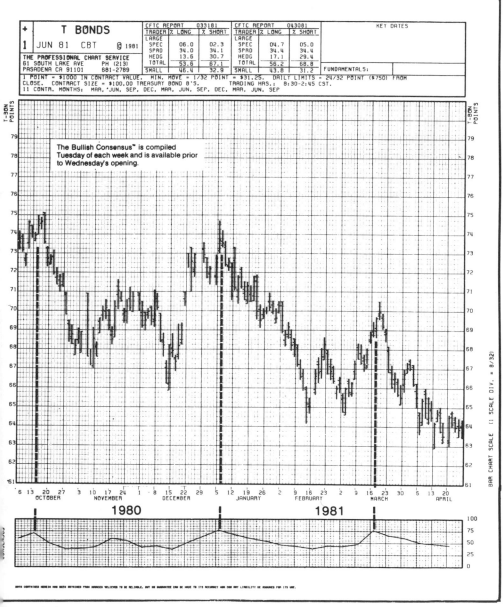

Figure 12-11. Daily Sentiment Index. *Three-day moving average vs. S&P 500 futures. Note how low DSI readings correspond to price lows, and vice-versa.*

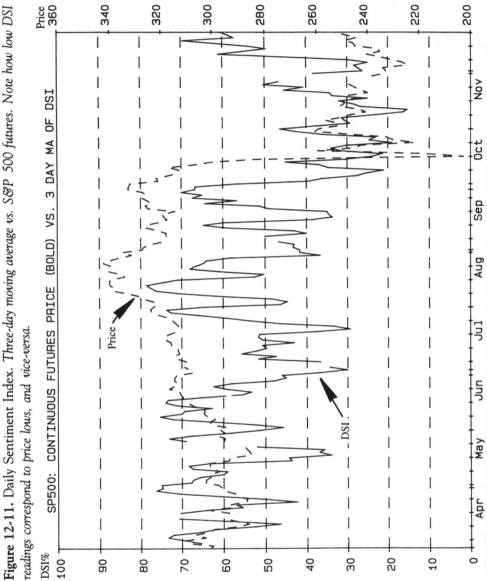

Figure 12.12. Daily Sentiment *five-day moving average vs. crude oil futures. Note correspondence of high and lows.*

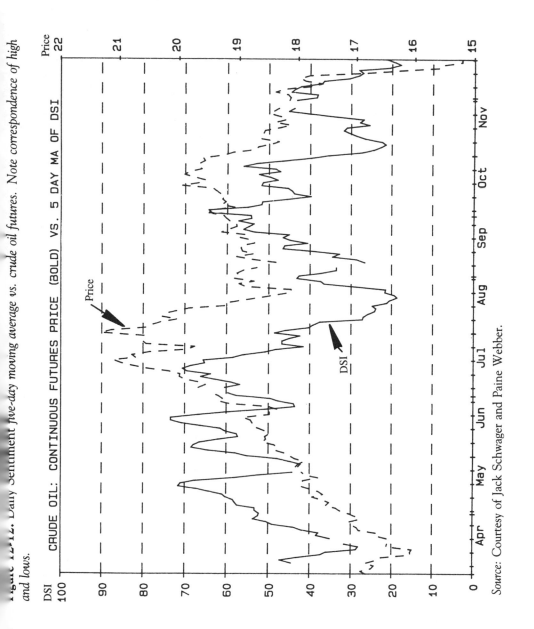

CRUDE OIL: CONTINUOUS FUTURES PRICE (BOLD) VS. 5 DAY MA OF DSI

Source: Courtesy of Jack Schwager and Paine Webber.

299

What does this have to do with the economy and the long wave? The answer should be obvious. When most people are the most negative, trends are likely to be bottoming. When most investors are excited, euphoric, and bullish, trends are likely to be topping. Take the time to conduct your private surveys. Call about twenty to fifty people from time to time and assess their opinions. When sentiment runs high (more than 75 percent agreement or disagreement), you are most likely to profit by taking action in the opposite direction. The greater the public positive sentiment, the more likely we are to be near an economic peak; the greater the public negativism, the more likely we are to be near an economic low. It's that simple. Though not infallible, the degree of sentiment is an important indicator, one I suggest you follow closely.

HOW DO TAXES ENTER INTO THE LONG-WAVE PICTURE?

There is no simple answer, yet there does appear to be a relationship between taxes and the economy. When taxes are low, the economy tends to grow, but high taxes tend to prohibit expansion. Growth slows or deteriorates. By raising or lowering taxes, government can either stimulate or slow down the economy. Ideally, taxes should be low at all times. They should be kept at a minimum so that investors and businesspersons will have more income that will, in turn, come back into the economy. Giving more money to government is useless; it supports the inefficient and squanderous machinery of a wasteful bureaucracy. Government, however, is often in a situation where it must keep taxes high in order to support its own uncontrollable spending. Whether the government spending is for military or social programs, it is likely to be excessive, ill advised, misdirected, and spurious. The less money we give to government, the better off we will be in terms of the long wave.

Governments must operate economically. Give governments too much power to tax the people and you will have waste, inefficiency, and graft. This is why taxes should, ideally, be kept as low as possible at all times.

WHAT'S THE ROLE OF "MONEY SUPPLY"?

Money supply consists of various measures. These are defined and redefined according to government wishes and needs. Definitions are changed from time to time, and different components are factored into the equation. Simply stated, money supply is the aggregate of money in circulation. When the available supply of money is expanded, interest rates can be artificially reduced (*i.e.*, the more money available, the lower the interest rates). When the money supply is decreased, interest rates can be influenced upward. The role of money-supply expansion and contraction is to either stimulate or retard the economy. If government suspects that the economy is growing too rapidly, it may tighten or pull in the purse strings, reducing the money supply and theoretically slowing growth. If growth is too slow and a recession appears to be developing, government may increase the money supply. This loosens credit, thereby stimulating business. The expansion and contraction of money supply tends to have a significant impact on economic trends and is, in part, responsible for the high economic volatility seen since the 1970s.

It should be noted that manipulation of the money supply can have a substantial impact on the U.S. economy: A "tight" monetary policy for too long a time can have a devastating effect on business, while a "loose" policy for too long can result in a sharp inflationary increase. The danger in money-supply manipulation is that it may result in an economy that is "out of control." By tightening for too long, government may precipitate a chain reaction of bankruptcies, whereas a policy of increasing money supply for too long could result in hyperinflation.

WHY IS THE GOVERNMENT SO INEPT AT MONEY MANAGEMENT?

Considering the size of the U.S. economic machine, government deserves some praise for the job it has done; however, given the resources, both financial and intellectual, that the United States has had at its disposal, the job has not been an admirable one. In a nation that boasts the greatest agricultural and intellectual resources in the world, there is no excuse for poverty, unemployment, or economic volatility. What has impaired the effective and efficient functioning of government? It is not one thing but many. Here are a few of my observations:

1. Government does not plan ahead.
2. Special-interest groups, Congressional lobbies, and political action groups have exerted a continuing and imbalanced influence on government officials and Congressional representatives. This has resulted in government policies that are established by power and influence but not necessarily by what's good or best.
3. There is gross inefficiency in the operation of government institutions. Waste is rampant in all levels of government and government programs.
4. Decisions are not made from a long-term orientation. For the most part, decisions are made with the next election in mind.
5. Government officials tend to have limited knowledge about economic history and/or theory. They rely on advisors and economists for guidance. Furthermore, their advice often falls on deaf ears. Their advisors tend to disagree amongst themselves.

These are only some of the reasons for government's inability to manage the economy effectively. There are many more. I'm certain you can think of numerous reasons I've not mentioned.

WHAT'S AHEAD IN THE AREA OF TECHNOLOGICAL BREAKTHROUGHS?

I've indicated in previous chapters that there has been a close relationship between technological breakthroughs and long-wave lows. There have been numerous research studies on this aspect of the long wave. There is strong evidence supporting this theory, but there is also evidence that the relationship is not as valid as claimed. The most recent studies support the finding that each long-wave low has been accompanied by important technological breakthroughs. Assuming that this is indeed the case, and looking ahead to the next long-wave lows, what might some of the breakthroughs be? Here are a few ideas about what may develop:

1. Genetic engineering is likely to be an important area of technological innovation. This might prove to be one of the most profitable investment areas when the long-wave lows come and perhaps even prior to the bottom of the long wave.

2. Routine space travel is likely to become a reality in the next ten to fifteen years. This opens an entirely new era of transportation and exploration. The possibilities are virtually boundless.

3. Computer technology is changing dramatically. "Artificial intelligence," computers that learn from their mistakes, is growing rapidly. In the coming years there will be quantum leaps. Recent innovations include so-called "neutral" computers that operate at incredibly fast speeds. Computer technology is likely to continue as a field of important innovation. I'd not be surprised to see a marriage of genetic engineering and computer technology, resulting in a machine that can outperform the human brain many times over.

4. Communications technology has remained in a relatively stagnant phase for many years. The coming long-wave lows may witness some new developments in communications technology using revolutionary methods and totally new technology.

It is important to keep in touch with areas of possibly new technology in order to capitalize on them with your investment dollars. Jay Forrester commented on innovations and the long wave in an interview with *Fortune* magazine. He was asked, "Do you have any idea of the technological basis for the next major wave?"

I am no more sure of the shape of the next technological wave than other people. I expect that energy will move toward renewable and more decentralized sources, not only because of the nature of new energy sources, but because of changes in our social system. If our society goes to still bigger and more centralized energy sources, as we have been doing in the past, we will produce a more and more vulnerable socioeconomic system. I expect that declining worldwide political stability with increasing unrest and sabotage will combine with the persuasiveness of decentralized energy sources—like solar and wind power and alcohol from farm products—to encourage decentralization. Energy networks with larger and larger power plants are not, I think, the wave of the future.

Likewise, I believe we are at the end of the pendulum swing toward a tightly integrated world economy. Many stresses are now arising from excessive international coupling. Countries will realize that they can't solve all their problems outside their borders. Hence, the natural drift of political forces will be toward more economic nationalism. Now that is not necessarily bad. It will bring problems down to a more manageable scale. If individual countries can't understand and manage their economies, I doubt the likelihood of managing all countries simultaneously. [*Fortune*, January 16, 1978, p. 148]

WHAT CAN THE AVERAGE INVESTOR DO TO PLAN FOR THE LONG TERM?

No one answer to this question will suffice. Each investor has his or her specific needs and abilities. Every individual has requirements which are a function of his or her age, occupation, and current investments. Here are some general suggestions and procedures for determining what's best for you.

1. Make an accurate assessment of your present financial status.
2. Determine how much capital you have available for investment.
3. Determine your debts, assets, liabilities, and potential income over the coming years.
4. Determine which area(s) of investment are best suited to your needs and abilities depending upon where things stand in the long-wave cycles at the time you are making your decisions.
5. Implement your plans only after research and clear direction have been established.
6. Don't be swayed from your decisions by others.
7. If you are tempted to change your mind about what's best for you, ask yourself how much you know in comparison to those who claim to know what is right for you.
8. Make your own decisions, and you will fare well.
9. Don't forget the basics of cyclic and long-wave philosophy.

WHAT CAN A YOUNG PERSON DO IN PREPARATION FOR THE LONG-WAVE PHASES?

Those who are in their teenage years or early twenties during the latter portion of the long-wave decline are in the best position of all to benefit from the next long-wave upswing. By the mid-1990s, resolution of the current long wave should be well underway. Indeed, an economic low may have been seen by then. This means that there will be abundant opportunities in virtually every investment area. The young person is in a particularly good position to take advantage of these opportunities because he or she will likely not be in debt. Therefore, the next several years should be seen by young people as an opportunity for saving as much cash as possible. This, of course, is not consistent with what most young people are doing nowadays. However, those who wish to become very wealthy when the next long wave enters its growth stage will plan ahead, taking advantage of the coming opportunities with cash they have accumulated well ahead of the long-wave upturn.

DOES THE AIDS EPIDEMIC MEAN ANYTHING IN TERMS OF THE LONG WAVE?

Yes. It may not be entirely "coincidence" that the AIDS epidemic comes at a time when sexual behavior is likely to change in the direction of extreme conservatism. It also may not be coincidental that the dim prospects of an AIDS cure or vaccine suggest a long and costly epidemic. This comes during the time frame of an economic down-swing, which typically results not only in increased conservatism but also in isolationism. There is a growing trend throughout the world for AIDS testing of foreign exchange students and foreign visitors. If the epidemic continues at an epidemic rate, then 25 percent of the world's population may be afflicted. In an attempt to avoid contact with those who are infected or with those who may be carriers, there may be a marked increase in isolationism. Countries will isolate themselves from one another, making international travel restrictive and visitors unwelcome. Furthermore, depending on how severe the epidemic becomes, and on what we learn about its epidemiology, people within countries may choose to isolate themselves. If, for example, people become concerned about acquiring AIDS through normal social interaction, or through eating in restaurants, then travel and entertainment activities could be curtailed. While it has been stated that AIDS is not communicable other than through intimate contact, public panic is possible because of ignorance and misinformation. Leisure industries may suffer, and with them the economy in general. Pharmaceutical ventures, however, may benefit markedly. Consider also the cost of treating the many who are likely to become afflicted. Who will pay? If the government pays, then there will be an added strain placed on vital economic resources during a time period when it can be least afforded. The AIDS epidemic may, therefore, have a marked impact on the economy, one that is consistent with long-wave expectations. While public education and medical research could help avert isolationism and "AIDS phobia," the fact remains that too much ignorance has already fostered unhealthy attitudes and ignorance has inspired fear.

WHAT POLITICAL CHANGES CAN WE EXPECT BY THE MID- TO LATE 1990s?

If the long-wave cyclic analysis I've presented in this book is correct, then the general tone of political changes should be in the direction of conservatism until the latter portion of the long-wave cyclic lows. In addition to the above, I'd expect to see the following:

1. decreased social welfare programs as budget strings are tightened
2. increased victories by conservative candidates on local, state, and federal levels
3. more support for conservative ideas and right-wing candidates
4. increased "isolationist" legislation such as tariffs and import quotas
5. increased spending restraint in all areas, including defense
6. growing mistrust of foreign diplomats to the United Nations likely to result in severe limitations on their travel and rights
7. a move toward conservatism in Supreme Court rulings and in Supreme Court appointments, and
8. increased activity among far right-wing and fascist organizations, such as the American Nazi Party and the John Birch Society.

IS A VIOLENT SOCIAL-CLASS REVOLUTION LIKELY IN THE UNITED STATES?

Anything is possible, but I consider the likelihood of revolution in America to be relatively remote. Although times are likely to become difficult, my studies do not suggest revolution or anything that approaches it. If there is a revolution, then it will likely be on a political or academic level rather than in the physical sense.

WHAT IS THE FATE OF THE U.S. DOLLAR?

History suggests that during disinflationary times, the dollar becomes strong. The student of economic history will, therefore, conclude that if a serious disinflationary or deflationary trend is to grip the U.S. economy until well into the 1990s, then the U.S. dollar will become strong, gaining on foreign currencies and reversing the trend of the 1970s and 1980s. There are many who do not expect this to happen. With the overwhelming strength in foreign currencies against the U.S. dollar, the vast majority of analysts point to U.S. budget deficits and declining balance of trade as factors that are likely to keep the U.S. dollar on the defensive. If, however, a disinflation takes hold in earnest, then foreign currencies and foreign economies are likely to suffer even more than in the U.S. economy. Hence, the dollar should gain strength in a disinflationary period.

IS CANADA THE "NEW FRONTIER" OF OPPORTUNITY?

My work on cycles in the Canadian dollar clearly suggests that both the Canadian dollar as well as the Canadian economy are rich with opportunity, even in the event of a long-term disinflation in the United States. There are a number of reasons for my opinion. Here are several of them:

1. Canada has a vast land mass that is, for the most part, still largely underdeveloped.
2. The country is rich in natural resources, such as minerals, petroleum, and agricultural commodities.
3. The Canadian government has become more liberal, and trade is expanding rapidly.

4. The population of Canada is very small compared with its land mass and resources. This suggests that per-capita income could rise dramatically if and when Canadian trade is more fully developed. The opportunities for foreign investment in Canada appear to be tremendous.

I am certain that there are many other reasons. I suggest that serious investors interested in long-term growth look to the north.

WILL THE INFLUENCE OF JAPAN DECLINE?

Japan has, for good reasons, been a dominant force in world trade for many years now. Its economy has grown by leaps and bounds. The Japanese are masters at competition. They are productive, hardworking, and technologically astute. However, their economy has grown very rapidly, overexpanding to the point of great concern. In the event of a significant recession or disinflation in the United States and Europe, demand for Japanese goods will decline substantially. Japanese plants will cut back, and there will be a chain reaction of failures the likes of which have never before been seen in Japan or even, perhaps, in the United States. The Japanese economy is highly vulnerable to a major economic peak unless measures are taken to scale back plants and resources and something is done to check the Japanese rate of inflation. But government controls are unlikely to work in Japan or anywhere else. I think that it's just a question of time before the Japanese economy begins a downturn that may make previous declines in the U.S. economy look tame by comparison.

IS REVOLUTION IN LATIN AMERICA INEVITABLE, AND HOW DOES THIS RELATE TO THE LONG WAVE?

Latin America is likely to undergo profound social and political change until well into the 1990s. The long-wave decline that should dominate most free-world economies is also likely to affect Latin America. The result could be more concern about survival than about social revolution. Following the long-wave lows, Latin America is likely to grow substantially as a world power, both in terms of political influence and of productivity. Latin America's natural resources are only now being developed. One hopes that this would not include the current trend toward deforestation and defoliation of vital jungle lands. This would have a serious environmental impact in the long run.

WHY IS DISCIPLINE IMPORTANT?

Much has been said in this book about virtually every aspect of the long wave and about economic cycles in general. I have provided myriad suggestions on how to protect your assets and how to help them grow in various economic climates. Yet I have said relatively little about discipline and its importance to the investor. This is such an important topic that several volumes would be needed to cover its many phases. In fact, I have already written two such books to which I refer you for further information (*The Investor's Quotient* and *Beyond the Investor's Quotient*, both published by Wiley and Sons, New York). Briefly, however, here are a few comments about discipline and its importance in a long-term investment program, particularly in times of crisis:

1. Any system, method, indicator, theory, advisory service, or investment program will be totally useless unless implemented with discipline and persistence.
2. Each individual must come to terms with his or her own discipline or lack thereof. There are many ways in which this can be achieved. Regardless of how you develop discipline, it is absolutely necessary that it be developed prior to the long-wave economic decline's taking full hold. Difficult times will severely test your discipline.
3. Inconsistency will cause you to make errors that may prove costly.
4. In order to avoid the errors that result from emotion and lack of discipline, develop an investing plan and follow it through.
5. Avoid falling prey to the influence of well-intentioned others, no matter how right they appear to be. Develop your own plan and implement it as closely to your ideal plan as possible.
6. Fear, greed, tension, guilt, euphoria, and doubt are all human qualities; however, they tend to be counterproductive in a successful investment program.

7. When the long wave is in full force, when markets are declining rapidly, when emotion reigns supreme, you will need to be in full control of yourself, implementing whatever plans you have made. To act on whim or emotion will more often than not produce losses.

   If you need more information on the above, then read my previously mentioned books on this subject. The time and money will be well spent, particularly if you know that discipline is one of your weak points.

WHAT CAN AN "EXPERT" DO FOR ME?

The odds are that an "expert" can't do anything for you that you cannot do for yourself. Although many individuals claim to be experts, they may learn otherwise when "the chips are really down." There is a growing tendency for people to visit financial planners and investment counselors. A majority of these individuals are not aware of the long-wave cycles, nor do they feel that the long-wave cycles could be an important factor in the years ahead. Therefore, unless you want stock answers, don't consult the "experts." If you feel that there is validity to the issues I've raised in this book, if you feel that the long wave could, in fact, become a serious force in the years ahead, then find an expert who feels as you do and investigate alternatives using some of the guidelines I've given you in this book.

IS THE U.S. BANKING SYSTEM SAFE?

What I've read and studied about the long wave has convinced me that the U.S. banking system and, perhaps, the world banking system are in serious trouble. Many major U.S. banks are plagued with loans to countries that are, for all intents and purposes, insolvent. These loans will never be repaid; they will eventually be written off as losses. In addition to uncollectable foreign loans, there are bad domestic loans, particularly by farm banks. Any further deterioration of the farm credit situation will result in default by many farmers. This will place additional pressure on the entire U.S. banking system.

The Federal Reserve System was created in order to avoid the problems that besieged the U.S. banking system during the last economic decline. Although the system does help provide some stability, it is doubtful that any serious chain reaction of bank failures or a major run on banks by depositors can be weathered by the system. In addition to bad foreign and domestic loans, the ratio of bank reserves to total obligations is dangerously low. If depositors run on the banks, demanding their money, then there will be very little ready capital to meet their demands.

In short, the U.S. banking system is in serious trouble. It's an accident waiting for a place to happen. The bank failures of the early to mid-1980s are likely to grow dramatically in the mid- to late 1990s.

WHAT OBJECTIVE CONDITIONS CAN YOU POINT TO AS INDICATIVE OF A FURTHER DECLINE IN THE U.S. ECONOMY?

Perhaps the best way I can summarize this is by again citing the excellent work of Donald Hoppe. In his February 1988 newsletter he noted the following conditions, all of which suggest a long-wave depression:

Conditions That Precede a Long-Wave Depression

1. Massive overbuilding in the capital goods sectors.
2. An unprecedented increase in debt at all levels, public, corporate and individual.
3. Severe problems in international debt.
4. An era of extremely reckless speculation followed by a stock market crash—"the worst crash in more than 50 years."
5. A boom and bust in agricultural commodities and farm land, resulting in great distress in the agricultural sector, with many failures and foreclosures.
6. Troubles in the banking system, with a rising curve of bank failures, beginning several years before the stock market crash.
7. A sharp rise in protectionist sentiment caused by increasing foreign competition and poor trade figures.
8. Producers of raw materials—oil, minerals and agricultural products—caught in a squeeze between high production costs and low

prices, aggravated by huge surpluses and excess productive capacity. Cartels (OPEC) and quota agreements prevalent in efforts to hold down production and hold up prices (they always fail in the end).

9. Retail stores jammed with merchandise, luxury items in heavy oversupply, price cutting and discounting rampant.

10. Huge rise in real estate prices during prior decade. Massive speculative building boom. Real estate market glutted with commercial and office properties.

11. Great increase in the number of people employed in the financial sector—stock brokers, bond salesmen, investment advisers, financial planners, fund managers, in-house traders, security analysts, etc. (Note: during the past five years, the number of registered stock brokers has more than doubled and now totals 440,000.)

12. Financial mania and speculative boom of prior decade not limited to one or two countries but worldwide. [February 1988, p. 17]

I conclude, as did Hoppe:

> In my opinion, the current period of apparent stability and recovery in the U.S. economy should be regarded only as the final opportunity to get one's financial affairs in order and to liquidate unsound, high risk or heavily mortgaged or marginal investments. . . . The current period of false optimism and false recovery is *exactly* parallel to what happened in the early months of 1930, following the Crash of 1929. [1988, p. 17]

WHAT'S A GOOD ALTERNATIVE TO PUTTING MONEY IN BANKS IF THE BANKING SYSTEM IS IN DANGER OF COLLAPSE?

Certainly, you could keep your money in a sock, or you could bury it in your backyard. However, there may be several more reasonable alternatives. Here are a few suggestions you might consider:

1. *U.S. Government Treasury bills* may not offer the highest possible percentage return, but they are likely to be among the safest of places for cash. In addition, you could consider Canadian Government Treasury bills. Generally speaking, any direct obligation of the U.S. Treasury should be relatively safe. If the government fails to honor

commitments on its direct obligations, then the country will most certainly fall prey to anarchy, and nothing will be safe.

2. *Money market mutual funds* that invest their shareholders' money in the various direct obligations of the U.S. Treasury can offer a slightly higher return. They should also be relatively safe from the problems that are likely to afflict the U.S. banking system.

3. *Funds in foreign currencies* might be considered an alternative; however, it is also likely that foreign economies will suffer if the U.S. economy is affected. Therefore, this might be a risky alternative at best.

4. *Gold and other precious metals mining stocks* might be a good place for a portion of your funds; however, they are just as likely to decline as are other investments unless legislation against the ownership of gold is enacted or decreed by government "crisis" measures.

5. *Futures trading* for those who are willing and able to accept the risk might be a reasonable place for a portion of funds. Although crises may force closing of some futures exchanges or suspension of trading, those who are nimble at speculation could profit handsomely by trading on the short side and/or by knowing when to jump into the markets in advance of short-lived, but potentially violent, corrective price upswings.

6. *Gold and precious metal bullion and/or coins* have already been discussed as vehicles that might make up a portion of your cash portfolio; however, as I've warned previously, they should not constitute the majority of your holdings. In fact, as things appear now, they should play only a secondary role in your overall investment strategy.

The issue of bank safety and the best possible place for funds is one that cannot fully be resolved at this time. So much depends upon government action, reaction, programs, and policies. If the past is any guide, then the foregoing suggestions will hold you in good stead. However, there is no telling what tricks the government may have up its sleeve or how desperate it will get. In the end, flexibility and adaptability are the best alternatives. They should be your main investment guidelines. The suggestions I've outlined here can be valuable;

however, they will not prove helpful in the event of a hyperinflationary blowoff (as previously discussed). This is why a balanced portfolio is advised.

IS HYPERINFLATION A POSSIBILITY?

It most certainly is! I doubt, however, that it will become reality. Although the U.S. government is gravely concerned about the current economic situation and is doing its best to resolve the massive budget deficit, it is well aware of the fact that to print its way out of debt is not a solution but rather a new problem. What it would be trying to do is to buy time by artificial expansion and contraction of the money supply and by the manipulation of interest rates. Though there is always the danger that during one of these manipulations government could lose control of the situation, causing a chain reaction of hyperinflation, the deflationary scenario is still of greater concern. Therefore, although hyperinflation is always a possibility, I do not see it as developing into a reality. History has shown that the danger of economic disinflation due to stringent and prolonged budget tightening is more of a concern than is hyperinflation.

HOW AND WHY DID YOU DECIDE ON THE TITLE OF THIS BOOK?

When I relax my mind allowing all I know about the economic situation to come to consciousness, I am stunned by a mental picture of the utter confusion, wild price gyrations, and hundreds of bureaucrats seated at their expensive desks, or in their budgetary meetings, all speaking different tongues. I think of the Tower of Babel, of a vehicle about to run off the edge of a cliff. I'm reminded also of the accompanying cartoon I saw recently in a local newspaper.

It appears very much to me that the U.S. economy is heading straight for the buzz saw, while the politicians argue. Once the damage has been done the foundation for a new order of prosperity will be in place. The "new prosperity" could very well provide unprecedented opportunities for profit and real economic growth.

Reprinted with permission of the Chicago Sun Times.

The problems I've discussed in this book are present, to varying degrees, in virtually every economy of the world—capitalist, socialist, and/or communist. They are correlators of "economic growth and progress." There is no nation, no leader, no people, no business, no market that will remain unaffected during the economic crises about to rip through all nations of the world. One by one, the economies of each nation will be called to the test. They will be tested more severely and thoroughly than ever before. Some will withstand the pressures and others will fail, plunging their populaces into confusion and their markets into turmoil.

I sincerely hope that my forecasts and analyses will not come to pass. Yet my brain tells me that hope is not the proper emotion. Hope is a sign that we are not dealing with a situation intellectually, that we may be denying reality. We must come to grips with reality, and we must be honest with ourselves. P. D. Ouspensky, the Russian philosopher whose work, like that of Kondratieff, has been rejected by many of his peers, made great sense when he wrote the following sage words about the way in which humankind can evolve to a higher psychology:

> The truth lies in the fact that before acquiring any *new* faculties or powers which man does not know and does not possess now, he must acquire faculties and powers he *also does not possess*, but which he ascribes to himself; that is, he thinks that he knows them and can use and control them.
>
> This is the missing link, and *this is the most important point.*
>
> By way of evolution, as described before, that is, a way based on effort and help, man must acquire qualities which he thinks he already possesses, but about which he deceives himself.
>
> In order to understand this better, and to know what are these faculties and powers which man can acquire, both quite new and unexpected and also those which he imagines that he already possesses, we must begin with man's general knowledge about himself. . . . [1974, p. 11]

We must admit to what we know is truth. Sooner or later there will come a day of economic reckoning. Those who are prepared will survive the flood, as did Noah. But in order to do so we will need to have our financial boat prepared, stocked, and ready to confront the waters. The economic storms have already started. The rain is still falling, but still lightly; however, in the not-too-distant future it is likely to grow to a torrent. Our economic system will be unable to bear the burden of the storm and may collapse, giving way to the flood waters. Our boat will need to be ready, but most of all, we will need to know where to guide it and how to navigate it. This book can help point you in several historically reliable directions, but only you can prepare, equip, and navigate your vehicle before the flood waters rage.

HOW HIGH MIGHT UNEMPLOYMENT GO?

If history is any guide to the future, then unemployment should rise dramatically, as layoff after layoff reverberates through world economies like waves of thunder. Many layoffs have already started. Large corporations have cut back on employees, laying off workers and eliminating middle-management positions. They recognize the fact that in order to survive they will need to be "lean." They will need to be conservative. They will need to cut back on spending in order to meet the challenge of reduced profits and sales. In the meantime, unemployment compensation provided by the government can go only so far to remedy the situation. Eventually the rising trend of unemployment should spread like an uncontrollable virus through every social class and stratum. Hardest hit will be the middle-management white-collar worker and the blue-collar worker. I suspect that unemployment could rise to all-time highs.

TO MAINTAIN A POSITION SUCH AS YOU HAVE DESCRIBED IN THIS BOOK IS BOTH UNPATRIOTIC AND LIKELY TO BECOME SELF-FULFILLING. WHAT'S YOUR RESPONSE?

What you have read in this book is merely one person's opinion. But it is an opinion based on many years of research and upon the writings of accomplished market analysts and economists. The founding principles upon which the United States and most so-called free-world governments are based include respect for truth and for the right to express opinions, no matter how contrary they may be to popularly accepted notions. A great majority of the world's most respected leaders have, at great personal risk, expressed opinions directly in opposition to popularly accepted opinions.

It is unpatriotic to sit idly by and watch the economic decay of the West while people the world over suffer as a consequence. Even here in the United States people want for food and shelter, a situation that should not exist in a nation with such vast agricultural and financial resources. To permit such inequities to continue is unpatriotic. To turn a deaf ear on the obvious sounds of an economy's "going under for the last time" is unpatriotic. But to express thoughts with honesty, clarity, and supporting evidence is a service both to country and to humanity.

Regarding the question of "self-fulfilling prophecies," the idea is absurd. If millions of investors the world over were to read this book, and if they were all to act on its ideas immediately, then there might be a minor reaction in the markets, and some of my forecasts might become self-fulfilling, but neither is likely to happen. The vast majority of those reading this book are likely to be victims of indolence. They will read my words, reacting with "That's interesting, but . . ." It will give them something to talk about at their next party or PTA meeting. Still another percentage of my readers will lack the discipline and/or organization to do anything about their personal financial situations. Then, of course, there will be disbelievers, the critics, and the detractors, who will not be swayed at all by what I have said.

Therefore, I conclude that the possibility of my forecasts becoming self-fulfilling is virtually nil. I cannot, through my words, create a negative situation. This situation has already been created by decades of government mismanagement and administration after administration of "buck passing" and political expediency. No, my friends, I cannot make things worse than they are. I can only hope that you will have the power, discipline, and motivation to make them better.

HOW CAN I HELP EFFECT MORE PERVASIVE CHANGE IN GOVERNMENT POLICY?

I'd like to tell you that it's not too late to do something on a federal or state level about the problems I've discussed. But alas, *I fear that it is too late.* I could easily give you a list of ideal cures or solutions to the problems that face us. Yet this would be a fruitless exercise. Why? Because only through concerted, prompt, and persistent action could anything be changed with sufficient dispatch. It is so very late in the game and in the cycle that only through a major shift in political action and strategy could anything be achieved. In other words, I'm saying that it is truly too late. I could tell you that our economic problems would be solved if the United States were to return to gold standard. I could tell you that the problems could be solved if a balanced budget became a reality. But even if it did, it would take time. Yet time is working against us because we have bought so much of it for so long that the supply is about gone, and the money with which to buy time is also gone. Consequently, I cannot recommend any concerted group or political action because I know it to be an idealistic thought. If there are individuals who have the power to act, if there are groups that can meaningfully affect government, thereby prompting swift legislation designed to change the underlying economic woes, then let them come forward! Let them take immediate action. But in the interim, I suggest that you straighten up your own house, resolving your personal finances and planning on your own. It's every person for him- or herself. And that's how it must be until and unless more pervasive actions are taken by government. But remember that the time to act is nearly gone!

HOW ACCURATE ARE THE CYCLES?

I have made every effort to portray cycles in realistic terms. The use of cycles for forecasting long-term and/or short-term trends is by no means a panacea to the problem of prediction. Cycles have their very clear limitations. They are not perfect, nor are they regular. Yet for all their limitations, cycles can allow the experienced practitioner to make some highly accurate forecasts about trends and about the potential for changes in trends within given time frames. If we know in advance that cycles are not the ultimate forecasting tool, then we can cope with their inaccuracies. The combination of cycles, timing, and history can, however, compensate for the inaccuracy of cycles. Although it may be tempting to ignore one of these three factors in preference to another, or to look only at those facts that support our expectations and wishes, neither makes good sense from an investment standpoint. Remember the following general guidelines in connection with cycles and you will not be disappointed by their performance:

1. *Cycles are accurate only within a given period of time or "time window."* They can be as much as 15 percent early or 15 percent late (at times even earlier or later than the 15 percent window). This, however, should not be a major concern if you use other methods of pinpointing a more precise time for entering or exiting given investments and/or markets.
2. *Never use cycles as the only factor in your investment timing.* The sole purpose of a long-term cycle is to get you near the anticipated time frame of a turn in trend.
3. *There are cycles in virtually every market*, every statistic, and every natural phenomenon. Don't restrict your study to only one cycle in one area; rather, attempt to become familiar with as many cycles as you possibly can.

4. *Study the interaction of cycles* and attempt to construct scenarios of future economic activity based on the interaction of different cycles.

5. *Remember that significant social, political, and military events* can and will alter both the timing and magnitude of cycles.

6. *Keep current on the latest in cyclic research.* Perhaps the most efficient and economical way to do this is by becoming a member of the Foundation for the Study of Cycles, or by reading their publication regularly.[2]

7. *Keep current on news events, government actions and policies, and on market activity.* Correlate these with the major cycles to see if the cycles are acting as expected.

8. *Remember that cyclic trends tend to change* when news and events are in a period of great change and high volatility. Opinions will often be the most optimistic at cyclic peaks and the most pessimistic at cyclic bottoms. Use this knowledge to your advantage.

HOW IMPORTANT IS IT TO MONITOR INTEREST RATE TRENDS?

Earlier in this book I indicated that long-term and short-term interest rates are important barometers of current and anticipated economic activity. This is particularly true when interest rates are at extreme highs or lows. I have given you some trend projections for short-term and long-term interest rates. Study these on your own in order to establish an understanding of the cycles and patterns. But beyond this, take the time to study each of the interest rate cycles as far back in time as you can, determining the correlates of rising, falling, and stagnating interest rates.

The early- and mid-decade patterns I've discussed in short-term and long-term interest rates can be very valuable to you. This is why I suggest that every investor study trends of interest rates as well as their cycles and patterns. By knowing when interest rate trends are about to change, you will be able to make more timely and well-planned invest-ments and business decisions. If you act on the emotion of interest rates, then you will be no better off than those who all around you are losing their heads.

[2]Foundation for the Study of Cycles, 3333 Michelson Drive #210, Irvine, CA 92715.

WHY IS ORGANIZATION IMPORTANT?

Though the answer is obvious, I cannot say enough about the importance and value of organization. Many investors approach their finances in a random and/or disorganized fashion. They make investments on the basis of whims, tips, or wishful thinking. Few investors are totally aware of their financial condition, assets, and/or liabilities at any given point in time. Such lack of awareness may not be detrimental in times of economic growth when all trends favor the long side, but in times of economic crisis, disorganization goes hand in hand with lack of discipline. The result is often confusion and indecision. If and when an economic crisis or series of crises develops, you will be unprepared to make fast decisions if you are disorganized. If you're not organized, then get organized. Here are some of the key elements of organization to assist you in attaining this important goal:

1. Keep an up-to-date portfolio of all your investments.
2. List the purchase price and current profit or loss of all investments.
3. List your objectives, either in time or price, for all investments.
4. Have a specific idea of your risk and where you plan to exit each investment if it fails to perform as anticipated.
5. Know how much of your assets are available for additional investment.
6. Know your liabilities—in particular, how much you owe and whom you owe it to.
7. Establish long-range, intermediate-range, and short-range investment goals.
8. Make certain you keep all records timely by updating them at least once weekly.
9. Refer to your list often.
10. Before you make any investment and/or commitment of cash, know where it fits into your plan, and know why you are making the investment. This will help verify your decisions.
11. If what you have decided is clearly not within the constraints of your program, then take this as an indication that you are probably off the track and may be making a mistake.

Organization is important, as it will keep you in line with your program. If, however, you are disorganized, you are more likely to act on impulse, on incomplete information, and out of fear or greed. These are all behaviors or emotions that will get you into trouble.

WHAT CAN I READ IF I WANT TO LEARN MORE ABOUT THE LONG-WAVE CYCLES?

Virtually any of the books I've referred to either in the chapters of this book or in the reference list will be valuable in your continuing long-wave education. I suggest that you begin with an understanding of history, however, inasmuch as this will allow you to fit events into the long-wave perspective. Read the *Cambridge Economic History of Europe*. Although it is a massive compilation of information contained in several volumes, it is *must reading* for serious students of economic history. You can then round out your studies with any of several books (see references at the end of this book) on U.S. economic history. You can take whatever direction you wish thereafter.

As you read on, you will find certain topics that interest you more than others. You can select your readings with deliberation, paying specific attention to the topics that most concern your investments; or you can meander through the many choices that await you. Regardless of what you decide, it will prove time well spent.

Finally, I suggest that you spend some time reading some of the more current writings of long-wave theorists such as Jay W. Forrester. I recommend highly *The Kondratieff Wave Analyst*, published regularly by Don Hoppe.[3] I am certain that many other questions may have occurred to you in the course of your reading this book. While I do not have the space to answer all relevant questions, I have covered a good majority of them in the preceding pages. If, however, there are still vital questions to which you cannot find answers, then please drop me a line and I will do my best to respond.[4] However, I suggest that you first attempt to find the answer(s) on your own, inasmuch as this will be the best way for you to learn.

[3]Hoppe, Donald J., *The Kondratieff Wave Analyst*, Box 977, Crystal Lake, IL 60014.

[4]Author can be reached at P.O. Box 353, Winnetka, IL 60093.

Chapter 13

Toward a New Prosperity

For it is my belief no man ever understands quite his own artful dodges to escape from the grim shadow of self-knowledge.

—Joseph Conrad
Lord Jim

The history of humankind teaches that attitudes, theories, and behavior are slow to change. Although science may generate findings that appear, on the surface, to have far-reaching implications, both beneficial and detrimental, changes are frequently slow in their development unless necessity dictates that they be faster. The AIDS crisis, for example, has prompted a host of investigatory responses in virtually all areas of medical and biological research. In order to discover a cure or preventive, new areas of science are being probed for answers. Ultimately, if an answer is to be found it will likely come from those involved in genetic engineering. Yet, were it not for the emerging epidemic and its serious implications for the human race, AIDS research would still be progressing at a relative snail's pace. But research in and of itself does not ensure that a cure will be discovered for AIDS any more than it has meant a cure for cancer. There is no one-to-one relationship between energy, cost expended, and results when it comes to medical progress.

The fact that we cannot find cures for these and other diseases does not mean that the cures do not exist or that they are not readily available with present technology and knowledge. Rather, it could very well be true that we have not put the pieces of the puzzle together correctly, or that we have the wrong pieces for the puzzle we are attempting to solve. When we consider economic history and its problems in the terms discussed above, then we may begin to think of past, present, and future as more closely related than commonly thought. Although contemporary economists may advance the notion that with increased computer power, advanced statistical methods, and new theories current economic woes as well as yesterday's severe conditions may be minimized, this is not necessarily true. If there were any truth to the contention that economics and social science were contributing to the growth of humankind, then crime would be on the decline, hunger would be virtually nonexistent, world economies would not be in a state of disarray, and domestic conditions would not be in their present disheveled state. "We need more research in order to get better answers," we are told by academia. "We need more money for more research," they tell us. And they have been getting both for many years now, but the results have been slow in coming and even slower in their implementation. Even if reasonably promising answers were being turned out by economists and their scientific peers, it is most likely that government, in its inefficient and politically inept condition, could not implement these changes with even the most minute degree of success.

Unfortunately, economics and social science are neither as operationally defined or as procedurally precise as are medicine and physical science. Hence, answers to problems are not as readily defined as they might be in medicine. Discovering the cure to a congenital disease is less of a guessing game than is the process of finding a cause for economic or social problems. Any economist, psychologist, political scientist, criminologist, or sociologist who claims that cures and causes are either definitive or operational is talking in his or her sleep, prompted by a Utopian dream. Any any government that claims to have the economy "under control" is deceiving itself and/or the public. Any politician who campaigns under the promise of a "balanced budget" or "near full employment" or, for that matter, any other of the many meaningless political epigrams is merely a demagogue in a business suit. The fact is, has been, and will probably always be that economics is not something we can control any more than we control the weather, public opinion, or the revolution of the planets. Efforts at control may have their momentary impact, yet depending on the force applied to effect the desired change, the ultimate result will usually be destructive.

Furthermore, any financial advisor, business analyst, financial planner, or market messiah who comes forward with "the" answer to "the problem" is, perhaps, even more dangerous than is the political bungler who in his or her own pathetic way makes promises and attempts to take actions that are misdirected, ineffectual, or totally unrelated to the problem(s). This is true whether we are talking about Keynesian economics, supply-side economics, Sarkar's Law, and/or Marxism. My studies of economics, history, sociology, religion, and psychology have led me to the conclusion that there has always been a vast schism between theory and practice when it comes to human issues such as those that affect virtually anything other than our medical and biological processes. While the physical sciences have been able to achieve a fairly advanced state of understanding and results based on cause and effect, the social sciences have not been able to attain such a status inasmuch as the "stuff" with which they deal is not primarily tangible. Rather, the essence of social science is psychological, emotional, political, and somewhat instinctual, as opposed to biological and/or chemical. It is interesting to note that even such processes as disease, which were once felt to be totally biological, are now coming to be seen as affected by the emotional and psychical. Since the 1960s there has been a growing body of medical, anecdotal, and psychological evidence that mind and body interact in ways heretofore unacknowledged or denied. *Love, Medicine and Miracles*,[1] the recent bestseller by Bernie Siegel, M.D., is merely one example of our expanding awareness of the mind–body interactive process. Siegel notes:

> Western science has only just begun to study the effects of meditation and visualization on disease, although the interrelationships among the brain, endocrine glands, and immune system . . . are probably the way these effects occur. Perhaps the most direct research was a 1976 pilot study by Gurucharan Singh Khalsa, founder of Boston's Kundalini Research Institute. The study, conducted at the Veterans Administration hospital in La Jolla, California, showed that regular yoga and meditation

[1]Siegel, B., M.D., *Love, Medicine and Miracles*, Harper & Row Publishers, NY, 1986, pp. 150–51.

increased blood levels of three important immune-system hormones by
100 percent. Unfortunately, this work could only be done with a few test
subjects, and funds have not yet been granted to follow it up.

All the research to date indicates that the power drive, with its
constant anxieties, continually activates the sympathetic (excitatory)
part of the body's nervous system, with a consequent deactivation of the
parasympathetic (calming) nerves. This in turn keeps the fight-or-flight
stress response of adrenaline continually switched on, diminishing the
body's ability to respond to another stress, such as illness. Harvard
psychology professor David C. McClelland recently found that individuals motivated by power had lower levels of immunoglobulin A in
their saliva than those motivated by concern for others. . . .

Mind affects body, and mind affects economic behavior. Most
theories of economics begin with the result and construct a model to
explain what has happened. They look at statistics rather than motivation; they examine government policies as opposed to the reasons for
those policies; they begin with a fixed idea of supply and demand
without consideration of intervening variables; they fail to treat economic systems as if they were biological systems; and this is where they
fail. Yet, I cannot claim that my understandings, interpretations, and
forecasts will be any more reliable than those that have come before.
Indeed, what I have proposed in this book is drawn from a variety of
sources and understandings. It is more holistic than theoretical; it has as
its core historical and human reality as opposed to academic ivy-tower
theory, dialectic determinism, or suggestions for change that emanate
from the teachings of an Eastern prophet. It is likely that every one of
these understandings has some truth in it, but it is also unlikely that any
single approach will provide a majority of the necessary answers. Virtually every theory, method, system analysis, or econometric analysis
has failed to stress the importance of the individual, the group, and mass
behavior. Few approaches have stressed the importance of cyclical
behavior, patterns, and price relationships. Even the analyses and
relationships I've explained in this book are still in their infancy and
remain somewhat incomplete. My hope is that the ideas in this book—
some of which are mine by origin, and others drawn from experts in
their own right—will inspire further research, analyses, and discovery.
And I hope that this will be done before too much more time has
elapsed, because time is now the single most valuable commodity in
existence, and it is a commodity we cannot possess or acquire. Past,
present, and future are all entwined into one process. Past becomes

present and future. Future will, in many respects, be like past and present. Cycles and patterns will repeat, once the players change. Although events may differ in their precise nature, timing, and interaction, economies will still grow, mature, degenerate, and regenerate in the age-old process they have exhibited since time immemorial. We cannot know as much about the "why" or the "wherefore" of this process as we would like. We cannot necessarily affect the process in the ways we would like. We cannot halt one stage or eliminate it in favor of lengthening or enhancing another any more than we can achieve eternal youth or unending bliss. A constantly growing economy with full employment, no poverty, limited inflation, and stable finances is a hedonistic dream. Such thoughts are dreams, wishes, hallucinations.

As long as we understand that we are dealing with chance and that there are no definitive laws or rules of economic behavior, we will fare well. Remember that what I have presented in this book consists of various patterns, ideas, relationships, and cycles. There are not guarantees, as I have repeatedly stated, that all of the ideas, forecasts, and opinions presented herein will be correct. Yet I have every confidence, every reason to believe, that within reasonable limits the general course of future events will be essentially similar to the expectations and forecasts I've given you. Tomorrow should be basically the same as yesterday, and today should be understood in terms of yesterday and in consideration of the economic life cycles and their stages. In writing the final pages of this long-range forecast, I'd like to leave you with the following ideas, hoping that you will take the time to evaluate them and, if you find them worthwhile, to integrate them with your investment policies and programs as best you can. Remember that although I do not feel that any economic theory, political party, or series of actions will prevent the ultimate economic collapse and restructure, I do know that you can take the necessary actions to protect yourself, your family, and your business. Indeed, the correct and proper actions at or close to the right times will allow you to prosper even while many of those around you are failing with the system that has bred their perception and behavior. Here are the essential principles and structural elements that I would like you to keep foremost in mind as you prepare to enter the age of the "new prosperity":

1. The international and domestic economic structures are in danger of total collapse in the 1990s. Whereas the deterioration that will ultimately lead to the anticipated collapse varies from one nation

to another and from one economy to another, it will eventually afflict all nations, first-, second-, and third-world alike, whether socialist, communist, or democratic.

2. There is virtually no way for governments, political leaders, or the public as a whole to avert the crises that await us in the years ahead. Although there was a time when appropriate and responsible actions could have been taken, years of excesses, procrastination, and political self-interest have been given primary consideration, and the time for preventive action has long passed.

3. Although governments appear to be responsible for the current extreme state of affairs, it is ultimately the people who elected these governments who must take the responsibility for what has come to pass. Yet the people cannot be admonished too harshly inasmuch as the process has been a slow and relentless one, just as is the process of erosion by water and wind on the geographical structures of the Earth.

4. The process of birth, growth, maturity, decline, decay, and eventual rebirth is a natural economic process that has been with us since prior to the beginning of recorded history. Evidence for this process can be found in the teachings, writings, and historical records of civilizations past and present. The future will likely be essentially similar to the present and the past in terms of the cycles, stages, and phases.

5. Whole economic history does appear to repeat itself, but it rarely repeats in precisely the same fashion, at precisely the same time, or with exactly the same degree of intensity of magnitude. Kondratieff and others have proposed theories built upon historical evidence and precedent that help delineate the various long-wave cycles and their stages. Though these theories and findings are subject to debate, as are most theories in the social sciences, they not only make sense, but they also have considerable statistical verification by Jay W. Forrester and others, and they make sense from a strictly pragmatic point of view. Ultimately, their value will be determined by their predictive validity.

6. Given the existence of cycles and patterns, both long term and intermediate term, it is reasonable to assume that timing and time are more important than price and price level. If, therefore, the approximate time to take action is right, then the price at which to

take action must also, therefore, be right, regardless of what that price may be. Investors would do better ultimately to pay more attention to timing rather than to price.

7. There are seasonal and cyclical patterns in virtually all prices, indicators, indices, and markets. Knowing these patterns in advance can provide valuable information on timing not only for the speculator and investor but for the businessperson as well. It behooves us, therefore, to be students of price patterns and price relationships, analyzing as much historical evidence and data as possible prior to taking decisive action.

8. The study of economic history is a quintessential aspect in the thorough understanding of current economic turmoil and in the mapping out of future economic policies and individual investment decisions.

9. It is highly unlikely that governments can act to prevent or minimize the events that I have forecast. This is due to a variety of reasons, not the least among which are self-interest, corruption, disorganization, lack of cohesive or rational policies, and a painfully slow response time.

10. Governments, whether socialist, communist, or democratic, no longer represent the will of the people. If they did, then there would be more cooperation, open dialogue among nations, and considerably more cooperation toward the goals of world peace, elimination of hunger by maximization of resources, and stable economic structures.

11. In view of the above, and in consideration of the cataclysmic economic events that are slowly but surely inching their way to realization, it is up to each and every individual to take the actions necessary to preserve capital and/or to prosper in spite of the coming economic upheaval.

12. Various ideas for specific investment strategies are presented with the understanding that each individual has different assets, liabilities, needs, objectives, and goals. Hence, no blanket statement about specific investments is possible. Instead, various guidelines and alternatives are given with the understanding that they must be adapted to each individual's situation. In so doing, such things as age, tax bracket, long-range needs, current liabilities and assets, and investments must be considered.

13. Until the long-wave economic cycle has bottomed, the primary goal of all investment strategies will be upon safety of funds. Should world economies experience a severe contraction such as the one described in previous chapters, then the stability of banks, currencies, and governments will be threatened. Many institutions and governments may fail. Many municipalities, individuals, businesses, and debtors will be unable to meet their obligations. The safety of invested funds will, therefore, be in jeopardy. Safety of funds must be the primary consideration during the current long-wave stage.

14. Cash is likely to be "king," as it has been in previous long-wave declining phases. Therefore, cash and cash equivalents, highly liquid investments, and deflation-responsive investments are the areas of choice. A number of these were discussed in this book; however, you can obtain considerably more information from your financial planner or advisor, provided he or she shares your expectations.

15. Economic realities and investments notwithstanding, emotion and psychology are equally important. Panic, fear, and financial uncertainty are likely to erode investor self-confidence and confidence in government and private financial institutions. The ensuing result will be felt on an emotional and psychological level as well as on an economic, social, and political level.

16. At this juncture it is entirely possible that the other alternative will be called into action—namely, that of hyperinflation. This is still considered a remote possibility, yet as remote as it may be, there are specific investment strategies designed to take advantage of this alternative. Several have been suggested here. The reader can easily determine the proper course of action in such an event.

17. There are many other ramifications—social, religious, political, and military—of the long wave. The "bottom war" looms ahead. Events are certainly pointing in this direction, and we can only hope and pray that the coming bottom war will not bring with it Armageddon.

18. Political events, international and domestic developments across a broad front, are likely to fall into place as forecast by the long-wave stage analysis I have presented herein. When events occur, don't ask, "Why?"; rather, ask, "What does this event tell us about the

current stage of the long wave?" I am certain that you will not be too surprised by any event once you know, based on the long-wave stages, what to expect.

There are many other things you will need to remember in the coming days, weeks, months, and years of turmoil, which, unfortunately, cannot be made more promising by virtually any unilateral government action. Although I have done my best to prepare you, the final actions and responses are up to you. You have a clear and unmistakable choice: Either you will react as governments do, or you will anticipate and plan as you should do. By being prepared you will avoid many unpleasant surprises. Tomorrow can bring with it destruction, grief, and financial ruin, or it can be the age of "new prosperity" for those who are courageous enough to act now and for those who have the staunch individualistic qualities that the new prosperity will require. To run with the crowd will be to run with the lemmings. To go against the popular misconceptions, to buck the tide of strong sentiment, will be difficult, but it will be the only logical choice, particularly when emotions run high, with panic as the result. But fear not what tomorrow will bring; whether inflation, disinflation, stagnation, "stagflation," hyperinflation, or depression, preparation, self-confidence, planning, organization, knowledge, and action will hold you in good stead. Once the cataclysm has come and gone, whether slow and erosive or quick and paroxysmal, the phoenix will rise from the ashes to be reborn, and the cycle will continue.

Finally, let's assume that I am wrong. Let's assume that the world economic situation will continue indefinitely in its present condition and on its present course. If this is to be the case, then I am certain you will still find the cycles, my historical perspective, and my investment strategies valid and suitable for the conservative investor. While I am not in a position, and never will be in the position to guarantee the future, I do know that understanding the past facilitates our ability to cope with and master the future.

Chapter 14

Epilogue

Since completion of *The New Prosperity* manuscript, there have been a number of domestic and international developments, all of which have added to or confirmed various aspects, forecasts, and/or expectations originally advanced in the chapters you have just read! As you can easily imagine, it is difficult—if not actually impossible—to keep a book such as this completely up-to-date. New conditions and events bring increasingly swift responses in the economic environment. A good majority of these will, I hope, be sufficiently close to the expectations I have given in the preceding pages. Some events may, at first blush, seem incongruous with the theory and forecasts I have presented. Yet, upon further study and examination, you may find them clearly consistent with what I have foretold on the basis of my studies.

Late 1988 and early 1989 have brought with them many events that are clearly consistent with my interpretations and expectations, based on the cyclical theories I described heretofore in this book. What follows is an update.

BUSH VICTORY LIKELY TO LEAD TO INCREASED CONSERVATISM

Long-wave theory, as I have explained and interpreted it, suggests that from the late 1980s through the mid-1990s the United States and, in fact, most "free-world" nations are likely to experience a trend in the direction of increased conservatism. Such conservatism has been in process and clearly evident in the United States since the early 1980s. There has been a significant diminution in vociferous civil rights movements, a marked increase in right-wing protests, and increased visibility by such groups as the American Nazi Party; rising protests against abortion and talk of repealing liberal abortion laws; considerable efforts to control illicit drug traffic as witnessed by "zero tolerance"; and growing conservative judge appointments to the Supreme Court. Could zero tolerance foreshadow the type of enforcement that sought to crush alcohol during the prohibition days? Based on recent events such as these, my forecast of a growing conservative trend is still valid.

WILL "PEACE" EFFORTS BRING WAR?

Late 1988 and early 1989 have witnessed a number of events that could bring the world closer to peace, or could they? These developments are as follows:

1. "Glasnost" in the Soviet Union has placed the Soviets on a course that could enhance their image and strength in international dealings. This could, therefore, increase their competitiveness among China, Central Europe, and the United States. The end result could be more conflict; conflict prompted by economic motivation as opposed to ideological disagreement. Economic conflict could lead to war just as easily as could other forms of conflict.

2. "Peace" efforts in the Mideast have seemingly been advanced by overtures of the PLO. Israel is likely to be pressured into negotiations that could lead it to make concessions that are not totally acceptable. The same could be true for the PLO and the Arab states. The resulting peace may be a "shaky" one at best. The end result could *increase* prospects for a war rather than *decrease* them. Participants who may be frustrated at possible failures or unexpected inequities in a new peace may be more apt to engage in armed conflict than they were previously. Frustration often leads to aggression.

3. Peace initiatives from Libya in early 1989 may prove to be nothing more than a Trojan Horse. Libyan terrorism and demagoguery are

among the most serious threats to world peace. The "bottom war" of which I have written could very well be precipitated by hostile Libyan actions against the United States.

4. As the economic power of Japan and the other Far Eastern nations increases, so do their imperialists' designs. The need for more land mass, more resources, and more labor is likely to prompt militaristic encroachment on neighboring nations. This could facilitate the necessary conditions for a bottom war. The positive elements of prosperity are not easily relinquished if threatened.

In my estimation, the power stalemate that existed from the 1960s to the early 1980s paradoxically may have been more conducive to keeping the peace than would the frustration of failed peace efforts.

JAPANESE ECONOMIC STABILITY

I have no doubt that Japan has become the leading world economic power. Not only have Japanese banking institutions taken control of a good portion of the free-world's capital, but they have also been a dominant leading force in the wave of U.S. leveraged buyouts.

Japanese holdings of U.S. real estate, U.S. manufacturing corporations, and U.S. financial institutions are increasing at a rapid pace. The statistics are staggering. What does that mean? As long as the Japanese economy continues to grow; as long as there is no credit or cash "crunch" in Japan, there will be few problems. But a reversal in the Japanese uptrend may bring with it a contraction that could cause Japanese investors to liquidate their holdings for whatever price they will bring. The resulting domino effect of declining prices could reverberate through the free-world economy, as Japanese investors liquidate in panic.

The Japanese stock market has remained strong into early 1989. Speculation is now on a significant upswing in Japan. Stock-manipulation scandals are on the increase. Japanese consumers are beginning to feel the "pinch" of inflation. With each passing day, the prospects of a Japanese economic and stock panic are increasing. Such a panic could rock the very foundation of other world economies as did the stock market "Crash of '87."

INTEREST RATES

Consistent with their 9–11-year cycle, interest rates have started an upswing (see Figures 14.1 and 14.2), which should peak in 1989 or in early 1990. The uptrend in interest rates is, therefore, not unexpected and suggests only a minor inflationary recovery. If the 50–60-year long-wave interest rate cycle is on schedule, interest rates should again begin to decline, penetrating their 1985 lows and bottoming again in the mid-1990s along with a host of other economic phenomena.

HYPERINFLATION OR DISINFLATION: AN UPDATE

I have mentioned earlier (Chapter 4) that the current massive U.S. debt situation can be liquidated in either of several ways. First, we can attempt to spend our way out of debt by furthering Keynesian policies, but this may eventually lead to a hyperinflation. Second, we can attempt to "balance the budget," cutting back on spending, wherever and whenever possible. This is not an untenable proposition. In fact, the new Bush administration has already indicated its intention to do so. Given the magnitude of debt, however, it would take severe and continuing austerity measures, which will not sit well either with the public or with politicians. Unless we are willing to"bite the bullet" for many years, making spending cuts, decreasing welfare programs across the board, eliminating most foreign aid, and curtailing new defense expenditures, this alternative is not viable.

Recently, the Treasury decided to bail out failing U.S. Savings and Loan Institutions, which will add billions of dollars to an already incomprehensible large national debt. This bailout merely compensates for problems that are the result of insolvencies created by the first wave of illiquidity, which occurred from the early to mid-1980s. What will they do when the next wave comes? Can economic austerity and a balanced budget be consistent with continued bank bailouts? Can a balanced budget be consistent with continued expansion and military spending and growing costs of the Social Security administration? Is the balanced budget, therefore, a realistic possibility? The third, and most unpalatable alternative is the liquidation of debts through default

Figure 14-1. *Upswing in short-term interest rates, 1985–1988.*

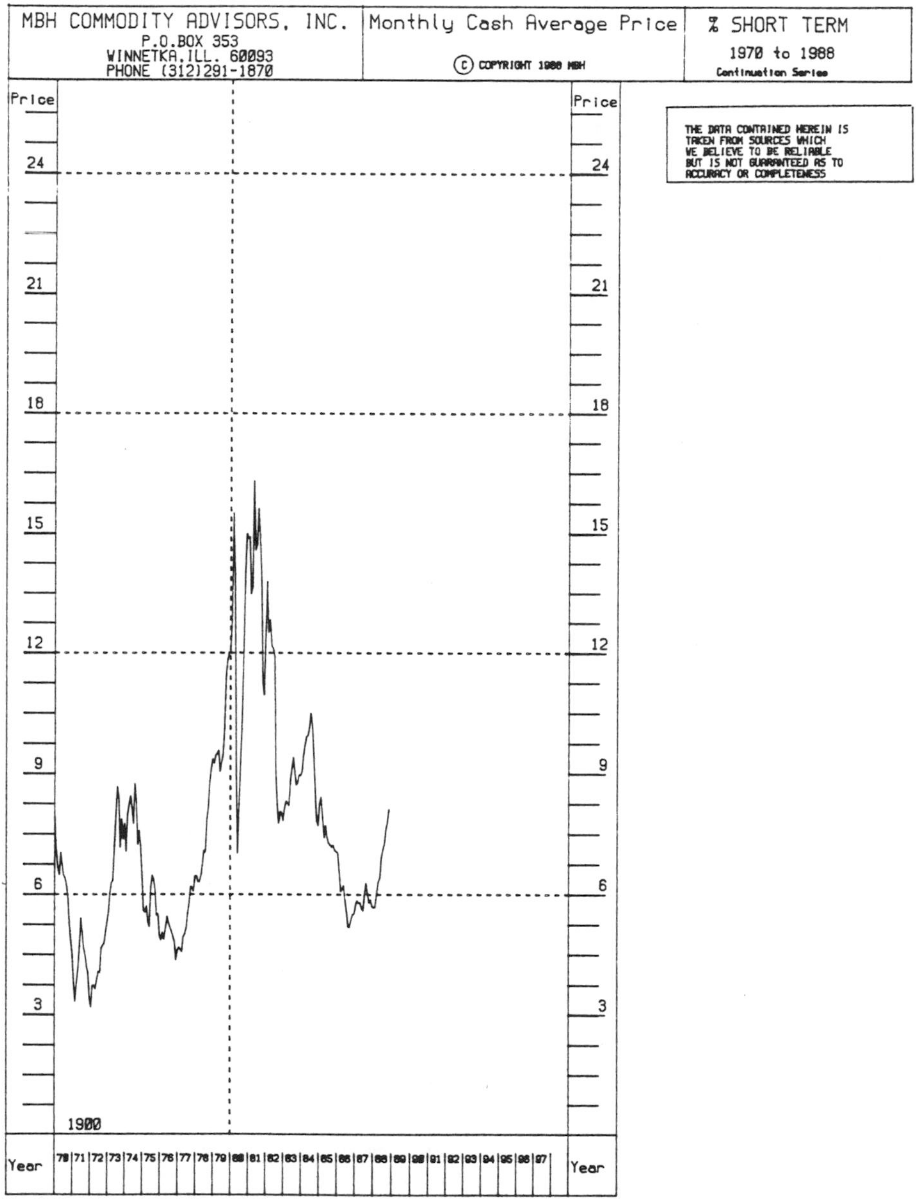
MBH COMMODITY ADVISORS, INC.
P.O.BOX 353
WINNETKA,ILL. 60093
PHONE (312)291-1870
Monthly Cash Average Price
© COPYRIGHT 1988 MBH
% SHORT TERM
1970 to 1988
Continuation Series
THE DATA CONTAINED HEREIN IS TAKEN FROM SOURCES WHICH WE BELIEVE TO BE RELIABLE BUT IS NOT GUARANTEED AS TO ACCURACY OR COMPLETENESS
Price
24
21
18
15
12
9
6
3
1900
Year
70 71 72 73 74 75 76 77 78 79 80 81 82 83 84 85 86 87 88 89 90 91 92 93 94 95 96 97

Figure 14-2. *Upswing in long-term interest rates, 1985–1988.*

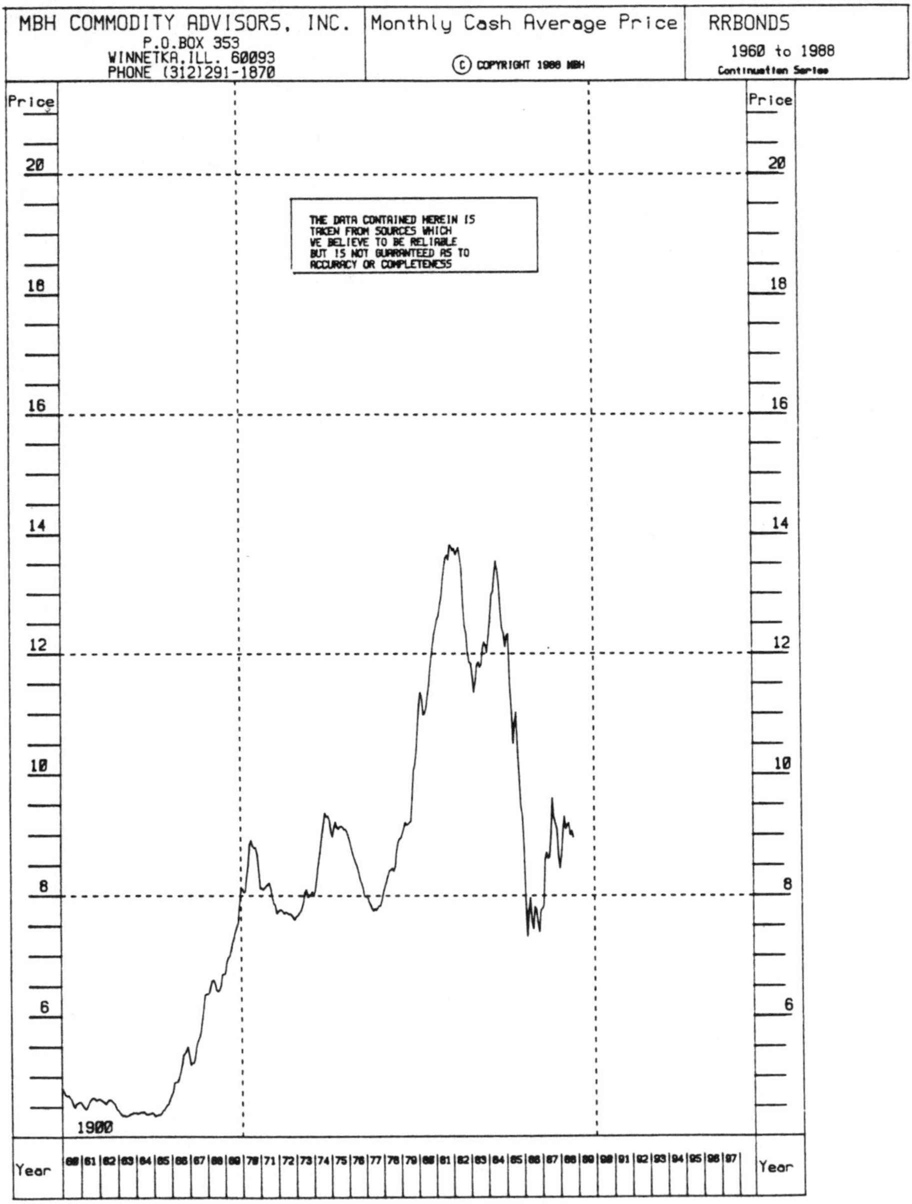

which is still the most likely possibility based on my understanding of the situation. Should the Bush administration demonstrate an unwillingness to continue its support of failing institutions, either in the private sector or in the banking industry, we will have ample initial evidence that a repudiation of debt has started.

Since I finished writing Chapters 1–13 of *The New Prosperity*, virtually nothing has changed for the better. Keep your eyes and ears open for events that fall into my pattern of expectation. Those who wish to remain abreast of my current thinking are encouraged to write me at P.O. Box 353, Winnetka, IL 60093 for information on my monthly K-Wave Tape Series, which is designed to keep my forecast and expectations current.

In closing I would like to leave you with a thought that comes from Don Hoppe's *Kondratieff Wave Analyst*, Volume IV, #1 (Box 977, Crystal Lake, IL 60014). I have long admired the work Don has been doing in economic cycles and historical patterns. His long-term perspective as well as his understanding of U.S. economic history are truly phenomenal. His January 1989 issue, which bears the title "Real Crash Still to Come," begins with the following quote:

> We are apparently finished and done with economic cycles as we know them.
> —Edward Simmons, President, NYSE, September 1929

For those who feel that we are done with cycles, historical price tendencies, and patterns, and for those who feel that Keynesian theory was the economic messiah that ushered in an era of unending economic growth, I suggest a long, hard look at the reality of the current worldwide situation.

Bibliography

Achinstein, Asher. *Introduction to Business Cycles.* New York: Thomas Y. Crowell, 1951.

Barr, Kenneth. "Long Waves: A Selective Annotated Bibliography." *Review* Vol. 2, No. 4. Spring, 1979: 675-718.

Berger, Joan. "Is the World Economy Riding a Long Wave to Prosperity?" *Business Week* May 5, 1986: 84-88.

Booth, Douglas E. *Regional Long Waves, Uneven Growth, and the Cooperative Alternative.* New York: Praeger, 1987.

Browder, Robert P. and Kerensky, Alexander F., eds. *The Russian Provisional Government 1917: Documents.* Stanford: Stanford University Press, 1961.

The Cambridge Economic History of Europe Vols. II and III. Cambridge, Mass.: Cambridge University Press, 1963.

Carr, Edward H. *The Bolshevik Revolution 1917–1923* Vol. 2. London: Macmillan & Co., 1963.

——— *Socialism in One Country 1924–1926* Vol. 3, Pt. 2. London: Macmillan, 1964.

Carr, Edward H. and Davies, R. W. *Foundations of a Planned Economy: 1926–1929* Vol. 1, Parts I & II; Vol. 2. London: Macmillan, 1969.

Clark, John, Freeman, Christopher, and Soete, Luc. "Long Waves, Inventions, and Innovations." *Futures* Vol. 13, No. 4. Aug., 1981: 308-322.

Clemence, Richard V. and Doody, Francis S. *The Schumpeterian System.* Cambridge, Mass.: Addison-Wesley, 1950.

Cole, G.D.H. *Introduction to Economic History 1750–1950.* Macmillan & Co. Ltd. New York: St. Martin's Press, 1954.

Craig, Paul P. and Watt, Kenneth E. F. "The Kondratieff Cycle and War: How Close Is the Connection?" *The Futurist* Vol. 19. April, 1985: 25-27.

Dauten, Carl A. and Valentine, Lloyd M. *Business Cycles and Forecasting.* 3rd ed. Cincinnati: South-Western Pub. Co., 1968.

Dawes, Charles G. *How Long Prosperity?* Chicago: A. N. Marquis Co., 1937.

Day, Richard B. "The Theory of the Long Cycle: Kondratieff, Trotsky, Mandel." *New Left Review* No. 99, Sept.-Oct., 1976: 67-82.

Dean, Phyllis and Cole, W. A., *British Economy Growth 1688–1959.* 2nd ed. Cambridge: Cambridge University Press, 1962.

Dean, Vera M. *Soviet Russia: 1917–1933.* World Affairs Pamphlets. No. 2. New York: Foreign Policy Association and Boston, World Peace Foundation, 1933.

Delbeke, Joseph. "Recent Long-Wave Theories." *Futures* Vol. 13, No. 4. Aug., 1981: 246-257.

Dewey, Edward R. *Cycles: Selected Writings.* Pittsburgh, PA: Foundation for the Study of Cycles, 1970.

Dewey, Edward R. and Dakin, Edwin F. *Cycles: The Science of Prediction.* New York: Henry Holt & Co., 1947.

Dorfman, Joseph. *The Economic Mind in American Civilization 1865–1918* Volume III. New York: Augustus M. Kelley, 1969.

Eklund, Klas. "Long Waves in the Development of Capitalism?" *Kyklos* Vol. 33, No. 3. 1980: 383-419.

Erickson, Scott W. "The Transition Between Eras." *The Futurist* Vol. 19. Aug., 1985: 40-44.

Fergusson, Adam. *When Money Dies: The Nightmare of the Weimar Collapse.* London: William Kimber, 1975.

Fisher, H. H. *The Famine in Soviet Russia 1919–1923.* New York: MacMillan, 1927.

Fisher, Irving. *The Stock Market Crash—and After.* New York: MacMillan, 1930.

Forrester, Jay W. "Economic Conditions Ahead: Understanding the Kondratieff Wave." *The Futurist* Vol. 19. June, 1985: 16-20.

———— "A Great Depression Ahead? Changing Economic Patterns." *The Futurist* Vol. 12, No. 6. Dec., 1978: 379-385.

————"Growth Cycles." *De Economist* Vol. 125, No. 4. 1977: 525-543.

———— "Innovation and Economic Change." *Futures* Vol. 13, No. 4. Aug., 1981: 323-331.

———— "We're Headed For Another Depression." *Fortune* Vol. 97, No. 1. Jan. 16, 1978: 145-148.

Freeman, Christopher. *Design, Innovation, and Long Cycles in Economic Development.* London: Frances Pinter, 1986.

———— ed. *Long Waves in the World Economy.* Dover, N.H.: Frances Pinter (Publishers), 1984.

Garvy, George. "Kondratieff, N.D." *International Encyclopedia of the Social Sciences.* Vol. 8. Macmillan, 1968: 443-444.

———— "Kondratieff's Theory of Long Cycles." *Review of Economic Statistics* Vol. 25, No. 4. Nov., 1943: 203-220.

Giarini, Orio. *Cycles, Value, and Employment.* New York: Pergamon Press, 1984.

Goodwin, Richard M., Kruger, Michael, and Vercelli, Alessandro, eds. *Nonlinear Models of Fluctuating Growth.* New York: Springer-Verlag, 1984.

Gordon, Robert J., ed. *The American Business Cycle.* Chicago: University of Chicago Press, 1986.

Guttman, William and Meehan, Patricia. *The Great Inflation: Germany 1919–23.* Westmeade, England: Saxonhouse, D.C. Heath Ltd., 1975.

Hall, Peter. "The Next Economic Boom." *World Press Review* Vol. 28. June, 1981: 23-25.

Holtfrerich, Carl-Ludwig. *The German Inflation 1914–1923: Causes and Effects in International Perspective.* Trans. by Theo Balderston. Berlin: Walter de Gruyter, 1986.

Kerensky, Alexander. *The Crucifixion of Liberty.* Trans. by G. Kerensky. New York: The John Day Co., 1934.

———— *Russia and History's Turning Point.* New York: Duell, Sloan & Pearce, 1965.

Kitchin, Joseph. "Cycles and Trends in Economic Factors." *Review of Economic Statistics* Vol. 5, No. 1. 1923: 10-16.

Kleinknecht, Alfred. "Observations on the Schumpeterian Swarming of Innovations." *Futures* Vol. 13, No. 4. Aug., 1981: 293-306.

Kochan, Lionel. *Russia in Revolution 1890–1918*. London: Wiedenfeld & Nicolson, 1966.

Kondratieff, Nikolai. *The Long Wave Cycle*. Trans. by Guy Daniels. Richardson & Snyder, 1984.

———— "The Conjuncture Institute at Moscow." *Quarterly Journal of Economics* Vol. 39. Feb., 1925: 320-324.

———— "The Long Waves in Economic Life." *Review of Economic Statistics* Vol. XVII, No. 6. Nov., 1935: 105-115.

———— "The Static and the Dynamic View of Economics." *Quarterly Journal of Economics* Vol. 39. Aug., 1925: 575-583.

Kuznets, Simon. "Long Swings in the Growth of Population and in Related Economic Variables." *Proceedings of The American Philosophical Society* Vol. 102, No. 1. Feb., 1958: 25-52.

Lincoln, W. Bruce. *In War's Dark Shadow*. New York: The Dial Press, 1983.

McCusker, John J. and Menard, Russell R. *The Economy of British America 1607–1789*. Chapel Hill & London: University of North Carolina Press, 1985.

Mager, Nathan H. *The Kondratieff Waves*. New York: Praeger, 1987.

Malle, Silvana. *The Economic Organization of War: Communism*. Cambridge: Cambridge University Press, 1985.

Mandel, Ernest. "Explaining Long Waves of Capitalist Development." *Futures* Vol. 13, No. 4. Aug., 1981: 332-338.

Marchal, André. "Juglar, Clément." *International Encyclopedia of the Social Sciences* Vol. 8. Macmillan, 1968: 324-326.

Martino, Joseph P. "Does the Kondratieff Wave Really Exist?" *The Futurist* Vol. 19. Feb., 1985: 23-25.

Melgunow, S. "The 'Red Terror' in Russia (1917–1927)," in *Ten Years of Bolshevik Domination*. Joseph Bickermann, ed. Berlin: Siegfried Scholem, 1928: 213-227.

Mermelstein, David. *The Economic Crisis Reader*. New York: Vintage Books, Random House, 1975.

Metz, Rainer. "Zur Empirischen Evidence 'Langer Wellen'." *Kyklos* Vol. 37, No. 2. 1984: 266-290.

Michaels, James W., Baldwin, William, and Minard, Lawrence. "Echoes from a Siberian Prison Camp." *Forbes* Vol. 128. 1984:164-174.

Nove, Alec. *Stalinism and After*. London: George Allen and Unwin, 1981.

Pope, David. "Rostow's Kondratieff Cycle in Australia." *Journal of Economic History* Vol. 44, No. 3. Sept., 1984: 729-753.

Readings in Business Cycle Theory. Philadelphia: The Blakiston Co., 1944. (Sel. by committee of The American Economic Assoc.)

Rosenberg, Nathan and Frischtak, Claudio R. "Technological Innovation and Long Waves." *Cambridge Journal of Economics* Vol. 8, No. 1. March, 1984: 7-24.

Rostow, W. W. *Why The Poor Get Richer and The Rich Slow Down.* Austin: University of Texas Press, 1980.

———— "Kondratieff, Schumpeter, and Kuznets: Trend Periods Revisited." *Journal of Economic History* Vol. 35, No. 4. Dec., 1975: 719-753.

———— *The World Economy. History & Prospect.* Austin & London: University of Texas Press, 1978.

Schumpeter, Joseph A. "The Analysis of Economic Change." *Review of Economic Statistics* XVII, No. 4. May, 1935: 2-10.

———— *Business Cycles.*

———— *Economic Doctrine and Method.* Trans. by R. Aris. New York: Oxford University Press, 1954.

———— *History of Economic Analysis.* Elizabeth Boody, ed. New York: Oxford University Press, 1954.

———— *The Theory of Economic Development: An Inquiry Into Profits, Capital, Credit, Interest, and the Business Cycle.* Trans. by Redvers Opie. New York: Oxford University Press, 1961.

Shuman, James B. and Rosenall, David. *The Kondratieff Wave.* New York: World Publishing, 1972.

Snyder, Julian M. "The Government and Economic Policy Decisions." *Vital Speeches of the Day* Vol. 48. April 1, 1982: 376-379.

Solomou, Solomos. "Non-Balanced Growth and Kondratieff Waves in the World Economy, 1850-1913." *Journal of Economic History* Vol. 46, No. 1. March, 1986: 165-169.

Solzhenitsyn, Aleksandr I. *The Gulag Archipelago.* Vol. 1. Trans. by Thomas P. Whitney. New York: Harper & Row, 1973.

Stipp, John L. *Soviet Russia Today: Patterns and Prospects.* New York: Harper & Bros., 1956.

Stoken, Dick A. *Cycles: What They Are, What They Mean, How to Profit by Them.* New York: McGraw-Hill, 1978.

Tinbergen, J. "Kondratiev Cycles and So-Called Long Waves: The Early Research." *Futures* Vol. 13, No. 4. 1982: 258-263.

Van Duijn, Jacob J. "Fluctuations in Innovations Over Time." *Futures*
    Vol. 13, No. 4. 1982: 264-275.
────── *The Long Wave in Economic Life.* London: George Allen &
    Unwin, 1983.
────── "The Long Wave in Economic Life." *De Economist* Vol. 125,
    No. 4. 1977: 544-576.
Van Ewijk, C. "The Long Wave—A Real Phenomenon?" *De Econo-
    mist* Vol. 129, No. 3. 1981: 324-372.
────── "A Spectral Analysis of the Kondratieff Cycle." *Kyklos* Vol. 35,
    No. 2. 1982: 468-499.
Volland, Craig S. "Kondratieff's Long-Wave Cycle." *The Futurist* Vol.
    19. Feb., 1985: 26-27.
Wallerstein, Immanuel. "Kondratieff Up or Kondratieff Down?" *Re-
    view* Vol. 2, No. 4. Spring, 1979: 663-673.
Zarnowitz, Victor, ed. *The Business Cycle Today.* New York: Columbia
    University Press, 1922.

Index